Tillie Olsen
and a Feminist Spiritual Vision

Tillie
Olsen

ELAINE NEIL ORR

For Nancy
Who taught me something
about Giving
and about being
a learner*

Love
Elaine Neil Orr

(* Olsen's unmarried name
is Lerner)

UNIVERSITY PRESS
OF MISSISSIPPI
JACKSON & LONDON

and a Feminist Spiritual Vision

Library of Congress Cataloging-in-Publication Data

Orr, Elaine Neil.
  Tillie Olsen and a feminist spiritual vision.

  Bibliography: p.
  Includes index.
  1. Olsen, Tillie—Criticism and interpretation.
2. Feminism in literature.   3. Religion in literature.
4. Feminism—Religious aspects.   I. Title.
PS3565.L82Z8   1987   813'.54   86-28925
ISBN 0-87805-300-X (alk. paper)

British Library Cataloging in Publication data is
available.

All excerpts from *Tell Me a Riddle, Yonnondio,* and
Silences printed by permission of the publisher Delacorte
Press/Seymour Lawrence and Tillie Olsen.

For Joel and Andy,
who live with me
beyond
the boundaries

A person who walks in only one direction, who receives only one gift, and who develops in a one-sided way cannot become a whole person. Remember the rainbow, the gift of fire, the gift of water, the gift of air, and the gift of earth. Remember the seven colors that, taken together, make up light. Remember that time after the flood; remember today and the beginnings of new life.

DOROTHEE SOELLE

Only help her to know—help make it so there is cause for her to know—that she is more than this dress on the ironing board, helpless before the iron.

TILLIE OLSEN

I have been born many times, a false
    Messiah,
but let me be born again
into something true.

ANNE SEXTON

We the darker ones come even now not altogether empty-handed.

W.E.B. DU BOIS

Contents

Preface

"[Women], like their characters, have been denied the legitimate evidence of their own experience." This sentence, by Joanne Frye in her study *Living Stories: Telling Lives*, encapsulates a central motivation guiding this book. In reading Tillie Olsen, I am seeking evidence in literature of women's experience as a woman writer has reflected it. The search will lead, I think, to establishing women's voices as authoritative of women's lives, both what they have been and what they may be. As a writer who is a woman and who gives artistic expression to women's experience (as mothers, wives, sisters, nurturers, seekers), Tillie Olsen is a particularly promising source for readers who seek in literature knowledge of realities, perspectives, and dreams other than those that have dominated Western literature.

The present study began in the confluence of several important events: an academic introduction into the ways language and story both reflect and create our reality; a discovery of feminist criticism; and the birth of my own child. The last of these was for a time the most consuming, and it was during the exigencies of that experience that I first read Tillie Olsen. It seemed to me that she wrote with rare honesty, compassion, and understanding about what is perhaps the most central and historical of women's experiences, that is, mothering.

In the spring of 1983, I met Tillie in San Antonio, Texas, where she was giving a reading. The meeting confirmed my determination to study her literature for the perspectives and truths it reveals about women's lives and for the sense of value it conveys to experiences we have commonly not regarded as revealing spiritual truth—for example, doing house work, preparing food, looking to the ordinary needs of children, and struggling for a self in those contexts. Tillie Olsen's work resonates with the promises and difficulties of mothering and with the immense holiness revealed in every child. Regarding her vision of women's lives and dreams, Olsen's working-class background, political activism, and mothering have lent her a different perspective from most American writers, even other women writers and feminist critics.

My study of Olsen's literature has confirmed my intuition that in seeking to correct the biases of male norms, feminist critics have for the most part largely ignored or undervalued many truths of women's childbearing and nurturing work. In particular, the feminist ideal of freedom for women has most often been interpreted as freedom from traditional women's experience. I have found little investigation into the values and achievements of those experiences. Only Olsen seems to be exploring as her primary interest the implications for culture and for being human of women's traditional caretaking roles.

Though I alone am responsible for errors and frailties in the book, many contributed to my work. I wish to thank Robert Detweiler, Ellen Umansky, Robert Paul, and William Beardslee, all of Emory University, who were true teachers and who were invaluable and sensitive critics of my writing and thought. Furthermore, I wish to express my deepest thanks to Robert Doty and Sena Naslund, teachers at the B.A. and M.A. level, who touched my spirit and my intellect and who laid the groundwork for later study. I am forever indebted to friends at Oakhurst Baptist Church in Atlanta and at Mercer University Atlanta who encouraged me in more ways than one. It was through a faculty development award from Mercer that I first met Olsen in 1983.

I am grateful to Belmont College for tangible encouragement of my work; in particular I wish to express thanks to John Paine and Robert Simmons. All of my colleagues in the Department of Literature and Language have lent moral support and have allowed me time to focus on this project while they carried on with more extended departmental duties. I wish as well to thank my students who give deeper meaning to this work.

John Bassett, Mike Awalt, and Jim Carnes graciously read revisions of chapters and made suggestions that led to clearer thought and writing. I am particularly indebted to Deborah Rosenfelt, who read the entire manuscript, offered excellent criticism, and then reread parts of the revised book. Seetha Srinivasan, my editor at the University Press of Mississippi, enthusiastically led me through the process of revision. Beth Walker graciously and carefully helped proofread.

I owe special thanks to friends and colleagues who have shared in the intellectual and religious discussions that have shaped my thought: Rosemary Magee, Granville Taylor, Elizabeth Barnes, Mel Williams, and Nancy Sehested. Virginia Neeley, Ann Bishop, and Lucy Duke typed the manuscript at different stages of the work; each was interested in my writing, careful in her work, and always encouraging.

This book would not have been written, perhaps not even conceived, without the work of feminist scholars who go before me and whose vision of the world and of the Divine has liberated me toward thinking in new ways about Spirit and humanity, especially Rosemary Ruether, Phyllis Trible, Dorothee Soelle, Elisabeth Schüssler Fiorenza, Carol Christ, and Judith Plaskow. I am indebted as well to feminist literary critics who have begun to ask new questions of literature and whose work in the last decade has sparked my own thought even when I have not agreed with them.

Family members—Anne and Lloyd Neil, Becky and Bob Albritton, Bonnie and Vester Orr, and Myra Orr—have encouraged and helped me in this endeavor and have made it possible for me to balance multiple duties and roles.

I am forever grateful to my parents for living lives that have inspired me. I wish to thank Joel Orr for offering daily correction to my often erroneous evaluations. He keeps me from concluding. My spouse, Andy Orr, is a long-suffering friend, an astute critic, and a co-worker in the task of raising a child. I offer him my deepest thanks.

Finally, Tillie Olsen has talked with me, written letters, shared notes, stayed up late at night over the phone and in person. Her spirit and faith give me hope.

Introduction

Perhaps . . . lost in the mists of time, there was . . . an
earlier cultural consciousness, where women appeared
as subjects of their own humanity, speaking of their
experience in their own name; . . . But . . . it is lost to
us.

   How then should we go about collecting the texts
for the doing of feminist theology?

ROSEMARY RUETHER
Womanguides

As a uniquely masculine image and language for
divinity loses credibility, so also the idea of a single
divine incarnation in a human being of the male sex
may give way in the religious consciousness to an
increased awareness of the power of Being in all
persons.

MARY DALY
Beyond God the Father

Once I saw a woman's throat open with a cry so great
the cry could not come to sound—as in an old person
who dies.

NELLE MORTON
The Journey Is Home

American writer Tillie Olsen limns the stories of working-class
women, men, and children.[1] She gives a voice to those whose
experience has been so unheard and unreflected that it has been

essentially silent and silenced. Her own voice was nearly lost to us. Because of her sex, because of political circumstances, because she had to work, she might not have published more than a few brief pieces in her twenties. To our great advantage, she has written more. Her three volumes of writing, a few essays and poems, and a later story are the subject of this book. They present a picture of the world as Olsen and her characters know it—sexist, racist, and classist; therefore broken, silenced, and defeated—and evoke a vision of the world as it should be. The picture and the vision come out of the almost destroyed spirits of Olsen's people and of Olsen herself.

Yet the vision of Tillie Olsen is a resounding affirmation of life. The questions this book asks are the questions Olsen's literature discloses: Who are we in light of this broken and abused world? And who are we in light of the human longing for re-creation and wholeness? In large measure, this book interprets what Olsen has sought to write, what inspires her. I have chosen to emphasize her accomplishment in disclosing a deep spiritual vision, believing that even where Olsen's texts appear to fail, they still evoke our sympathy and compel us to listen.

I begin with the premise that creative literature discloses ways of knowing and being in the world, which have implications for who we are and what our purpose is in existing. Stories have always been central to our understanding of the divine and of the human. Mythic stories like Oedipus's search for identity as well as religious stories like the Exodus of the Hebrews from Israel offer their audiences a way of knowing themselves in light of the narratives. This book, through an in-depth interpretation of the work of one woman writer, suggests that literature by women is a particularly fecund source for women's and men's present search for meaning and identity.

In the past, in literary and religious ponderings, we have understood our world and our destiny through meanings that arise primarily in relation to men's lives and perspectives.[2] In reading women's literature, women and men may begin to see their destiny in a new light, that is, in light of the worlds women create in poem and story, worlds often disclosed through the perspectives of female characters. While there are no firm boundaries between literature by men and literature by women, we might imagine them as neighboring countries sharing some common territories. The borders are not visible (we may even quarrel over them), but when we get far enough into one or the other, we notice a change of tastes and smells, of geography, setting, people, and interests. I take as a starting point that in women's literature we find world visions that are different from those dreamed of and designed by men; in reading

literature by women, we may begin to imagine human destiny in
terms of women's lives. As Tillie Olsen's writing shows, such
imagining leads to new and sometimes radical rethinking of human
values, needs, and aspirations. It may even lead to revising our very
ways of thinking about such things and thus to changes in the
language we use to express and symbolize human nature and
destiny. The potential for awakening to new comprehensions of life
through women's literature, then, is the broadest inquiry of this
study.

A second premise informing this study is that the appropriation
of a text's vision or world may be a religious act. This is not to say
that literary texts are intrinsically or primarily religious. Rather,
coherent and serious works of literature invite conversation about
being human and possibilities for transcendence.[3] Some texts, more
than others, evoke such conversation. These texts bring us into an
awareness of healing and perhaps transcending presence in human
experience, or they compel us toward moral contemplation in their
presentation of a way or mode of being in the world. Olsen's
literature invites a religious engagement in both of these senses. In
our reading of her fiction, we sense longings and dreams that give
rise to an envisioned world of harmony, nurturance, and fulfillment.
The human infant as well as the exhausted mother of children is
emblematic in Olsen's world of the hoped for and healing experience
of human to human unfolding and becoming. When, in her last
published fiction, Olsen describes an orphaned boy's emotional
resurrection, she points vividly to this vision through its beginnings
in concrete experience: The miracle of life, of renaissance and
transformation, is rooted in the human necessities of caretaking,
nurturance, and encouragement. Knit of broken and abused lives,
the hoped-for world this literature evokes is apocalyptic. It is a
transformed world, celebrant of child and of the sacred powers of life
and creativity. This vision is Olsen's transcending message,
transcending because it offers deep connection and hope. In her
world, we as readers begin to comprehend ourselves as moral beings
whose destinies are connected with the characters'. We see our own
history and future in light of theirs.

Thus this book is a religious interpretation of Tillie Olsen's
literature. Beginning with a small group of poems and essays written
in the thirties and her unfinished novel, *Yonnondio*, through Olsen's
middle period *(Tell Me a Riddle)*, and to her latest publications
(including a work of prose titled *Silences*), the study examines
Olsen's writing for what it suggests about the human situation in
light of the transcending vision it evokes.

Though most article-length studies of Olsen's writing refer to a mystical healing, a powerful faith, or an enduring power in her fiction and prose, this is the first interpretation to give sustained attention to the implications of her work as a whole for our understanding of the human situation and of religious consciousness. Yet her relatively small canon is written to communicate a vision for human existence, a vision rooted in her family's Russian Jewish heritage and in her own history as an American worker, a Communist party member, a humanist, a feminist, and a mother. What I will show is that a religious comprehension of her texts enhances others' interpretations of her writing.[4]

As it has evolved from the 1920s to the present, Olsen's writing requires a religious comprehension not only because of the life-affirming vision it discloses but because it is based on hope. A new world is possible, not because God dictates it, but because human longing gives rise to it. As feminist theologian Nelle Morton points out, the "religious" words "spiritual" and "transcending" both were originally understood as referring to the "rising up out of what already is."[5] Applied to Olsen's hoped-for world, these definitions lead me to say that the religious meanings and understandings we glean from her writing arise out of what already is, out of scarred lives desirous of a new beginning, out of silence hoping for hearing and speech.

The mystery of Olsen's central paradox—the riddle of depletion and renewing life—is another invitation to religious interpretation. Her hope for rebirth takes the unlikely form of a search among absences, silences, discontinuities, and brokenness.[6] Even in such conditions and circumstances, drawing her vision in images characterized by muteness and partiality, she finds reason to believe in a transformed world. In bringing the dark to light or the speechless to speech, Olsen's literature reveals the presence of miraculous powers in life. While the texts do not unfold any systematic religious program, they point to faith in transforming possibilities, which are inexplicable by reason alone.

My method of reading Olsen's work will be through an analysis of the smallest and largest units of a piece of literature, through metaphor (word) as it illumines and is illumined by the entire written text.[7] Employing key images, which cluster to form metaphors, Olsen offers throughout her texts "miniature poems" (Monroe Beardsley's phrase), which give rise to certain understandings. These image clusters or metaphors offer an entrance into the whole work. Thus the multiple allusions in the

stories to buds, flowers, and blossoming gather in our reading and
cause us to see the narratives of abused and unopened lives in the
context of how the world *should be*, that is, in relation to the
flower's opening. In this way, metaphors of wholeness and coherence
are interpretive clues for reading Olsen's world. At the same time,
each discrete text, in its consistent engagement with certain kinds
of people, compels us to read the metaphors in light of the stories.
Thus we are always returned to the reality of these lives and to their
as-yet-unrealized hopes.

If the metaphors are luminous signs of another and better world,
they are still developed within the contexts of the shaped lives and
circumstances that make the work. Thus, the story of the eldest
daughter in "I Stand Here Ironing" gives particular meaning to the
blossoming Olsen's texts desire. The home environment, the soil of
earliest growth, becomes the focus of our attention and we realize
that actual circumstances, more than dreams, may determine what
this particular life can be. If a young girl is like a blighted flower,
what else matters to her or to her mother? How can one dream
beyond the borders of a wasted garden? As a consequence we are
made to ponder promise and dream within the contexts of silenced
and thwarted lives.

Olsen is visionary, but not by ignoring or underestimating the
realities of suffering. She is neither a harsh realist nor a romantic
escapist. Instead she makes blessing of necessity, showing that
transcending hope is cognizant of acute pain, loss, and brokenness,
and that only out of such awareness can a vision for humanity be
woven. Her portraits of weary workers and mothers, of children, of
an expiring sailor, of a black churchwoman, present us with a new
and compelling world view: a world hoped for in tension with the
world these characters inhabit. The stories create a chorus as Olsen
speaks for women and other outsiders. As the black mother, Alva,
says in "O Yes," the singing comes from "a hope in their blood,
their bones. . . . They [are] singing," she explains, "songs every
word that's real to them, . . . every word out of they own life."[8]

Beginning with the dirge of *Yonnondio* and through the
miraculous rebirth of Stevie in "Requa," Olsen's language and texts
express her central meaning, the miracle and sanctity of each
human life, and give witness to her enduring hope. Her narratives
depict what harms in life, to quicken our desire for the unfolding of
the divine human spark born daily into the world. The mystery of
hope and the possibility for renewal are the subjects of Olsen's art
and must be the frame for our interpretation. Literature is, as Henry

James once said, a kind of teaching. What Olsen teaches is the possibility and necessity for a harmonious and flowering world where "every life shall be a song."[9]

Olsen's art may also be teaching us "brave new words and old words used in fresh ways . . . [to] create new realities."[10] She may be speaking a new word out of the depths of women's experience, knowledge, and being which will surpass the words used here like "transcendence," "spirit," and "religious," words all fraught with patriarchal meanings. Part of our search in her world is for a new language for the human experience of and desire for transformation and fulfillment, *for the experience of the fullness of who we really are.*

One of the great gifts of literature is its ability not merely to reflect the past in a clearer light but its tendency to create something new and to distill different ways of being and knowing. In reading, we are awakened to possibilities that are often more than the writer intended. When readers meet texts with the expectation of learning, miracles still occur. Through Olsen's art, we encounter a vision for humanity that is ultimately transformative, calling us into truer identity and purpose. My goal is to interpret the vision and perhaps, in interpreting, to expand it.[11]

1. Though it is not my primary purpose in this book to study Olsen as an American writer, I do see her within the tradition of American literature. Some secondary themes of this study address Olsen's place in our national letters. Primarily, however, Olsen is read here as a writer in an as-yet minority tradition of those representing in literature the perspectives of women, of the working class, and of children. For an approach to Olsen as an American and Western writer see Abigail Martin.

2. The overflowing preoccupation in literature and literary theory alike with the hero, with male experience, with male spheres and points of view, with male gods, is a commonplace observation by now. A glance at a volume like Hazard Adams's *Critical Theory since Plato* (New York: Harcourt, Brace, Jovanovich, 1971) illustrates the prevailing absence of critics who are women in the Western literary tradition. Almost any volume of theological essays used in divinity schools makes the same point in terms of religious thinkers.

3. I borrow the notion of conversing with texts from Hans-Georg Gadamer's *Philosophical Hermeneutics,* trans. ed. David E. Linge (Berkeley: University of California Press, 1976).

4. I am indebted to many sensitive critics of Olsen's work whose articles, reviews, and interviews were inspirational and instructive for this book. See the Bibliography, Section II. The dissertation by Linda Marguerite Park-Fuller includes a chapter surveying Olsen criticism.

5. *The Journey Is Home* (Boston: Beacon Press, 1985), p. 89.

6. Olsen has been effective in bringing back into print (in collaboration with The Feminist Press) the works of Rebecca Harding Davis, Charlotte Perkins Gilman, and Agnes Smedley, among others. Thus, she breaks the silences of unsung women writers as well as the silences of her own heroines and heroes.

7. This method is spelled out more thoroughly in Chapter I.

8. In *Tell Me a Riddle*, p. 60.

9. The phrase is from the title novella in the *Tell Me a Riddle* collection. It comes from a socialist hymn, which the dying protagonist, Eva, whispers in her death. The phrase provides a touchstone for understanding Olsen's vision.

10. Morton, *The Journey Is Home*, p. 88.

11. In Chapter 11, I draw from several articles on Olsen by other critics, from personal and telephone interviews conducted with Olsen 1983–86, and from books, e.g., Irving Howe, *World of Our Fathers* (New York: Simon and Schuster, Touchstone, 1976); Charlotte Baum, Paula Hyman, and Sonya Michel, *The Jewish Woman in America* (New York: Plume paperback, New American Library, 1976); and Nathan Glazer, *American Judaism*, 2d ed. rev. (Chicago: The University of Chicago Press, 1972). In their article, Burkom and Williams divide Olsen's writing into three periods: 1933–34, 1953–56, and 1959 to the present (Selma Burkom and Margaret Williams, "De-Riddling Tillie Olsen's Writing"). They include *Yonnondio* in the last period. I place it in the first, because all of the actual writing was accomplished then and it therefore reflects Olsen's early comprehension and style. I draw the lines less rigidly and include years when Olsen was writing, if not publishing. The dates are approximate. Thus, for me the first period spans 1930–36; the second, 1953–60; and the last, from the sixties forward.

Tillie Olsen
and a Feminist Spiritual Vision

Toward a Feminist Religious Reading

Mazie felt the strange happiness in her mother's body, happiness that had nought to do with them, with her; happiness and farness and selfness.

> I saw a ship a sailing
> And on that ship was me.

The fingers stroked, spun a web, cocooned Mazie into happiness and intactness and selfness. Soft wove the bliss round hurt and fear and want and shame—the old worn fragile bliss, a new frail selfness bliss, healing, transforming. Up from the grasses, from the earth, from the broad tree trunk at their back, latent life streamed and seeded. The air and self shone boundless. Absently, her mother stroked; stroked unfolding, wingedness, boundlessness.

TILLIE OLSEN
Yonnondio

Were the human community taken with dead seriousness in our theologizing, there would be no more temple—for God would be in the midst of the people. The personal could be recognized for the political it is and the political the personal. A new heaven and a new earth would indeed appear . . . for the old patriarchal heaven and earth are already disappearing.

NELLE MORTON
The Journey Is Home

It is time for asking wholly new questions.

MARY DALY
Beyond God the Father

T he present engagement of many readers with religious meanings in literature and the thought that literature may be our most fecund source for knowledge of the spiritual depths of being in modern life have various sources and expressions.[1] The recent interest in narrative, for example, stems from the rather contemporary need (in view of the crisis in traditional religious language) to find some bedrock for theological discourse and expresses the ancient human penchant for knowing through myth and story.[2] Two moments in recent thought contribute to the interpretive investigation I make in this book. While the second is more directly related to Olsen's literature, the first must be understood in order that the significance of literature to modern theological or religious discourse may be fully appreciated.

The first is what may be called the "shaking of the foundations" of religious discourse. As Langdon Gilkey points out in *Naming the Whirlwind: The Renewal of God-Language,* the question of the adequacy of theological language has been replaced by the question of whether there is any transcendence about which to speak.[3] We may use the categories of Paul Ricoeur to illustrate Gilkey's point.[4] Those of us in religious studies are no longer asking for the *sense* that religious language makes (the plot, the point), or which language makes the most sense, but whether there is any *reference* for this language. Is religious language *about* anything?

Some comfort may be felt in knowing that the problem of the reference of language is shared by all the disciplines that focus on meaning and language, including, of course, literary criticism. The deconstructionist movement has, in fact, flourished upon this very possibility—that there may be nothing beneath our word games.[5] The depth of the crisis for theology is felt in its dependence on the referent (in traditional language, on God) to make its sense. Theology has more often than not begun with the assurance of ultimates from which it has worked deductively, often drawing a dichotomy between the Ultimate Referent (God) and the human. Gilkey writes about this crisis and points to the fact that in our age, theologians may be required to proceed by a more inductive method: "If the question of *God* is raised, theology literally must begin from the beginning, it must deal with its own most basic foundations. . . . that means starting as best one can on one's own and at the level of concrete experience. This is an upheaval that has thrown us all quite back to the beginnings of religious reflection."[6]

Gilkey's allusion to the "beginnings" and to "one's own . . . experience" brings us to a second moment in recent experience and thought: that is, many women's awakening to the false consciousness that has shaped their lives and their consequent search for more authentic identify and meaning.[7] For a significant number of women, traditional definitions of their personhood and the various texts and interpretations that have governed cultural expectations and associations regarding women no longer have meaning. If the work of women scholars and writers like Adrienne Rich, Mary Daly, Nelle Morton, Anne Wilson Schaef, and Carol Christ gives voice to contemporary women's feminist experience, many women are beginning "on their own" and "at the beginning" in the search for meaning and purpose.[8] In a way, their loss of faith in the culturally circumscribed traditions of womanhood, motherhood, and femininity is analogous to the theologians' dilemma. Both groups face the possibility that there is no meaning where they had expected it, that they have placed their faith in nothingness. Mary Daly begins her feminist theology on this experience of awakening to nothingness. In her analysis, women experience the Void as they tear away the "masks of sexist society and . . . confront the horrifying fact of [women's] own alienation from [their] authentic sel[ves]."[9]

However, the creative work of many feminist theologians and writers testifies to a difference between the crisis in traditional theological discourse and the crisis women face in becoming alert to the falseness of their former lives. Women (as scholars, poets, and theologians) are embracing concrete and personal experience as an avenue for self and transcending knowledge. Like liberation theologians in general, they demonstrate a lively faith in a spiritual reality that springs from experience. What feminist theologians and feminist critics have lost faith in, by and large, is not the possibility for religious experience and knowledge, but the adequacy of masculine language, symbol systems, and interpretations to disclose the whole truth about humanity and about transcendent possibilities. For those feminists who have lost faith in the possibility of religious experience, the loss results from the failed viability of the masculine symbol system, from the accompanying sense of subjugation and dehumanization fostered by that symbol system, and an inability to creatively break through the old symbols in order to create new wineskins to contain the outpouring of the new wine. Perhaps at the heart of the larger theological crisis is the inadequacy of masculine language. If so, those feminists who are seeking a new and expanded language for ultimacy may be the leaders in religious thought today.

Writing out of their own and other women's personal experience, some feminist scholars indicate that women are awakening to the depths of their own souls and are learning to hear themselves and the truths of their experience for the first time. Nelle Morton's recent book, *The Journey Is Home,* for example, bears testimony to women's spiritual awakening since the late 1960s. Calling into question the modes of thinking and being handed them by the dominant religious and secular cultures and the symbol systems that construct them, the women Morton writes about and for are gaining authentic knowledge of themselves and of spiritual being as it is present in their lives. Morton describes this process as she has witnessed it:

> Our tongues were loosened and we experienced ourselves speaking a new speech—boldly, perhaps, or haltingly, but authentically for the first time in our lives. We experienced a speech that follows hearing, as opposed to the going logic that demands precise speech for more accurate hearing to take place. Hearing, for us, became a personally transitive verb that evoked speech. We heard the person before the word was spoken. In that sense we can say we were heard to our own speech— to new creation. . . . It was not the word from the sky or from the patriarchal interpreter. The word was our word—our most human word. The word was ourselves. We heard one another to our own word—to our own self-birth.[10]

One source of women's awakening and a guide to feminist moral mapping is women's literature. A suggestion of this engagement with literature is that reflections of women's worlds in written texts have implications for the interpretation of ourselves. We are not saying that there is some core and unmediated women's experience that shines through the text and is *the truth.* Rather, this engagement with literature assumes in Aristotelian fashion that the written text makes new meanings and discloses deeper understanding than we may have in the "natural" and unmediated world.

This claim, that women's texts may disclose important re-visions of our traditional ways of thinking and valuing, beginning with re-visions of ourselves, is akin to the feminist theological proposal that women's own experience is a primary source of understanding and knowledge about transcendence. As Rosemary Ruether points out in her book, *Sexism and God-Talk,* all interpretation begins and ends with experience.[11] We all understand out of our own lives. Of course, this insight is not exclusively feminist. Hans-Georg Gadamer writes provocatively about the prejudices of experience, which we all bring to interpretation.[12] And yet, we might say that the recognition of the centrality of experience to interpretation and meaning is a contribution many feminist scholars make to current religious discourse and to cultural and literary criticism.

Noncritical individualism can, of course, lead to anarchy in letters as well as in life. Whose truth is the truest? Which texts reveal the fullest comprehensions of who we are and of the nature of transcending knowledge? Michael Goldberg has raised this criticism in regard to Carol Christ's work on women's stories, *Diving Deep and Surfacing: Women Writers on Spiritual Quest,* remarking that she leaves open the question of which stories reveal the ultimate truth.[13] His criticism may be premature. We may need to listen to the stories of the traditionally voiceless for a long time before we begin to establish categories and hierarchies of truth. At the same time, evaluations have already begun. The community of feminist scholars serves itself as an evaluative audience for current scholarship. Reading one another's work and bringing women's literature into the purview of critical and religious thinking, these scholars, like a band of searching believers, test texts and interpretations for their adequacy in presenting possibilities for a transformed and just humanity. For this reason, I do not find it necessary to categorize women's literature according to rubrics like "traditional" or "feminist." We need to read writers who are women for what we may learn of alternative perspectives and for new ways of knowing and being. Together, as we appropriate these meanings, we will evaluate what we find.

In regard to the two moments named above, we can conclude that in both, interpretive communities are searching for new avenues of faith, belief, and understanding. Thus, the concern of this book with the disclosure in literature of transcending vision and moral comprehension.

Olsen does not define herself as a religious writer, of course, and she was influenced in part by a socialist/Marxist tradition that rejected "religion." Yet, it is my understanding of the Marxist (also Nietzschean, Freudian) critique of religion that what is questioned is the practice of religion as a mask for more fearsome or threatening realities (including the possibility that there is no divine reality, nothing but oneself and one's illusions).[14] For Marx, religion served to dupe the masses into submissive acceptance of economic injustice. Religion was a tool of the state. This is probably the understanding of religion that Olsen's parents had as socialist Russian Jews. Olsen recreates the passionate rejection of religion in her character Eva (in "Tell Me a Riddle") who declares almost venomously that her religion is "none."[15]

Marxist criticism, then, is less interested in the sources of religious expression than it is concerned with religion as an outward structure of society. Its focus is less upon human imagination and human experience than upon the corrupt uses of religion as an institution.

As Paul Ricoeur points out in "The Critique of Religion," the positive contribution of Marx, Freud, and Nietzsche to religious thought is that they demystify traditional religion, making it possible for us to listen again to "the eruption of something from the other side, from the totally other into our culture." In their fight "against idols, that is, against the gods or the God of men," these thinkers require us to hearken back to our most fundamental experiences and to search for our most profound knowledge.[16] Thus, these three bequeath to religious investigation a healthy skepticism, a realization that all corporate religious expression has already entered the culture and become a part of it.

The feminist criticism of religion is akin to the Marxist in its analysis of religious oppressions, though it focuses on gender rather than class, looking particularly at women's submission to men within patriarchal religion and at the effects of this coerced submission upon women's self-understanding. In both Judaism and Christianity, sacred texts and traditionally authoritative interpretations have placed women in positions of subjection and inferiority to men. Women have been oppressed in their being and identity, according to writers like Daly. Women have been falsely named evil (as Eve, the initiator of sin in the world) and have thus suffered the burden of negative identification. Women, says Daly, must rename themselves to counteract the false naming of women by men.[17] What has been strongly criticized in religious traditions by Marxists and feminists alike, then, is *the use of religion to oppress*. The masks of religion (the gods or God whose rule and judgment are invoked to make inequality a divine ordinance) give rise to images, texts, traditions, and beliefs that actually keep people in darkness, or weakness.

The feminist critique of religion has been leveled at patriarchal language in particular.[18] For this reason, some feminists are very skeptical about the use of any religious language—perhaps even the categories of "the religious," or "the spiritual"—in feminist discourse. I use these terms as Nelle Morton does, tentatively. Our purpose, as Morton writes, is to see "the rise of spiritual interest [among women] . . . as a possible rebellion against patriarchy . . . as a search for alternative life sources."[19]

A fuller discussion of my use of terms like "transcendence," "otherness," and "moral" may be helpful in defining my own notions of spirituality and arguing my claim for the specifically spiritual power in Olsen's writing.

Giles Gunn has written that "since the Enlightenment . . . it has been assumed that the key to ultimate reality no longer resides in the spiritual divinities that shape our ends but in the spiritual attributes that define our nature as human beings."[20] I think most readers will agree that Olsen's writing communicates a vision of the enduring and divine attributes of human being. Gunn's statement, though not as radical as Gilkey's assessment of theological discourse and the problem of God, does suggest that religious investigation can no longer afford to be deductive, from God to human; it must begin and focus upon how human being discloses divine being. Certainly strains of neo-orthodox theology continue, but Gunn describes, I think, a dominant method in the current discourse of religious thought.

The continuation of any talk of religious dimensions, modes of being, or unconditional and ultimate truths and realities, begins with the position that the human voice gives witness to some qualitatively different and transforming experiences both in our collective and individual histories. Various theologians refer to such experiences as the "more," the "miraculous" or "paradoxical," or "the holy other." Paul Tillich referred to this dimension of experience as Ultimate Reality, the phrase borrowed by Gunn, or as the Unconditional, or as the Ground of Being. In the last case, Tillich's language reflects an attempt to do away with traditional notions of spiritual presence as above and beyond (transcendence coming down to us) or as a divinity thought of as a Supreme Human (a god or God) and instead to imagine spiritual reality as transcending from below (the *Ground)* and as divine movement and quality in time and experience, as verb (the Ground of *Being).*[21]

Thus Tillich's language makes it possible for theology to be

imagined without deductive or dichotomous terminology. Nelle
Morton takes this pivotal position and uses it in speaking of
women's experience and the new religious awareness women are
trying to express. In her own struggle with language, she began an
investigation into the word "spiritual," looking for its origins and
earliest meanings. What she discovered, as others may who use their
dictionaries, was that "the earliest meaning of spirit that we can
trace derives from the word *breath* . . . then later *wind* of the
cosmos." (One popular dictionary translates the Latin word *spiritus*
as "breath or to breathe.") Morton's research shows that both
meanings were connected with the feminine (the mother), since
mothers were imagined to breathe into the child the breath of life.
Thus, in early conceptualizing of the creation of life and spirit, "the
body is not separated from spirit, nor spirit separated from woman,
nor history separated from nature." Instead, the roots of the word
spiritual are material. Morton further comments that "of the same
movement [body to life or spirit] derives *transcending*—rising up out
of what already is."[22] In light of these insights, Morton shuns the
static noun "transcendence," which has been used hierarchically to
suggest " 'down from up above,' " and instead reinstates the sense of
the original meanings, " 'up from down under,' " by using the
"moving verb *transcending*." Employing a traditional metaphor, she
writes that "dove (spirit) descending suggests power over; dove
(spirit) ascending—as the phoenix—suggests life out of the heart of a
struggling people."[23]

To speak of the religious in the postmodern world is to imagine
the universe and our being dialogically, not dichotomously. That is,
our experience reveals to us some ultimate order, truth, or mode of
being that is binding in the world, and we understand ourselves in
light of it; we understand ourselves *to be like* transcendent Being, in
the metaphorical sense of striking similarity in difference, rather
than ourselves as fundamentally and categorically separate and
different from transcendence. We also speak of truth, justice, and
love to our children, suggesting that what we feel deeply is rooted in
the universe itself. Works of literature, some more than others, may
disclose such principles. Narrative texts especially seem to invite
conversation about being and truth since they establish a complex
and peopled world rooted in certain "sense making" principles and
ask us to enter it. Thus there is an ongoing dialogue between
humanity and the miraculous beginning in us; the "beyond,"
apprehended in the experienced world, echoes and expands the
truths we come to in struggling for justice, meaning, and
fulfillment. To hope, as Olsen does, in another world, transformed

in terms of the values she holds sacred, is to attest that certain ways of being and believing lead to transcendence. We might say that the hope pervading Olsen's texts creates an awareness that certain claims extend even beyond death and historical defeat. These claims—in human creativity, in the divine spark in the human infant, in wellness and wholeness, in the power of solidarity—are "transcending" in that they propel us to belief regarding what finally is ultimate, true, and enduring.

Experiences of transcendence have the power to transform not merely one value among many, or one aspect of life, but identity itself.[24] We are reinvented, made new creatures, through experiences that call us into new undersandings of the world and of who we really are. Insofar as the experience has power to inform our lives—in how we perceive our identity and purpose—and to bring us to act upon that knowledge, it is moral. Interpretation becomes moral as it suggests what texts have to say about how we should live. Here we are returned to the notion of didacticism in literary criticism.[25] In the final analysis, my interpretation of Olsen's writing *is* didactic. It appropriates her vision as it has implications for a new way of living in *our* world.

We have said that transcending experience is characterized by radical insight, which rises out of what already is. Transcending experience answers the question, "For what was I born?" Giles Gunn speaks of the experience of transcendence in terms of otherness or strangeness. In "The Moral Imagination in Modern American Criticism," he remarks:

> In a world no longer dominated by essentialist assumptions about reality and the passion they generate for a correspondent theory of truth, the aim of cultural discourse [including literary], of the conversation that constitutes culture, ceases to be the attainment of ontological certitude or discovery of an unprivileged hierarchy of values and becomes instead . . . "to take us out of our old selves by the power of strangeness, to aid us in becoming new beings."[26]

By "otherness," then, is meant the power of strangeness, of something new, which confronts us and has the potential to transform us. Many feminist theologians, like Morton, show that this sense of strangeness is less something apart from us coming down—or even from "the other side," as Ricoeur imagines it—than something already in us being born into its fullness. While women have been "the other" in male language and symbols, women discovering their otherness may be making connection with their transcendence, which is at once strange and familiar. In any case, this otherness of which I speak is for women not a function they fulfill for men but an awareness of the sacred connecting them with powers and possibilities in the universe.

The strangeness of transcending experience among women as Morton discusses it comes when what we already intuit or are groping toward is echoed by other women in community. We gain new knowledge about our old selves when we are heard (by ourselves and others) in our deepest being. If we follow this thinking, transcendence may be the remembrance of who we are meant to be but have forgotten or the re-creation of our potential in birth to be new beings. Thus, transcendence may be understood as the condition of human and divine wholeness in being, as the affirmative calling of people who struggle together toward the realization of their most authentic and creative selves. This is not a state of being but a mode or process of being in which we are led toward our greatest possibilities.

Strangeness is what makes metaphor, and as Paul Ricoeur, Sallie McFague, and others have shown, metaphor is a way of knowing and perceiving very close to religious experience itself. Furthermore, it is another way of knowing grounded in the concrete and familiar. What occurs when ordinary associations or expectations are met with extraordinary, strange, or "other" ones, is radically new insight. Yet these are insights evoked through the use of knowledge we already have. It is the combination of dissimilar things already appropriated in our experience that discloses the insight. New associations give birth to new meanings. Through metaphor we see things new; and not just that, but we are changed in light of this new knowledge or way of seeing. Thus, the strange that breaks out in metaphor is like the religious experience of otherness as I describe it; it rises from the ground or from the concrete. The strange or the other disclosed by metaphor, says McFague, "returns us to ourselves with new insight."[27]

Using these definitions, developed in relation to human experience in general and relating them to the particular focused activity of reading and interpretation, we can say that moments of awakening to transcendence may occur as we are met by or find ourselves in the world of the text, that these confrontations may act upon us as radically other or new and as revealing of some profound insight in the light of which we interpret ourselves, recognizing our true or ultimate and therefore divine nature. The echoing in literature, or the fleshing out of our own deepest sense of self has the potential for drawing us toward our purposes in existence.

Reading Olsen's work, we perceive something about ourselves

that confronts us as ultimate. This experience is like the experience of religious awakening to an unconditional reality. In Olsen's world, the awakening is to human lives that trail the mystery of creation in the midst of brokenness, pain, and despair. Olsen's voice for humanity, drawn from impoverished lives, is a message of miracle and thus of otherness that brings us into contact with present realities and future hopes. The transformation to which the texts point—from brokenness to well-being—intimates a divine plan and power surging in the universe, a power and plan inexplicable in purely human terms, though it springs from concrete experience.

Reading the transcendent in Olsen's work, then, means giving attention to the surprising hopes and dreams that break upon us through her characters entwined with the figure of the narrator (often a clearly autobiographical persona). It is something like the song on the radio that frightens Carol in Olsen's short story "O Yes." The song frightens her so badly, in fact, that she can at first only run from it. In the end, however, she hears the truth, that the painful experience of her black childhood friend offers her connection with her own values and pains, and that she may drown in her knowledge if she does not embrace it. Reading ourselves in light of Olsen's transcendent otherness (the experiences of the poor, the broken, of harrassed women and listless children, all of which remind us of our own loss and pain), we are confronted with knowledge of life's most uncompromising requirements and the most fundamental of human hopes. By metaphorically counterposing that which hurts with that which heals, Olsen's work elicits a vision for a transformed humanity. "What has not been destroyed" in Tillie Olsen, Sandy Bouncher has written, "is that largeness of belief in the human Spirit, her vision of the future in which the miracle of human life will be born into a world in which human life is a miracle."[28]

Theological purists might complain that we are speaking only penultimately to speak of human needs and dreams. The book will have to argue itself. My thesis is that Olsen's characters and the language that represents their lives acquaint us with transcendence by drawing us into "the heart of a struggling people" and gives witness, though miraculously, and perhaps scandalously, that human and divine are knit in being and destiny.

It remains for me to spell out more clearly how my interpretation proceeds and to draw some distinctions between this work and other feminist scholars' engagements with the religious implications of women's texts. Because most of the literature of traditional religion (and for that matter of the dominant culture) has not presented women's experience and knowledge from women's perspectives, feminist scholars have looked to women's texts— including poetry, fiction, diaries, and letters—for clues to women's comprehensions of value, truth, and belief.

Judith Plaskow, Carol Christ, and Ellen Umansky, to name a few, have come to women's texts out of particular religious traditions and contexts.[29] For these scholars, literature by women is correlated with certain (traditional or nontraditional) categories. Plaskow and Umansky seek ways of reinterpreting Judaism in light of women's lives and stories. Christ uses Mary Daly's categories for interpreting women's stories in *Diving Deep and Surfacing*. Another theologian, Rosemary Ruether, searches for texts by women (and men) that may serve as alternate religious texts (if not a canon) for women in her book *Womanguides: Readings toward a Feminist Theology*. In *The Sacred and the Feminine: Toward a Theology of Housework*, Kathryn Rabuzzi shows herself to be one of many feminist scholars who draws heavily from women's texts to illustrate their theses about the nature of women's traditional and feminist experience. In her weighty volume *In Memory of Her*, New Testament scholar Elisabeth Schüssler Fiorenza argues that certain canonical texts may have been written by women, since they reflect alternate themes and understandings closer to the experience of women in the early church.[30]

In all of these cases, the tendency is either to correlate religious categories or theses with the literary texts, or to uncover women's religious texts (works intended for religious use or brought into religious use by a community of readers). A dominant method in these investigations is to bring the text(s) into alignment with systematic theological and religious categories. This scholarship has accomplished a radical revision of the standard interpretations of traditional theological and religious language and categories. Plaskow, for example, illustrates how women's experience, as reflected in literature, may relativize the claims of male-centered theology. Introducing new categories for analyzing religious experience, Christ makes a strong case for difference between men's and women's spiritual consciousness. Like Mary Daly and Nelle Morton, Christ suggests that a new language may be needed to speak adequately about what women's texts disclose about human and divine Being.

My own interpretation is inspired by this last thought. However, my method is different from Christ's. I am not bringing categories of traditional or feminist religious discourse to Olsen's literature and searching her texts for how they enlighten (perhaps disprove, relativize, or affirm) that language. Neither am I calling her works religious texts. I am seeking to appropriate Olsen's writing as literature which has implications for religious understanding. Beginning with history as a window into the texts, I seek to discover how the texts offer their own interpretation. Once an image or metaphor from the writing achieves authority in a story, we may use it to reflect back upon the whole work. At the same time, the text continues to give meaning to the metaphors. The paradigmatic metaphors I read as disclosing Olsen's vision are ones she establishes and uses herself.

Further, my method is not a models approach, a search for heroines or for women questers and leaders. Neither is this work primarily a study of the images of women in women's literature, an approach largely developed by feminist literary criticism and also used by theologians like Ruether.[31] While a model for being emerges in Chapter VI, it does not point to any particular character or type of character in Olsen's literature but to a transformative mode of being that informs her world vision as a whole. Thus we are looking not for characters to pattern lives after, but for ways of being and knowing that quicken our awareness of the possibilities for a new humanity.

Tillie Olsen's world is informed by a dual impulse toward women's liberation from limiting human circumstances and toward the careful evaluation of women's values and understandings as they arise from their traditional roles in culture. Not always in spite of, but often because of their mothering and caretaking roles, women characters (Olsen's "essential angels") are capable of far deeper contemplation of the sacredness of human life than they might otherwise be. My interpretation has more to do with how we see ourselves in light of women's traditionally defined lives than with how Olsen's women characters see themselves. Some of Olsen's less weary mothers, for example Alva and Helen in "O Yes," suggest—though they do not seem self-conscious of it—that mothering can be a creative force in human valuations and visions. Regardless of whether we wish to emulate their lives, we must ask what their knowledge means for us.

The study begins with an examination of the writer's life and crucial historical influences: Olsen's parents' Russian Jewish heritage, their American socialism, and Olsen's participation in the American Communist Party in the 1930s. This history is given in order that we may have enough knowledge of "the cultural horizons" of her work to make reasonable historical connections in the process of reading the texts. If the interpretation proceeds as a close reading, it is, in Phyllis Trible's words, reading "wholly upon the text rather than wholly within the text."[32] Books, or at least their meanings, do not exist in isolation from history, writer, or reader. Rather, responsible readership has an awareness of the author's life (if possible) and of the influences upon it. The function of such awareness is to guide us toward establishing tentative interpretations, which are rethought in light of the meanings the texts begin to make among themselves. Terry Eagleton summarizes this method when he writes that "the novel will gradually construct the context."[33]

Paul Ricoeur defines my understanding of interpretation as it arises from the texts themselves. His thinking accords nicely with Gunn's notion of transcending otherness and with our description of the "strangeness" of metaphor, which gives rise to transformative insight. Gunn, in fact, describes his own critical position in regard to literary and religious investigation in terms of Ricoeur:

> I would still share with Dorothy Van Ghent and Paul Ricoeur the conviction that the fullest portion of any work's meaning lies, . . . to continue the awkward figure, out in front of it, in the hypothetical world—or, better, hypothetical way of looking at the world and orienting oneself within it—which the work is designed both to project and through some alchemy of its own devising, to assess.[34]

He goes on to connect this understanding of meaning as "out in front of" the work with the concept of otherness. "So conceived, literature's function is always that of mediating a form of otherness, a sense of things not quite our own, which it does by inviting us, at least for its own duration, to think accordingly."[35] As we have said, women's reading of women's literature may show that otherness deepens a sense of things *our own*, which are only now coming to speech.

Ricoeur's analysis of metaphor and hermeneutics argues that because the meaning of the text is out in front, our appropriation is not merely subjective. Instead, "the coming to language of the sense and the reference is the coming to language of a world" disclosed by the work. Interpreting is the articulation of the world of the text. Ricoeur calls this "appropriation" the counterpart of "disclosure." Thus, he remarks, the reader does not project himself or herself upon the text; rather "the reader understands him [her] self before the text, before the world of the work." This is the interpretive method I seek in relation to Olsen. As Ricoeur writes further on, "Interpretation is the process by which the disclosure of new modes *of being*—or if you prefer Wittgenstein to Heidegger, of new 'forms of life'—gives to the subject a new capacity of knowing him [her] self."[36]

Ricoeur's description of interpretation is very useful to my description of the religious, since I have said that what may be disclosed by some texts is the awareness of modes of being which have significant and life-changing implications for who we are and how we live.

For Ricoeur, hermeneutics is the analysis of the work in its interaction of metaphor and text (what I referred to earlier as the largest and smallest units of discourse in written works). "The explication of metaphor as a local event in the text," he writes, "contributes to the interpretation itself of the work as a whole." At the same time the metaphor gains its meaning in the text, so that "the power of metaphor proceeds from that of the poem [or text] as a whole."[37] Clearly, this understanding is useful in appropriating Olsen's texts (the stories) in her own language (her own metaphors). Each will be understood in light of the other, and our discourse about them is an attempt to articulate the world they disclose and ourselves in light of it. The surprise or strangeness of metaphor is like the presentation of otherness or transcendence emerging from the text as a whole. Thus, Olsen's metaphors and texts, in bringing news to us of possibilities for a humane and fully blossoming world, may lead us to transcend our former selves and to be reinvented according to the needs and dreams of the lives Olsen represents.

Learning through literature to imagine an alternate world is a highly moral activity, calling us out of complacency toward new possibilities. Imagining ourselves in terms of others' lives may be the greatest human act of which we are capable. Even if we are women who mother, the particular exigencies of the mother's life in Olsen's story "I Stand Here Ironing" requires us to understand the world on her terms, and these are not our own until we enter fully into the world she inhabits. Thus, meeting with another perspective in literature is not simply learning about one foreign to us or simply seeing reflections of ourselves. Rather, it is the experience of meeting ourselves anew, as if we were this one, or as if the world, were like this. Thus, literature by women reflective of women's perspectives does not merely tell women what we already know about our experience but draws us into a world *where we begin to know ourselves* in relation to the vision of the author. Between writer, text, and reader breaks the possibility for new meanings and hence a new creation of ourselves.[38]

1. Dietrich Bonhoeffer, in *Letters and Papers from Prison*, ed. Eberhard Bethge (New York: Macmillan Publishing Co., 1975), says that our only avenue to theology is that of radical openness to the world and an affirmative attitude toward our time. Since World War II, the interest in literature as an avenue to religious comprehensions has risen sharply. Clearly, this interest parallels a rising skepticism toward traditional theological discourse. Giles Gunn goes so far as to say that except for the category of language itself, religious interest is perhaps the primary interest brought to creative literature. Gunn, "The Literary and Cultural Study of Religion: Problems and Prospects," *Journal of the American Academy of Religion* 53 (December 85): 625.

Works by modern and postmodern writers who are clearly influenced by traditional religious comprehensions, from T. S. Eliot to Flannery O'Connor, have often been interpreted in a religious light. This book is sparked by the conviction that visionary, though not necessarily traditionally religious, texts by women writers like Virginia Woolf, Olsen, Adrienne Rich, Doris Lessing, and Alice Walker offer alternative world visions in which we encounter news of transforming possibilities for humanity. I would add that this is true of some modern and contemporary men's literature.

2. I could not hope to document even a representative sample of the recent engagements of literary and religious scholars with narrative. See Michael Goldberg, *Theology and Narrative: A Critical Introduction* (Nashville, Tenn.: Abingdon, 1981). Stephen Crite's article, "The Narrative Quality of Experience," *Journal of the American Academy of Religion* 39 (September 1971): 291–311, is a cornerstone study in this area.

3. (Indianapolis: The Bobbs-Merrill Company, 1969), p. 13. Again, the scholarship in this area is vast. Gilkey's book is a good introduction to the problem.

4. "Metaphor and the Main Problem of Hermeneutics," in *The Philosophy of Paul Ricoeur: An Anthology of His Work*, ed. Charles E. Reagan and David Steward (Boston: Beacon Press, 1978), pp. 134–148.

5. As an example of feminist deconstructionist criticism, see Barbara Johnson, *The Critical Difference: Essays in the Contemporary Rhetoric of Reading* (Baltimore: The Johns Hopkins University Press, 1980).

6. *Naming the Whirlwind*, p. 11.

7. For a discussion of women's awakening to false consciousness, see Kathryn Rabuzzi, *The Sacred and the Feminine: Toward a Theology of Housework* (New York: The Seabury Press, 1982), pp. 8–12. All of Mary Daly's work beginning with *Beyond God the Father* (Boston: Beacon Press, 1972) has been an attempt to write about and to create a language for woman's consciousness.

8. Adrienne Rich, *On Lies, Secrets and Silence: Selected Prose 1966–1978* (New York: W. W. Norton & Co., 1979); Mary Daly, *Gyn/Ecology: The Metaethics of Radical Feminism* (Boston: Beacon Press, 1978); Nelle Morton, *The Journey Is Home* (Boston: Beacon Press, 1985); Anne Wilson Schaef, *Women's Reality* (Minneapolis, Minn.: Winston Press, 1981); Carol Christ, *Diving Deep and Surfacing: Women Writers on Spiritual Quest* (Boston: Beacon Press, 1980).

9. *Beyond God the Father*, p. 8.

10. *Journey Is Home*, p. 99.

11. *Sexism and God-Talk: Toward a Feminist Theology* (Boston: Beacon Press, 1984), pp. 12–13. For another inductive attempt to do theology and talk about transcendence, see Peter Berger, *A Rumor of Angels* (Garden City, N.Y.: Doubleday & Co., 1970) and his more recent and expansive *Facing Up to Modernity: Excursions in Society, Politics, and Religion* (New York: Basic Books, 1977).

12. *Philosophical Hermeneutics*, trans. and ed. David E. Linge (Berkeley: University of California Press, 1976).

13. Goldberg, *Theology and Narrative*, pp. 12–15.

14. See Paul Ricoeur's essay "The Critique of Religion," in *Philosophy of Ricoeur*, pp. 213–22. Also see Rosemary Ruether's analysis of Marxism in *The Radical Kingdom: The Western Experience of Messianic Hope* (New York: Harper & Row, 1970).

15. P. 89.
16. P. 219.
17. *Beyond God the Father*, pp. 44–68.
18. Along with Daly and Morton, see Naomi Goldenberg, *Changing of the Gods* (Boston: Beacon Press, 1979).
19. *Journey Is Home*, pp. 87–88. For a sampling of how women writers are reinterpreting spirituality and politics, see *The Politics of Women's Spirituality: Essays on the Rise of Spiritual Power within the Feminist Movement*, ed. Charlene Spretnak (Garden City, N.Y.: Anchor Books, 1982).
20. "Literary and Cultural Study of Religion," 62.
21. Paul Tillich, *Theology of Culture* (1959). Reprint. London: Oxford University Press, 1978.
22. *Journey Is Home*, p. 89.
23. Ibid., pp. 90–91.
24. Nelle Morton writes that if the women's movement "says nothing else to us, as church people, it can call us to question the source of our identity." Ibid., p. 8.
25. While didactic criticism is not exactly in vogue these days, it can be argued that feminist criticism is essentially moral and didactic. See Josephine Donovan's "Beyond the Net: Feminist Criticism as a Moral Criticism," *Denver Quarterly* 17 (Winter 1983): 40–57. One can draw the conclusion from Terry Eagleton's *Literary Theory: An Introduction* (Minneapolis: University of Minnesota Press, 1983) that all types of criticism are, in the last analysis, didactic. They seek to further their own notions of "right reading," if not "right acting." Henry James once wrote that "every out-and-out realist who provokes serious meditation may claim that he [sic] is a moralist: for that, after all, is the most that the moralists can do for us. They sow the seeds of virtue; they can hardly pretend to raise the crop." In *Theory of Fiction: Henry James*, ed. James E. Miller, Jr. (Lincoln: University of Nebraska Press, 1972), p. 304.
26. In *Modern American Cultural Criticism: Proceedings of the Conference, March 17–18, 1983*, ed. Mark Johnson (Warrensburg: Central Missouri State University, 1983), p. 36.
27. *Speaking in Parables* (Philadelphia: Fortress Press, 1975); see also her second book, *Metaphorical Theology* (Philadelphia: Fortress Press, 1982).
28. Quoted in Sally Cunneen, "Tillie Olsen: Storyteller of Working America," 573.
29. For creative reflection upon how "secular" and women's experience may reinterpret the "sacred," see Judith Plaskow's "The Coming of Lilith: Toward a Feminist Theology," in *Womanspirit Rising: A Feminist Reader in Religion*, ed. Carol Christ and Judith Plaskow (San Francisco: Harper & Row, 1979), pp. 198–209. See Plaskow's other essays in the same collection, as well as her book, *Sex, Sin, and Grace: Women's Experience and the Theologies of Reinhold Niebuhr and Paul Tillich* (Washington, D.C.: University Press of America, 1980); and Ellen Umansky, *Lily Montagu and the Advancement of Liberal Judaism: From Vision to Vocation* (Lewiston, N.Y.: E. Mellen Press, 1984).
30. Christ's and Rabuzzi's books are noted in notes 8 and 7, respectively. Rosemary Ruether, *Womanguides: Readings toward a Feminist Theology* (New York: Beacon Press, 1985). Elisabeth Schüssler Fiorenza, *In Memory of Her: A Feminist Theological Reconstruction of Early Christian Origins* (New York: Crossroads, 1983).
31. Josephine Donovan's essay, "Beyond the Net," exemplifies the focus on images of women in literature. See *Religion and Sexism: Images of Women in the Jewish and Christian Traditions*, ed. Rosemary Ruether (New York: Simon and Schuster, 1974), for a religiously engaged use of the method. As an example of the various strategies employed by feminist literary critics, see *Writing and Sexual Difference*, ed. Elizabeth Abel (Chicago: The University of Chicago Press, 1982).
32. *Texts of Terror: Literary Feminist Readings of Biblical Narratives* (Philadelphia: Fortress Press, 1984), p. 3. I am much in debt to Trible's scholarship. Though my area of investigation is different from hers, I have learned much from her

readings, and her method of discovering muted themes through language connections is a methodological guide for this book.

33. *Literary Theory*, p. 88.

34. "Threading the Eye of the Needle: The Place of the Literary Critic in Religious Studies," *Journal of the American Academy of Religion"* 43 (June 75): 191.

35. Ibid.

36. "Metaphor and the Main Problem of Hermeneutics," *Philosophy of Paul Ricoeur*, p. 145.

37. Ibid. p. 147.

38. For the reader who is primarily a feminist literary critic, these remarks should help place this work. Like Judith Fetterley, I assume that literary criticism "is a political act whose aim is not simply to interpret the world but to change it by changing the consciousness of those who read and their relation to what they read." Clearly, I am also assuming, as Elaine Showalter does in her own "gynocriticism," that we must read women's literary worlds through female-centered consciousness. This study participates in two strands of feminist literary criticism: women writers and depictions of women in literature. Fetterley is quoted in Sydney Janet Kaplan, "Varieties of Feminist Criticism," in *Making a Difference: Feminist Literary Criticism*, ed. Gayle Greene and Coppélia Kahn (New York: Methuen, 1985), p. 40. See Showalter's article in Abel, ed., *Writing and Sexual Difference.*

History and Identity

The Hope for Change

As we discover, we remember; remembering, we
discover, and most intensely do we experience this
when our separate journeys converge.

EUDORA WELTY
One Writer's Beginnings

There are words like *Liberty*
That almost make me cry.
If you had known what I know
You would know why.

LANGSTON HUGHES
Selected Poems

Ultimately, the goals of spirituality and of revolutionary
politics are the same: to create a world in which love,
equality, freedom, and fulfillment of individual and
collective potential is possible.

HALLIE IGLEHART
"The Unnatural Divorce of
Spirituality and Politics"

A brief introduction into the historical events and circumstances that have shaped Olsen will provide a "cultural horizon" for our reading of her literature and will acquaint us with some specific historical touchstones that have given rise to her vision.[1] Born in Nebraska in 1912 or 1913, Tillie Olsen lived as a youngster first in South, and later in North Omaha; her world was the American Midwest. A first-generation American, she came to know the United States both as a place of promise and as a country economically, socially, racially, and sexually divided. Around her she saw farmers suffering from a depressed agricultural industry and miners and packinghouse workers (among them her father) who were beginning to organize against management. Thus her first memories were colored by labor struggles, the realities of the workplace, the desire of laborers for a job and dignity, and a growing American socialism. She heard speeches by visiting political orators like Eugene Debs, educated herself in the city library, and knew the personal threat of capitalism when her father was blacklisted after the failure of a packinghouse strike in the early twenties.

Olsen's parents, Samuel and Ida Lerner (her mother's unmarried name was Beber), had been revolutionary Jews in Russia who were making a new life in America. Woven into Olsen's young consciousness then was also her parents' immigrant identity, the Yiddish ideal of enlightenment they embodied, and a spirit of hope, for freedom and justice that had imbued their lives in Russia. The young Lerner saw in her parents' lives and in the lives of American workers and socialists action undertaken for the purpose of gaining dignity for all people, in phrases of the day, for a living wage, for bread and roses.

From the writing Olsen was to create as an adult, we might conclude that she was especially fortunate in that her early experience was grounded in the particular exigencies of an American time and place and yet was also touched by a larger, more universal awareness of other worlds where people struggled for liberty. Though she did not grow up in an Orthodox Jewish family by any means (her parents were self-proclaimed atheists), Olsen received the socialist and Yiddish influence of her parents as a profound international concern. She has said her parents chose what they would keep of a Jewish identity, and it was largely the humanism of Yiddishkeit. Socialism provided the political lens for viewing the severe inequities of life in Russia and later in the United States and gave people like the Lerners a means of uniting with others to fight aggressively for change.

Born close to the time of the 1881-82 Russian pogroms, Olsen's parents belonged to a generation in rapid transition. They were active in the 1905 revolution against the czar. When it was crushed, they, like many others, fled to the United States. According to Olsen, her father escaped the night before he was to march to Siberia and almost certain death. From her comments in talks and interviews and from a recent essay about her mother, we know that their early life was characterized by economic extremity, by physical and personal restriction (Jews could not travel freely or enter professions of their choice), and by fear of pogroms.[2] In speaking about that past and Orthodox Judaism, Olsen acknowledges that the old ways made it possible for Jews to survive in a hostile environment and lent them the "strength to continue living."[3] Her parents' dream, however, was for more than survival.

With nineteenth-century industrialization, Russian life had begun to change. A time came when Jews could leave the ghetto. The Jewish Enlightenment or *Haskalah* was born as circumstances began to make it possible to imagine a different future. Many, like Olsen's parents, broke with traditional religion, a structure of life so tied with the old constrictions. They began to ask, in Olsen's words, "'That old, old way? Is it now the way?'"[4] And though it was anguishing for their parents, they answered "no."

For centuries, Russian Jews had had little choice but to hope in the Messiah. Believing in a power beyond their own, they waited for deliverance. But as people gained some power over their lives, they began to think that they might initiate their own liberation. Indeed, the old God seemed one who denied justice, learning, and freedom by requiring endless waiting. Emerging Yiddish culture, on the other hand, suggested that the true way for Jews was to work for greater economic justice, learning, and human expansiveness in this world.

Olsen has expressed the character of this new way in an interview, saying that in the Bund—an organization of Russian Jews influenced by socialism and committed to realizing the basic human freedoms—was "worked out a different way of keeping faith." To be a Jew "was to eradicate, uproot, rid the world of the breeding grounds for its hatreds, it injustices, its wants and ignorance."[5] Thus the idea dawned that a people must be its own messiah, an idea that would also grow indigenously among American workers when Tillie Lerner was growing up.

Once in America, Olsen's father traveled west to Nebraska on the promise of farm work. He and Ida were married after their arrival and lived for a short time on a farm when Olsen was very small. The second of six children, Tillie was born on 14 January 1912 or 1913 (Olsen says she comes from a family that didn't have birth certificates), probably in Omaha. Her father worked at paper hanging and in the packinghouses and become active in the state's Socialist party, holding office as state secretary. Her mother labored at raising the children. For the Lerners, the American labor movement now became the focus for defining a politically committed life, though always, as Olsen has said, it was not ideological rhetoric but "how they lived" that infused her with a socialist sensibility. She tells, for example, of how her father helped organize a caravan of men to go to Tulsa, Oklahoma, where they would rebuild blacks' homes after a particularly violent race riot in the twenties. According to Olsen, the black section of town had been almost entirely burned to the ground.[6]

We sense the continuation of the Lerners' determination that the world be a place for more flowering life throughout Olsen's writing. Rather than focusing upon custom and tradition, the Yiddishkeit that had influenced them as young people rose out of people's present needs and experiences and gave expression to their vision for a new life. The literature that came out of this new Jewishness, like the stories of Isaac Loeb Peretz, was faithful to the enduring values of the past (including knowledge of harms to humanity and community cooperation and sharing) and a hungry searching for enlightened ways of enhancing ordinary people's lives. As the heroine Eva says in Olsen's novella, "Tell Me a Riddle," what must be taught is human oneness, not separations and divisions. Olsen's early socialist writing found its best expression in a commuity identity, which declared the dignity and value of workers' lives and dreamed of a world of shared beauties as well as fair wages.

The decade before Olsen's birth was one of political and social ferment in the States. Rapidly expanding socialist and proletarian politics were superseding middle-class reformist movements like populism. The change had to do very largely with the industrialization of agriculture and industry. From 1850 to 1900, the number of factory workers increased ten times.[7] Working conditions were often hazardous to health and certainly indifferent to the individual. Confrontations like the Chicago Haymarket affair (1886), the homestead strike against Carnegie Steel (1892), and the Pullman strike in Chicago (led by Debs; 1894) began to create solidarity among workers and align them against soldiers and police.

Extreme instances of inhumane working conditions like the Triangle Waist Company fire of 1911 (which killed 146 workers, mostly women, as the result of numerous violations of fire codes), and of violence against workers like the Ludlow massacre (resulting in the deaths of women and children), stirred socialist passion not merely for reform but for a new society.[8] Increasingly, workers learned through experience that individual action could be crushed; only through unified action could they hope for change. Debs led the American Socialist party (formed in 1905), the workings of which Olsen knew personally through her father. In her memory, Debs was a visionary as well as an activist. She recalls that he gave imagistic description to the twin values of individuality and community by comparing an envisioned future with a symphony. Each person would play his or her own instrument, and together all would create a great harmony.[9]

Like Debs, Big Bill Haywood (leader of the radical Industrial Workers of the World, formed in 1905), was a prominent radical leader whose character helped establish the Left as Olsen knew it growing up. His experience as a miner, who saw the ghastly effects of lead poisoning on miners and determined to fight against the dehumanizations fostered by capitalistic industry, illustrates how working conditions in the States gave rise to radical activism.[10] Haywood preached that where working men and women were reduced to a function, they were indeed cogs in a machine; clearly, their lives were not thought worth protecting, and for all of their hardship and labor, they were vastly underpaid. Growing up in the Midwest when Haywood was organizing Wobblies, Olsen knew stories of mining community hardships and injustices. The mining experience we see depicted at the beginning of Olsen's thirties novel, Yonnondio, and in Agnes Smedley's Daughter of Earth, for example, came to be as the result of capitalistic industrialization. What these two novels reflect is how it was for the women who tried to create and sustain life in these inhumane circumstances. Both writers show that exhausted and defeated men often vented their rage at women and children who had even less power than the miners to bring about change in their lives. Later, in her novel, The

Dollmaker, Harriette Arnow was to depict a similar circumstance, in which women followed men to the factories of Detroit, losing their dreams and even their lives or their chidren's to the factories, the railroad yards, and the streets.[11]

The literature of working America had a long foreground for Olsen. She had read Rebecca Harding Davis, Theodore Dreiser, Jack London, Upton Sinclair, and Willa Cather, among others. Thus, when Rideout describes early socialist novels in his book *The Radical Novel in the United States 1900-1954*, he delineates an American genre which reached new heights and gained a larger audience as Olsen was growing up, though it was not a new development for Olsen herself:

> Against the workers, both native and immigrant, stands the corporate power of capitalism, a system which, as novel after novel insists, not only creates war as a means to market its surplus products, but is itself a state of war. The death and injuries of men and women in industry are the steady attritional casualties. There are no noncombatants; war is carried to the young and old of the slums in the form of poverty and disease. Strikes are the open fighting, and when these occur, capitalism throws off all pretenses of benevolence and brings naked opposition to bear on the workers.[12]

We do find certain motifs of working class literature in Olsen's novel, *Yonnondio*, composed in the thirties and describing life in the twenties: injury to labor, the diseases of poverty and poverty as a disease, strikes and strikers. But Olsen was to portray not only the violence and the degredation that characterized so many workers' lives; she also represented the valor and beauty of working people's struggles for education, art, and family harmony. In detailing one heroine's life, for example, she tells of a broken prism placed in the window, which brings the beauty and miracle of the rainbow into the woman's kitchen. Her early writing is a blend of realism— exposing the "terrible face of things beneath the capitalist mask"[13]—and romanticism—showing what could be the noble and divine face of the worker, the mother, and the child.

Olsen's own early life was a blend of limiting realities and visionary influences. As her critics have noted, she grew up in the alliance of American socialism and leftist writers, of workers and political orators that emerged early in the century. Economic necessity required that Olsen drop out of high school after the eleventh grade to go to work. And while she now points out that this was more education than most women of her generation received and that she "crossed the tracks" in Omaha to go to a good school, Tillie Lerner also grew up knowing from experience that money or the lack of it was a great determiner of life. As Deborah Rosenfelt recounts, Olsen's youth included work a a tie presser, hack writer, model, mother's helper, ice-cream packer, book clerk, waitress, and punch-press operator.[14] As illustrated in Olsen's earliest fiction, the Midwest acquainted the young girl with other workers: miners, slaughterhouse workers, and sharecroppers.

Though economically struggling, the family was nevertheless rich in asociations. Growing up in an integrated Omaha neighborhood, even visiting the black church on the corner, Olsen was able later to write "O Yes," the story of a friendship between a black girl and a white. She remembers that when Carl Sandburg came to Omaha to read and play his guitar, a special teacher made sure she was there.[15] As state secretary of the Nebraska Socialist party, Samuel Lerner often brought party leaders to the house when they came to town. One can imagine that as a girl, Olsen often fell asleep to the music of mingled immigrant, Midwestern, and political voices, mixing strategies for socialist action with memories of the old country.

Olsen's Omaha childhood was also rich in reading, although academic learning could not always be a priority; even before quitting school, she did odd jobs to contribute to the family income, like shelling peanuts after school. She first read modern poetry in a Haldeman-Julius 5¢ Blue Book published in Kansas and made to fit in a workingman's pocket. In the fiction category, she read almost through the M's in the Omaha library before she was interrupted by adult responsibilities. Thus much of Olsen's learning was self-won through early discipline. When she was in school, she learned—as others did—through recitation, so that she knew poets like Longfellow and Whittier by heart. And she has remarked that part of her early education was derived from texts of the popular culture like blues music and movies. According to Olsen, she was touched by eloquent language expressions—in oral speech, in classical literature, in song—that were a unique gift of being an American in that time and place. She expresses a sense of deep gratitude for her literary and linguistic heritage in Nebraska: among different kinds of people and workers, in the library, at political meetings, and in school.[16]

As she grew, bound volumes of the *Comrade,* and contemporary magazines like *Modern Quarterly,* the *Liberator,* and later *New Masses* (carrying articles by writers like Mike Gold and John Dos Passos), as well as socialist and communist pamphlets "'laying around [the] house'" were a part of Olsen's reading.[17] As she

explains in her Notes to the Feminist Press edition (1972) of Davis's
Life in the Iron Mills, that story—from a bound, water-stained, and
coverless volume of the *Atlantic Monthly* bought in an Omaha
junkshop when she was fifteen—commissioned her, saying:
"Literature can be made out of the lives of despised people. . . . You,
too, must write."[18] Though Olsen's reading was by no means
exclusively leftist, her interests were particularly toward writers "'of
social concern.'" Among these and in addition to the American
realists named earlier, were "Walt Whitman; European social critics
like Ibsen and Hugo . . . black writers like W. E. B. Du Bois and
Langston Hughes; American women realists like Elizabeth Madox
Roberts . . . and Ellen Glasgow; as well as Leftists like . . . John Dos
Passos, Mike Gold . . . and social feminists like Olive Schreiner."[19]

Together, the reading, her girlhood in the American working
class, and the political climate of her household prepared Olsen to
ask questions about the intersection of political ideology and artistic
expression. In the thirties, she would struggle with the relation of
politics to literature, entertaining thoughts of art by the masses,
asking, with other leftist writers, How can art be effectively used for
social and political causes?[20] Very early, she faced ethical dilemmas
that elicited from her political and literary ponderings; for example,
the disadvantages faced by black neighbors were not only the
limitations of poor schooling, poor jobs, and limited opportunity, but
loss of dignity and injury to self-definition and self-worth.

During her teens, Olsen recorded her experience in journals. An
excerpt from one reveals her already universalist concerns:

> Have been reading Nietzsche and *Modern Quarterly.* I must write out,
> clearly & concisely, my ideas on things. I vascillate so easily. And I am
> so-so sloppy in my mental thinking. What are my *true* opinions, for
> instance, on socialism, what life should be, the future of literature, true
> art, the relations between the sexes, where are we going. . . .
>
> Yes, I must write it out. . . .
>
> Later: That's quite simple to say, but there are so few things one can be
> sure & definite about—so often I am pulled both ways.[21]

The passage emphasizes the future: "What life should be," "the
future of literature," "where are we going." We notice the young
writer's questioning tone in this personal inventory. Her later
writing poses the same question to readers—"where are we going"—
asking the audience to participate in the struggle for a democratic
and flowering world. The tone of the pondering in these early entries
is evaluative, the impulse of the thought toward establishing
consistent values for a life.[22]

The American depression of the 1930s and the Communist party were the historical catalysts for Olsen's budding consciousness.[23] In the early years of that decade, Tillie Lerner became a political activist, a writer, and a mother.

Her experience in the party grew out of her socialist inheritance (though she notes that her brothers and sisters did not join), and was also born of necessity. Like many others, she joined for economic as well as ideological reasons. She could no longer depend on parents and needed a community of support. The Young Communist League gave Olsen a sense of commuity, a place to belong, and though it valued political message over artistic concerns, she might not have become the writer she is without the party's encouragement and the avenues it offered for publishing.[24] The primary attraction of the Y. C. L. for Olsen was its aggressiveness in addressing the problems of the time, expecially workers' isolation and vulnerability.

Diversity characterized the radical movement as Olsen knew it, for while the communists established the far Left in the thirties, many contributed to the cause: intellectuals who had been influenced by progressivism and socialism, farmers and factory workers learning the value of unionizing, the poor and the college graduate out of work. Some abandoned liberal morality and the laissez faire of the status quo while others, like Olsen, had grown up with socialist values. A spokesman for far Left writers throughout the thrities, Michael Gold attacked the heart of the capitalist system: competition and profit. "'One must decide now between two worlds—cooperative or competitive, proletarian or capitalist,'" he wrote.[25] The words will find resonance in our reading of Olsen, since she is still imagining in her latest writing the beginnings of a cooperative world, a world that has never yet been, but which is really our only choice if we wish to survive.

Certainly, one notion criticized by the proletarian literature emerging before and during Olsen's young adulthood was the mythology of rugged individualism.[26] Like its economic counterparts of private ownership and private profit, the idea of isolated self-betterment seemed clearly outdated and was being replaced by visions, like Debs', of collective identity. In writing and in political activism, the Left espoused the values of community good, integration, common responsibility, and human fellowship, themes we recognize in Olsen's writing from the fifties and sixties. For Olsen, the thematic emphasis on community arose largely from her focus upon women and children. In her penetrating portrayals of domestic situations in her first and second periods, she represents the interconnectedness of the characters' destinies. A loss to one is a loss to all.

Concerning Olsen's artistic sensibility and the thirties, Edmund Wilson's position, neither Marxist nor liberal, is instructive. He criticized the literary Right for inventing as its theoretical ideal a nonexistent past and the Left for locating the ideal in the future. Neither realized that "'art is something that has to grow out of the actual present substance of life to meet life's immediate needs.'"[27] Having grown up in the working class and among the less socially and politically advantaged, Olsen knew of inherited injustices as well as of plans and dreams for a different kind of experience. Thus her materials were drawn from the "present substance of life." In a similar way, her experiences as a woman and a mother as she was beginning her first fiction would mean personal acquaintance with the demands of child, home, and work, so that her feminist vision is one filtered through many traditional female realities. Her sense of life and its needs arises largely from actual circumstances, which have so characterized and limited women's lives.

Joining the Young Communist League, Olsen attended the party school in Kansas City, worked to support her compatriots, and was jailed for passing out leaflets to packinghouse workers. She picketed, walked with strikers, and wrote essays for communist publications. An illness in 1932 sent her home, where she began to write the novel, *Yonnondio: From the Thirties.*[28] The month she began, she was also pregnant with her first child, who was born before Olsen turned twenty. In an article on Olsen and the thirties, Erica Duncan records Olsen's own evaluation of the intersection of personal and national events. Political activism, mothering, and writing, she wrote, "burst . . . the thick wall of self," giving her a sense of the realities that allowed her to see "how social forces and social circumstances limit and shape what one can do."[29] She worked on the novel for several years but never completed it.

In 1933, Tillie met Jack Olsen, a fellow communist and Union printer whom she would later marry. By 1934, both were in San Francisco, where they were involved in maritime politics. She and Jack, along with other Y. C. L. members, were arrested for "vagrancy," and out of that experience she wrote one of her essays from this period. Political activism and caretaking reponsibilities began to eclipse the literary activity Olsen had managed in the important years of 1932–34. What emerged for Tillie Olsen was the three-faceted life that would be hers for the next two decades: mothering, political and paid work, and lastly, writing. The first two provided crucial knowledge and understanding that inspired the writing, and yet the realities and demands of work (domestic, paid, political) also eclipsed it.

Placing Olsen among other writers who began in or wrote about the thirties, we notice some distinguishing characteristics.[30] Olsen was occupied in her own life with rearing a child and making a living at the same time that she was intensely involved in political action. In conversation, Olsen has remarked that she sometimes took her young daughter Karla with her when she went to the waterfront where political organizing was going on. Even when Karla was away with relatives, Olsen was emotionally and intellectually preoccupied with her well-being. At the same time, this mother/writer was aware of human struggles all over the globe: in the Philippines, Spain especially, Guatemala, Africa, Chile, China. Being of working-class origin, Olsen always felt like something of an oddity in literary society. She was certainly never in the mainstream. Instead she was as inclined to identify with the literature of minority culture as with established greats on the Left, as her work with the Federal Writers Project exemplifies. In California in the mid-thirties, she recorded the life stories, songs, and dreams of Slavs, Filipinos, and Mexicans.[31]

Finally, while women were welcomed as co-workers in the party, and writers like Gold came from working-class backgrounds, women were not the editors of leftist magazines and their voices were not heard as often or with as much authority as were men's. As Baum, Hyman, and Michel remark; "In the literature of the thirties, women were much more likely to be indirectly connected with artistic, intellectual, or political circles as the helpmates of male figures."[32]

Thus an array of human realities, of opportunities and foreshortenings, perhaps most immediate her own mothering, converged in Olsen's life and gave matter to her artistic sensibility. Living through the depression rearing a young child, Olsen had an experience different from that reflected by the better-known writers on the Left or male Communist-party members. If her perspective, as she describes it, was often "trespass vision" in relation to the political and working worlds, many writers of the thirties had less access to, or were less convinced of, the crucial need to tell about the circumstances and realities in the home, where children were born and reared and mothers struggled to make a meal or turn a quilt into a coat.[33] Although a writer like Henry Roth offers description of home life, it is still a boy's perspective, that is, the perspective of one who will leave home. Similarly, a writer like Alfred Kazin, writing lovingly of his mother, is able to romanticize the sound of her sewing machine because he did not and would never sit for hours at such a machine.[34] Olsen's perspective was intimately familial, and she saw the decade from a vantage point largely dictated by the combination of her sex and working-class background. As Olsen has written in a letter, "In the 30's, as well as in the 40's, 50's, all was rooted for me in the family and workplace."[35]

In the 1940s and early 1950s, Tillie Olsen, with Jack, was rearing four daughters and working to support them.[36] The blankness of that time in sketches Olsen provides of her life may symbolize the dearth of writing. In *Silences*, Olsen's collection of prose essays analyzing the circumstances of writers and why they don't write, she offers a self-portrait of those years:

> In the twenty years I bore and reared my children, usually had to work on a paid job as well, the simplest circumstances for creation did not exist. Nevertheless writing, the hope of it, was "the air I breathed, so long as I shall breathe at all." In that hope, there was conscious storing, snatched reading, beginnings of writing, and always "the secret rootlets of reconnaissance."

> When the youngest of our four was in school, the beginnings struggled toward endings. . . .

> Bliss of movement. A full extended family life; the world of my job (transcriber in a dairy-equipment company); and the writing, which I was somehow able to carry around with me through work, through home. Time on the bus . . . the stolen moments at work . . . deep night hours . . .

> In such snatches of time I wrote what I did in those years, but there came a time when this triple life was no longer possible.[37]

The emphasis in the passage is on the years (mid 1950s) near the time when Olsen was awarded her first writing grant, allowing time off from work to write. What Olsen does not specifically mention here and what few of her critics have emphasized is the influence of 1940s political and international circumstances on her life and especially her literary vision. She has experienced great personal and political anguish over the American bombs dropped on Japan and the Cold War that followed World War II. Though the American Communist party had been forced to retreat and though Olsen's daily focus had, of necessity, turned more and more toward the domestic sphere, the bomb became a lasting personal emblem, spurring her on to begin writing again, to say to readers: There is another way, the human way of making change to enhance, not destroy, life.[38]

Later in the same period, Olsen began to work on the stories in the *Tell Me a Riddle* collection. Concerns with racial injustice since girlhood found expression in "O Yes." The story, whose roots

precede the civil rights movement (beginning in 1955-56 when
Central High of Little Rock, Arkansas, was in the news) is prophetic
in its portrayal of the crucial ways in which racism is perpetuated
among children. It and the other stories of *Tell Me a Riddle* were
writen in and around the political atmosphere of McCarthyism,
which touched her family directly.

In 1956 Tillie Olsen applied for and was awarded a Stanford
University Creative Writing Fellowship, and in 1959 she received a
Ford Foundation Grant in Literature. She became what she calls in
Silences "a writing writer." Other awards and opportunities
followed, but, as Olsen has said, time awarded for creative work does
not always coincide with the time of fullness when the work could
have been most fruitfully pursued.[39]

Two of the essays later to be included in *Silences* were composed
in the sixties, a decade that saw a climax of the civil rights
movement as well as the birth of the modern women's movement.
The new focus upon female authors elicited Olsen's writing during
this period. Her childhood and adult reading had included important
and sometimes undervalued women writers, and thus, when she was
invited to talk about literature by women by a session of the
Modern Language Association, she was able to draw from a long
education. As interest grew in the subjects of gender and language
and "women's topics" in literature, interest grew in Olsen's writing
as well, bringing enthusiastic readers to her stories.

For many women in the movement (readers and writers), Tillie
Olsen became a leading advocate for recovering women's voices and
making heard the experiences of women. What distinguishes her
feminist impulse from many others is her acute interest in what
women have known about life through traditionally defined
experiences of caretaking and domestic work. Speaking about the
women who led the feminist movement of the seventies, and their
disdain for their mothers' lives, Olsen has said, "There was nothing
[in writing] to tell them what the true content of their mother's life
was. . . . There was no way to see what the real achievement in
motherhood is."[40]

Olsen's vision, shaped by her parents' socialism, by an Omaha
girlhood, by American communism, by postwar threats and
continued injustices, is at once personal and political and has been
lifelong. These influences have moved her to approach spiritual
questions of value, action, and belief through situations traditionally
thought of as secular, especially the workplace and home. The
optimism discernable in her writing may also be traced in particular
to American socialism and to the Yiddishkeit focus on

enlightenment. Filtered through the historical realities of American working-class life, Olsen's literary vision, as begun in the thirties, suggests a fervent hope for dignity and freedom that immigrants shared with American workers. In Olsen the vision is expanded by a diverse cast of characters: blacks, Asians, Jews, working-class whites.[41]

Olsen has chosen, through critical reevaluation, to memorialize the accomplishments of her subjects—farm workers, mothers, immigrants, children—and to weave the desire for a better world out of their longings. Her writing stems from a political atmosphere and from lives lived according to ideals she knew as a girl and young woman, not from her acquaintance with novel or alternative philosophies she encountered later. (She did not need to read Marx, for example, to understand a socialist economic argument.) As a writer, she exemplifies a largely unacclaimed American tradition of discovery and invention through necessity. Like the women of earlier generations who created quilts out of discarded clothes and other remnants, she brings a new comprehension of life and its possibilities out of histories and hopes that appear hopeless or beyond repair.

While the 1930s were for Olsen a shaping period, offering the experience of communal struggle for the common good, she remained firmly on the Left, even after the exigencies of that decade had passed and the party had lost power. In the forties and fifties and to the present, she has found sufficient cause and belief to remain sure of the values of her upbringing, though her focus has become more specifically feminist.

Indeed, Olsen's experiences as a woman have profoundly shaped her writing and thus her world vision. Though not exclusively, she most often remarks upon her inheritance matrilineally, in terms of her mother's and her grandmothers' lives. Her most acclaimed work, "Tell Me a Riddle," was written "to celebrate a generation of revolutionaries . . . women particularly," who were active in the Bund making "the first great breaks with the past."[42]

The history Olsen draws from to make her literature has been, as she so eloquently states in the Preface to Silences, almost lost to memory because those who made it were and remain circumstantially unable to write their own stories or to record their poetry and song. She must have listened well as a girl and young woman to remembrances of Russian life, to immigrants in San Francisco, to farmers out of work in the twenties and thirties, to her own children, in order to create years later the lives in the Tell Me a Riddle collection.

Olsen's first pregnancy, conjoining personal economic struggle, active participation in the Y. C. L., and her first published writing, symbolizes the limiting female circumstances of her life at the same time that it suggests the perspective (the working mother's) and the concerns (sustaining and nurturing human life; human creativity; the hope for a better future) that are central in her writing. Thus, Olsen's writing contributes in a unique way to our insight about working-class and immigrant women's lives. If women have not been able to write about traditionally male realities (which in present history textbooks seem to be the most crucial to human civilization), few men have cared to write about common family realities in the lives of lower-class working women, and few women who knew those realities have had circumstances allowing them to write. And yet those familial contexts, and the dreams arising from them, may reflect invaluable truths about being human and whole, which must be understood if we are to envision the redemption of individual experience and the objective world.

Looking at Olsen's canon—a partial novel, a thin book of three short stories and a novella, a prose book of reflections on the subject of silence, a later partial novella, and an essay on her mother—we sense that she has not yet told all. While she is still writing, we will never have what she might have written as a young woman if she had been given more encouraging circumstances for artistic expression. On the other hand, part of the riddle of Tillie Olsen is the way in which her brevity and partiality engender so much response from other readers and writers. She seems to pose the questions that engage us most deeply, and in painting a few rare yet universal portraits, she provokes deep meditation in us. Thus, her writing engenders writing, and discloses more than seems actually to be there in the books themselves. To read Tillie Olsen, then, is to read her published work in order to perceive the greater vision that is out in front of it, to use Gunn's terminology. This book is a reading of the envisioned world desired by the characters whose lives, though often spiritless and depleted, miraculously create in us a hunger for more.

When in her notes Olsen writes, "[It] is through having known babies, my own and those of others, my profound belief comes in what is in the human being to be," she reflects an attitude that may be called religious and political.[43] Her vision is born essentially from experience and grounded in a personal history of struggle. Not because her writing advocates religious propositions but because its primary witness is to human courage, pain, and hope, it engages us spiritually. Like parables, her stories present to the reader dilemmas and questions of ultimate significance: Who is one's neighbor? To whom is one bound? What human attainments are of value and what, after all, is true attainment? What is possible when people believe? Who or what is worthy of faith? What hopes inspire our struggle and give us power?

1. This chapter draws heavily on a conversation with Tillie Olsen on 1 June 1986. Factual knowledge was gained from Olsen and from her critics. See, for example, Deborah Rosenfelt, "From the Thirties: Tillie Olsen and the Radical Tradition"; Erika Duncan, "Coming of Age in the Thirties: A Portrait of Tillie Olsen"; and Selma Burkom and Margaret Williams, "De-Riddling Tillie Olsen's Writing," *San Jose Studies* 2 (1976): 65–83.

2. Tillie Olsen, "Dream-Vision."

3. Quoted by Naomi Rubin, "A Riddle of History for the Future." For a fuller discussion of the Russian Jewish contexts, consult Irving Howe, *World of Our Fathers* (New York: Simon and Schuster, Touchstone, 1976), and Baum, Hyman, and Michel, *The Jewish Woman in America* (New York: Plume paperback, New American Library, 1976). Olsen recommends the stories of Isaac Loeb Peretz for an understanding of conditions in the last part of the nineteenth and in the early twentieth century for Russian Jews.

4. Quoted in Rubin, "Riddle of History."

5. Ibid.

6. From conversations with Tillie Olsen, 1983–86.

7. Walter Rideout, *The Radical Novel in the United States, 1900–1954* (Cambridge: Harvard University Press, 1956), p. 6.

8. For fuller understanding of how these kinds of incidents affected the labor movement, see a study like Philip Taft's *Organized Labor in American History* (New York: Harper and Row, 1964). For a study of greater scope, see Philip Foner's *History of the Labor Movement in the United States*, 6 vols. (International Publishing Company, 1947–1986).

9. Related by Duncan, "Coming of Age," 209.

10. See Joseph R. Conlin, *Big Bill Haywood and the Radical Union Movement* (Syracuse University Press, 1969), p. 11.

11. Tillie Olsen, *Yonnondio: From the Thirties.* Agnes Smedley, *Daughter of Earth* (1943). Reprint. Old Westbury, N.Y.: The Feminist Press, 1976. Harriette Arnow, *The Dollmaker* (1954). Reprint. New York: Avon Books, 1972.

12. Rideout, *The Radical Novel*, pp. 81–82.

13. Ibid.

14. Rosenfelt, "From the Thirties," 376.

15. Duncan, "Coming of Age," 209.

16. Most of the information in this paragraph comes from conversations with Olsen, 1983–86. Some of the same facts are reflected in other articles on Olsen.

17. The phrase "laying around [the] house" is the young Tillie Lerner's. Quoted by Rosenfelt, "From the Thirties," 376.

18. Tillie Olsen, *Silences*, p. 117.

19. Rosenfelt, "From the Thirties," 376.

20. These thoughts are reflected in the Rosenfelt article.

21. Quoted by Rosenfelt, "From the Thirties," 377–78.

22. Written twenty-five years later, Olsen's autobiographical story "I Stand Here Ironing" reflects the same impulse toward understanding an amalgam of interrelated events and subjects, personal, national, and international. The journal excerpt illustrates a driving motivation in Olsen's life, later reflected in the story: the desire to understand both how humans have come to be what they are and how, out of their histories and their human talents, they may begin more humanely.

23. "Requa," Olsen's latest story, is set in the thirties.

24. See Rosenfelt's article "From the Thirties" for an in-depth discussion of how the party hindered and helped Olsen's early career.

25. Quoted in Richard Pells, *Radical Visions and American Dreams* (New York: Harper and Row, Publishers, 1973), p. 76.

26. See Mike Gold's credo, "Toward Proletarian Art," discussed by Rideout, *Radical Novel*, pp. 122–31. See also Gold's essay, "Prize-Fights vs. Color Organs," *Liberator* 5 (March 1922): 26–27.

27. Quoted in Daniel Aaron, *Writers on the Left: Episodes in American Literary Communism* (New York: Harcourt, Brace, and World, 1961), p. 178.

28. The story "The Iron Throat," appeared in *Partisan Review* and later became the first chapter of *Yonnondio.*

29. Quoted in Duncan, "Coming of Age," 37.

30. Among women writers of the time with whom we might compare Olsen are Anzia Yezierska, Meridel LeSueur, Grace Lumpkin, and Josephine Herbst. A study has not been made showing how these women's political activities, mothering (or not), and writing experiences led to different expressions. It could be said that none of them has enjoyed the same critical attention as, say, Theodore Dreiser, Nathanael West, or Langston Hughes.

31. Susan Ware, *Holding Their Own: American Women in the 1930s* (Boston: Twayne Publishers, 1982), p. 147.

32. Baum, Hyman, and Michel, *Jewish Woman in America*, p. 231.

33. Among other places, Olsen uses the concept of "trespass vision" in her analysis of Rebecca Harding Davis, *Silences*, p. 62.

34. Henry Roth, *Call It Sleep* (1934). Reprint. New York: Avon Books, 1962. This book is still considered a classic of the American thirties. His career illustrates what Olsen calls, in *Silences*, a "one-book silence." Alfred Kazin's memory of his mother's sewing, from *A Walker in the City* (New York: Harcourt, Brace, 1951), is quoted in Baum, Hyman, and Michel, *Jewish Woman in America*, p. 247.

35. Tillie Olsen, letter to Elaine Orr, 12 May 1984.

36. Olsen is reserved regarding the intimate details of her marriage. She has not spoken of her first love affair, which gave her Karla, her first daughter. One can conjecture that she remained a single parent for a few years but that she and Jack lived together before they were married in Grace Cathedral in 1944, just before Jack entered the service. One senses in speaking with Olsen her high regard and affection for Jack and for his father, a person, she says, who was very important to her.

37. Olsen, *Silences*, pp. 19–20.

38. Olsen has said that "I Stand Here Ironing" was written during the Stockholm peace initiative to stop nuclear proliferation and the Cold War.

39. *Silences*, p. 41. Other awards, fellowships, and grants include the O. Henry Award for "Tell Me a Riddle" as best story of the year (1961), National Endowment for the Arts, Grant in Literature (1967), Guggenheim Fellowship (1975–76), Unitarian Women's Federation annual "Ministry to Women" Award (1980), May 18th proclaimed "Tillie Olsen Day" in San Francisco (1981), as well as four honorary doctoral degrees. Olsen has taught at Amherst College, Stanford University, M.I.T., and the Universities of Massachusetts and California, and was International Visiting Scholar to Norway.

40. Tillie Olsen, personal interview with the author, San Antonio, Texas, April 1983.

41. If we include Olsen's first poem, "I Want You Women Up North to Know," Olsen's canon includes a significant character from every race.

42. Quoted in the Rubin article.

43. From Olsen's personal files. The dates of Olsen's daughters' births are 1932, 1938, 1943, and 1948.

A Moral View of Representation

Giving Reflection to the Struggle

What was the good of trying to keep your own if when they grew up their days were like your own.
                                        HARRIETTE ARNOW
                                        The Dollmaker

Vision itself can be pregnant, enabling the onlooker to see through the "four eyes" of mother and child at once. The mother opposes "single meaning." There is always the child to take into account—the child in the sentence, the hidden meaning.
                                        NOR HALL
                        The Moon and the Virgin

As a person, woman is a transcendental being, a consciousness and a voice "taking her part in the duet."
                                        NELLY FURMAN
                        "The Politics of Language"

B egun in the 1930s, Tillie Olsen's writing career springs
largely from her sense that working-class people have the
need for and the right to literary representation. Her
conviction that truth may be elicited from the lives of
"despised people," who are without the means and circumstance for
giving voice to their own stories, leads her to write for the sake of
their memory and hope.[1] *Yonnondio: From the Thirties*, her novel
from this period, draws its title from Walt Whitman's poem, part of
which is reprinted as an epigraph:

> Race of the woods, the landscapes free and the falls.
> No picture, poem, statement, passing them to the
>   future:
> Yonnondio! Yonnondio!—unlimn'd they disappear;
> To-day gives place, and fades—the cities, farms,
>   factories fade;
> A muffled sonorous sound, a wailing word is borne
>   through the air for a moment,
> Then blank and gone and still, and utterly lost.

"Yonnondio" is an Iroquois term; used in the poem, it means a
"lament for the aborigines." Published almost four decades after it
was written, Olsen's novel is her attempt to give some voice to the
largely vanished lives of American workers in the 1920s and 1930s,
and thus, in part, an attempt to overcome the loss of history
mourned by Whitman's poem. Her perseverance as a writer has been
fueled by an understanding that she writes for many who might
remain mute without her, their experience "unlimn'd . . . blank and
gone and still, and utterly lost."

Olsen's early work, spanning the years 1930–36 or 1937, can be
interpreted in terms of her moral sense of responsibility for the lives
of forgotten people. By inheritance, by early life experience, and
later, through political activism, she was bound with those whose
worlds she began to write of in her poems, essays, and early fiction:

41

the world of workers, strikers, children, and women. She wrote out of compassion for and identification with their reality. Furthermore, as one whose Jewish ancestors' lives were largely vanished or vanishing, she felt a particular call to remember the past.[2] That sense of commitment and her working life as a writer suggest a particular interpretation of the literary concept of representation.[3]

Since Aristotle, representation has been broadly defined as the reflective and creative redescription of the world out of action, image, setting, character, and plot. In ordinary usage, we mean by the term a depiction of a possible world, a literary drawing of people, circumstance, and choice. In our criticism, we may stress the artist's role as one that gives representation to a time or to a class of people, or we may focus upon a text as a "re-presentation" of human existence, as the portrayal in words of a hypothetical world with consequences for our own.[4]

Elicited by Olsen's writing, the concept of representation can be understood as a moral act of speaking for others through literary visions called forth by their own experience. This definition not only gives attention to the role of writer as the one who shapes the text, but introduces the ethical dimension of the writer's work. Henry James has written that any realist who causes us to meditate deeply about the subject is a moralist.[5] In Olsen's case, her conviction about the value of her subject certainly suggests a moral dimension. Furthermore, her use of Whitman and themes developed throughout her writing suggest her understanding of the working classes in America and elsewhere, as well as turn-of-the-century immigrants and women of all classes, as largely voiceless people. Her writing seeks to limn their experience, to draw it upon the reader's consciousness and thus to effect change in attitudes and habits.

In relation to Olsen's work, the concept of representation just defined also gives attention to the text's disclosure of a vision (a world) from the experiences of its subjects. Thus, while Olsen's work is sparked by a sense of responsibility for voicing certain experiences, within the texts, the world comprehension that we meet as readers evolves through the characters themselves, their circumstances, actions, needs, and hopes. Often, as we will see in Yonnondio, the characters represent one another by carrying memory and concern for other persons in their thoughts. Thus, the concept also arises from within the texts as a way of conceiving one's self in relation with others. As we see in the novel, representing another can have the effect of literally keeping that one alive. In shared or mutual thought on each other's behalf, human beings may transcend the limiting circumstances that hinder their fullest being, Olsen suggests, since concerted efforts toward freedom and blossoming disencumber us of the burdens of competition and greed and liberate our imaginations to create better worlds.

In her early poems and essays, Olsen provides an authorial voice for the struggles of the economically disadvantaged. In reading these pieces, we are struck with the writer's role of representing her subject. In the novel, however, she adopts a more complex form, speaking from the combined perspectives of a mother and daughter and allowing the characters to share the responsibility of representing their own reality and thus of voicing their own hopes. The longer fictive work, then, suggests a focus upon the text as "re-presenting" for us a world and an understanding of human relationships as seen through the eyes of the characters.

From the beginning, Tillie Olsen's art and morality dovetail in the act of writing. A look at the moral code of American leftists and of immigrant Russian Jews in the early decades of the century offers us a historical entrance into Olsen's first period writing. A comprehension of the personal responsibility to represent each other inbued the lives of those in both of these groups. Basically, both recognized the need for solidarity and both interpreted life communally, understanding that the stronger and better off are responsible for the weaker and less fortunate. Leftist and immigrant writers were guided by such attitudes. When Henry Roth and Anzia Yezierska wrote, for example, they were inspired by the conviction that their stories of struggle and poverty might be catalysts for bettering Jewish life in America. Similarly, when Mike Gold wrote his flamboyant essays, he, like the intellectual who took to the streets with the strikers, felt he was voicing the oppressions and aspirations of working-class men and women. Historical experience reflected in literature should lead to change and the envisioning of a better society. Following in a tradition begun by Walt Whitman, what writers like these were trying to do was to enlarge the scope of their moral comprehension so that America as a whole, and not just minority immigrants and leftists, would understand that the well-being of the least powerful must be held equal with that of the powerful.

In writing about the American leftist experience during the period, Richard Pells has characterized "the radical view of the world [as] emphasiz[ing] man's [sic] natural harmony with and dependence on other people." "Community," he writes, "came to mean not only planning and socialism but also a spirit of mutuality, sharing, cooperation, brotherhood and inner peace."[6] A resemblance in Russian Jewish immigrant understanding is clearly reflected in Baum's, Hyman's, and Michel's study of Jewish women in America:

"Eastern European Jewish immigrants were . . . bonded compatriots. Every one of them had a friend or relative in need."[7] The systems of Jewish cooperative help that had originated in Russia were brought to America, where they were strengthened by joining with the labor movement. In a description of Yiddish morality, Joseph Landis offers further reflection to the understanding of community responsibility characteristic of immigrant Jews. Yiddish, he proposes, is "the language of human relatedness in action, of the insistence of man's obligation to be his brother's keeper [sic]."[8]

What all of this suggests in relation to young Tillie Lerner is a moral inheritance, from Russian and American experience, from Jewish and working-class identity, and an example from other writers that perhaps literature could be an agent of change.

As a young woman, Olsen felt a powerful call to action on behalf of the working class, a calling rooted in her Yiddish and working-class inheritance, and the stirring within of literary talents, the exercise of which would need meditation and time. In her first period, Olsen worked toward a solution. Drawing her subjects from history, she offered her voice on behalf of their struggle. When political activism and family responsibility silenced her, before the end of the 1930s, it was the victory of circumstances over vision. Olsen did not choose to stop writing. Rather, her motivation, then as now, was to write "what [would] help change that which is harmful . . . in our time." In her hands, a representation of poverty in America would become a transcending vision of hope, a representation from the perspectives of working-class people of spiritual longing, of the desire for value and wholeness in one's lifetime.[9]

At first polemical and didactic, Olsen's early poems and essays develop the themes of working-class poverty, of capitalistic exploitation, of class struggle, and of revolution. *Yonnondio*, however, begun before these pieces and worked on through 1936 or '37, offers through the characters a vision of human need and love that transcends political program. In her first published poem, "I Want You Women Up North to Know," Olsen transforms history into poetry, and in so doing amplifies rather than romanticizes the debilitating effects of mass production upon the laborer.[10] The poem depicts a mechanistic and capitalistic world in which the lives of many are sacrificed to a few. In the poem, women's flesh and blood are substitutes for thread and dye:[11]

> i want you women up north to know
> how those dainty children's dresses you buy
>   at macy's, wannamakers, gimbels, marshall fields,

are dyed in blood, are stitched in wasting flesh,
down in San Antonio, "where sunshine spends the winter."

I want you women up north to see
the obsequious smile, the salesladies trill
    "exquisite work, madame, exquisite pleats"
vanish into a bloated face, ordering more dresses,
    gouging the wages down,
dissolve into maria, ambrosa, catalina,
    stitching these dresses from dawn to night,
    in blood, in wasting flesh.

The poem invites a Marxist reading. The dresses illustrate alienated labor, since the mothers' work is not for their own children but for the mothers and daughters of the north, who in actuality purchase the time and lifeblood of the mothers down south. The radical depersonalization of capitalistic work suggested by Marx is clearly evident further in the poem. "Maria, ambrosa, catalina"—workers— are the same woman, the same hands, fingers, the same labor, ultimately the same product. Like "Catalina Rodriguez, 24,/ . . . / last stages of consumption," they weave their own deaths. Their value is slight and arbitrarily set: "Three dollars a week,/ two fifty-five,/ seventy cents a week."

The poem was based on a letter by a worker, Felipe Ibarro, appearing in *New Masses* (9 January 1934). Thus, Olsen's voice draws from the many women who experience such debilitating work, through the voice of Ibarro, finally becoming the authorial "I" that opens the poetic address: "I want you women up north to know." The voice becomes a force of solidarity seeking to uphold the women whose work destroys them. Fused in Olsen's representational "I," the multiple experiences of the women stand against the unraveling, dehumanizing, and finally, deadly work created by a capitalistic market. Paradoxically, the voice seems to gain strength as the poem progresses even though the story of overwork told by the voice reveals greater and greater horrors. Unfortunately, perhaps, the voice adopts the declarative mode at the end: " . . . I want you to know,/ I tell you this can't last forever./ I swear it won't." More powerful than the threat is the authorial "I" developed in the poem as a plural voice of many women brought to written expression. This most unabashedly political voice, then, already points to the narrative perspective Olsen will develop in the more subtle art of telling stories from a perspective within the literary world of the work.

Twenty-one or twenty-two when she wrote this poem, Olsen takes a critical stance toward the religion that appears to rob

"Ambrosa Espinoza." She gives her pennies to the church, "to keep the priest in wine," "to keep [her] god incarnate." Given Espinoza's world, the criticism does not seem naive, but in retrospect the authorial insertion later in the poem—heaven "was brought to / earth in 1917 in Russia"—does. What the poem suggests in our discussion is a redefinition of true morality, hence, of true spirituality, which begins in connection with people's actual circumstances.

The second poem, "There Is a Lesson," is another poetizing of politics, this time European.[12] The poem is preceded by a newspaper excerpt:

"All Austrian schools, meanwhile, were closed for an indefinite period under a government decree issued to keep children off the hazardous streets" (15 February 1934, *San Francisco Chronicle*).

The poem follows immediately:

Keep the children off the streets,
    Dollfuss,
there is an alphabet written in blood
    for them to learn,
there is a lesson thundered by collapsed
    books of bodies.

They might be riddled by the bullets
    of knowledge
. . .

there is a volume written with three
    thousand bodies that can never
    be hidden,
there is a sentence spelled by the
    grim faces of bereaved women
there is a message, inescapable, that
    vibrates the air with voices of
    heroes.

In the earlier poem, two materials coalesce; bodies and cloth. Here the bodies weave a message of revolt against fascism. The poem seems to indicate the dire but necessary costs of revolution. Yet the vision is ambiguous, for the images, like those of the earlier poem, are haunting: "riddled by . . . bullets," "grim faces of bereaved women," "deadly gas of revolution." The men's bodies stack in metonymic similarity, while the faces of the women, an image we will see again in *Yonnondio*, elicit the archetypal image of grieving woman.

The central transformation of the poem is the creation of

language, and therefore, of a message, out of death and violence. Blood makes an alphabet; bodies are texts that tell of terror; faces of mourning write a sentence.

This poem, like the earlier one, builds upon another text, a newspaper account of hazardous Austrian streets following Hitler's attempt to annex the country. Though the men, women, and children do not speak in the poem, we sense that it is their experience that gives rise to the voice of protest. In giving written reflection to the voice, Olsen attempts a corporate address, as she did in the earlier poem. The persona echoes the "voices of heroes," letting the fighters for freedom, rather than the personal "I," carry the banner of revolt described in the poem as finally overcoming oppression. Their voices are in the air like a power of nature that cannot be escaped. Olsen seems to be struggling in Whitmanesque fashion, drawing her voice from the masses, making it her personal poetic voice, and yet giving the voice back to the people.

In both poems, a voice of solidarity is raised against the conditions of war (including work that kills). Images of devastation, violence, and death dominate, but through articulation of people's struggle, the voice gains strength. This paradox will become a primary characteristic of Olsen's later work. Significant to our interpretation is the backdrop of destruction out of which Olsen, with historical personages, weaves a representation of struggle. The effect is something like that achieved in the central chapters of Frederick Douglass's *Narrative of the Life of an American Slave*. Though there is no triumph within the texts, we feel the currents of revolt alive in the writer's voice and echoed in the words of the poems. What is missing in these early pieces is a vision of what an alternate and better world might actually be.

Olsen's two essays of this period came out of her own involvement in the Young Communist League and her witness to labor's movement toward unionization. "Bloody Thursday" and the General Strike of 1934, the first general strike in America since 1919, offer the particular context for "The Strike."[13] Among those arrested for picketing was Tillie Lerner. "Thousand Dollar Vagrant" is Olsen's first-person narrative account of her arrest along with three men, including Jack Olsen, who are suspected of Communist party activities.[14]

"Thousand Dollar Vagrant" is prefaced by this remark:

> It was Lincoln Steffens who commanded me to write this story. "People don't know," he informed me, "how they arrest you, what they say, what happens in court. Tell them. Write it just as you told me about it." So here it is.

The young Lerner was asked to write in part because of her story, "The Iron Throat," which had come out in *Partisan Review* just before the strike.[15] Recalling the events of those days, Olsen says she and her friends were among about three hundred arrested and that she wrote not only to tell about her arrest but to tell about the others too. She resented the special treatment that her writer's identity gave her. Yet the story of the arrest, in its textual form, is encouraged by a voice of inspiration, Lincoln Steffens's, undergirding the essay itself.

The narrative begins with the authorial "I," this time clearly the writer herself, yet the essay evolves in the manner of a fiction, with narrative background, conversation between "characters," and summary of events. The writer never assumes a voice or identity outside the story. Instead, she is within the text, as are the men and the police who arrest them all.

A rather simplistic polarization characterizes the essay, a characteristic that we recognize through the first chapters of *Yonnondio*, separating the comrades from the brutalizing police. As a woman, the writer appears less harassed than the men, and freer to observe the inhumane treatment they receive: "Words were lurching out of the head bull's mouth. His small pig eyes floated in red puddles. I gathered he was telling us to move over against the wall. Dave wasn't fast enough for him. He whipped out a blackjack and beat Dave over the head and chest."

Though the essay is an example of political reportage, a genre characterized by its desire to tell, to educate, it is colored by emotion. The personal engagement is further witness to Olsen's early tendency to create, out of political events, a morally inspired representation of dehumanizing situations that both reflects the actual experience and gives voice to those who are exploited and silenced. Olsen has remarked that when she looks back now, the act of police brutality she remembers most vividly was the intentional destruction of a typewriter belonging to a young man who wanted to write and had invested all of his money in the machine.[16]

In the course of the essay, we are told that the writer refused to give her correct name when questioned. She gives her address as "37 Grove," the Western Worker address. Though clearly her secrecy is motivated by a desire to protect family and home from police invasion, in the text her deception is significant for other reasons. By refusing her actual name, she ignores her personal identity and becomes identifiable instead through her solidarity with the cause. The address suggests such an interpretation. In giving it, the young woman places her fate and identity with the strikers. Thus, the personal voice transcends personal identity, and the "I" of the essay represents the workers as a whole.

In "The Strike," Olsen begins by questioning her ability to construct an adequate literary representation. The persona seems to struggle with questions of literary form and duty to her subject, and in the struggling creates a more aesthetic essay. How does one respond to injustice and violence? If in words, what kind of writing is suitable? As opposed to the earlier essay, Olsen's voice seems in conflict with the political causes that require her talents for their expression:

> Do not ask me to write of the strike and the terror. I am on a battlefield, and the increasing stench and smoke sting my eyes so it is impossible to turn them back into the past. You leave me only this night to drop the bloody garment of Todays, to cleave through the gigantic events that have crashed one upon the other, to the first beginning. If I could go away for a while, if there were time and quiet, perhaps I could do it. All that has happened might resolve into order and sequence, fall into neat patterns of words. I could stumble back into the past and slowly, painfully rear the structure in all its towering magnificence, so that the beauty and heroism, the terror and significance of those days, would enter your heart and sear it forever with the vision.

The voice implies an internal conflict between the task of political reporting and the more complex work of giving vision to the whole body of events, desires, provocations, and struggles that resulted in the strike. It is a conflict between historical necessity and artistic invention. Although both before and after writing this essay Olsen sought to reconcile the struggle by creating her art out of historical movements for freedom, at this point in her life, she expresses a feeling of irreconcilable conflict between the two demands.

For our present interest, the passage suggests the need for literary representation that is more than mere factual reporting. Instead, the voice longs to create for an audience a portrait of a people's deepest sense of truth, commitment, and need, a vision in words of the circumstances, beliefs, and values that give rise to action and expression. The desire to "rear the structure in all its towering magnificence" and to "sear [the reader's heart] forever with the vision" suggests the hope for transformation. In this piece, then, we feel the young writer's grasping for literary expression of a just world, though it will take her writing in fiction to bring that vision fully before us.

The imagery of the piece is similar to that of the two poems and the short story that come from the same period ("The Iron Throat"). "The lesson of moving bodies," "letters of blood and hate," "fists of our bodies," for example, are images clearly reflective of "There Is a Lesson." The day described in the essay as "corpse gray, an enormous dead eyelid shutting down on the world" is similar to the archetypal use of dark imagery in "The Iron Throat." In every case, however, the writer infuses the deadly contexts with the voice of solidarity and the light of hope for freedom: "Spurts of song flaming up from downstairs, answered by us, echoed across the gallery," the young journalist exclaims, "solidarity *weaving us all into one being*" (italics mine). In this last phrase we are given a glimpse of Olsen's spiritual vision, of transcending being that comes through shared hearing and shared voice.

Thus, while the journalist persona struggles with the form of her report, the voice remains sure of its source in many voices. A sentence later, she announces: "And for blocks around they hear OUR voice."

The writer's dilemma seems at the end to find its answer in portraiture. One is the composite portrait of two dead strikers, the second is of a pregnant woman who might be any woman. The first is given to the writer by a "voice" rising "from the submerged hearts of the world," by our definition, a spiritual voice:

> The story was the story of any worker's life, of the thousand small deprivations and frustrations suffered, of the courage forged out of the cold and darkness of poverty, of the determination welded out of the helpless anger scalding the heart, the plodding hours of labor and weariness, of the life, given simply, . . . that the things which he had suffered should not be, must not be.

Taking the perspective of the men and women whom her essay is written to remember, Olsen gives expression to a vision of possibility. She describes the paradoxical learning of strength through weakness and the metaphorical shaping of a world out of a dream that will not allow present injustices to continue.

In the second portrait, a woman speaks:

> There was a pregnant woman standing on a corner, outlined against the sky, and she might have been a marble, rigid, eternal, expressing some vast and nameless sorrow. But her face was a flame, and I heard her say after a while dispassionately, as if it had been said so many times no accent was needed, "We'll not forget that. We'll pay it back . . . someday."

The voice of this woman recalls the authorial voice of the poem, "I Want You Women Up North to Know," determined to halt injustice. While her vocal expression is without feeling, the woman's face gives accent to her anger and determination. Her pregnancy seems not to make her more vulnerable but to strengthen her "marble" figure, prophesying the coming of new generations who will take up the fight.

In these portraits, the essayist's voice finds its fullest expression by forsaking the singular "I" who struggles with her writer's dilemma and becoming the voice of the people. Though by purely aesthetic standards, there are moments of emotional excess in both essays, the effect is advantageous historically since we gain a feeling for the terror and intensity of the time. Furthermore, there is something almost sermonlike in the narrative exhortation accompanying the portraits, an energy flowing from depths of feeling that appears to us to gain strength out of apparent defeat. The resolution Olsen came to in these early pieces—making her voice the voice of the working class—finds fulfillment in *Yonnondio*, though the novel was never finished and was only recovered, by accident, decades later.

Composed between 1932 and 1936, *Yonnondio: From the Thirties* is Olsen's lengthiest fictive work. The first chapter, as we have seen, was actually published just before the essays, and was then called by Robert Cantwell "a work of early genius."[17] When Olsen recovered the manuscript decades after writing it, most of the next three chapters were also in final form, but the rest was incomplete or unfinished. In "A Note about the Book," printed as an afterword, Olsen writes:

> This book, conceived primarily as a novel of the 1930's, was begun in 1932 in Faribault, Minnesota, when the author was nineteen, and worked on intermittently into 1936 or perhaps 1937 in Omaha, Stockton, Venice (Calif.), Los Angeles, and San Francisco.
>
> . . . .
>   . . . The first four chapters, in final or near-final form when fitted together, presented only minor problems. The succeeding pages were increasingly difficult to reclaim. There were usually two to fourteen versions to work from: 38 to 41 year old penciled-over scrawls and fragments to decipher and piece together.

Thus, when the novel came out in 1972, it had been edited but there was no new writing. The last chapters of the book, while more fragmented than the first, are also more mature, presenting a family's, the Holbrooks', situation in increasingly complex terms, which blame capitalism less than the early chapters do and instead seek to locate the mystery still residing in these lives. Mazie, the young heroine, offers a shaping consciousness at the beginning of the story. As the novel develops, however, the perspective becomes more and more that of the mother, Anna. To my mind, the development of girl-to-woman consciousness in the novel reflects the concurrent change in perspective in the writer's own life. Thus, the fictive voice emerging in the Holbrooks' story springs from the conjoined mother/daughter consciousness of Olsen and of her characters. Beginning in *Yonnondio*, we have in Tillie Olsen's work a shaping maternal consciousness, a political and spiritual voice arising from mothering realities.

The novel offers a realistic description of poverty in America. Olsen's representation of slaughterhouse realities, for example, is a significant historical reflection of working conditions in America in the twenties and thirties. But the artistry of the work resides in the text's visionary evocation of love, caring, and grace out of desperate and unfulfilled lives. Descending with the characters into the basest of life conditions—illness, poverty, and human-inflicted pain— readers are witnesses to the paradoxical beauty and strength of lives that refuse to be overcome. The force of the vision is the shared perspective between characters who, in solidarity with one another, keep hope alive. Emerging primarily from the points of view of Mazie and Anna, the text's voice suggests that representation engenders hope. Through the characters' thoughts of each other, a sense of ultimate responsibility for other lives is suggested, giving rise not to despair but to a quickening desire for wholeness and harmony. The effect of the narrative is a prayerful solicitation for readers' compassion and a lyrical and transcending vision of solidarity. At moments, even rebirth seems possible, miraculously engendered in the circumstances of brokenness and defeat that characterize the Holbrooks' existence.

Olsen began this writing as a protest novel, to show, in her words, "what the system does to human beings and their unarticulated ways of resisting dehumanization." She wanted to make clear the need for change and to show how and why people like the Holbrooks are capable of and deserving of a better life.[18] Developing, in the course of writing, a dual consciousness of mother and daughter, Olsen chose to use women's experience as the lens for presenting the worker's situation.[19] Thus, unlike the essays, which focus on political realities in the streets and courtroom, the settings and circumstances of *Yonnondio* are more, though not exclusively, familial and domestic. The result is a preoccupation in the novel with traditional female work: caring for the sick, preparing food, cleaning the house, clothing children, putting out the wash, canning, being present for a husband, soothing hurts. Mazie is shown growing into the same roles her mother fills. At six, she can diaper the baby. Later, she will complain that her brother Will can play while she must help with housework and cooking. And she learns that her body cannot be used as expressively as a boy's.

The story suggests that the traditional roles are limiting and unjust, but at the same time clearly reflects Anna's (and Mazie's) work as essential to the family's well-being. A dominant feeling with which Olsen imbues her mother figure is the feeling of hope for her children. One is reminded of the mother in Agnes Smedley's *Daughter of Earth*, whose existence, while greatly limited, also deepens our understanding of what heroism is. Both that mother and Anna try to keep their families clean and to provide for them. Both want to see their children go to school. Olsen's portrait of Anna exposes the limited circumstances of her life and expresses the love that undergirds her work.[20] Part of Mazie's learning as a young girl is the paradoxical nature of her mother's life. Out of fear and disgust, the girl often abandons the kitchen, running from Anna or shirking the household responsibilities that befall her at such an early age. "Why couldn't *I* get borned a boy?" she laments (142). But she also reciprocates Anna's care, thinking at crucial moments of her mother's well-being and even, when fearful, responding to her mother's need.

The novel, then, discloses a sense of responsibility learned primarily out of shared circumstances and hope for change, which continues despite injustices and limitations. As with the poems and essays, the voice of the narrator twines with those of the characters to express the human feelings of commitment to and desire for self's and others' restoration and repair. Out of the circumstances of the characters—in particular, the female circumstances faced by Mazie and Anna—comes a sense of human interconnectedness that is the foundation of religious consciousness in Olsen's work.

In *Yonnondio*, the authorial voice that has dominated in Olsen's poems and essays becomes more and more the voice of the characters as they think on behalf of each other. Anna's poignant reflection as she stands in the children's room offers illustration of the transformation in perspective:

> It was not that the clothes were beyond or almost beyond mending and that there were none others and no money to buy more; not that four children slept here in this closet bedroom, three on a mattress on the floor; not that in the corners dust curled in feathers . . . not that one of her children had stood a few minutes ago (ah, which hurt more, the earlier averted face or this?) looking at her with pain and fear and pity in her eyes.
>
> It was not any and it was all of these things that brought her now to swaying in the middle of the floor, twisting and twisting the rompers in

soundless anguish. It was that she felt so worn, so helpless; that it loomed gigantic beyond her, impossible ever to achieve, beyond, beyond any effort or doing of hers: that task of making a better life for her children to which her being was bound [105].

The actual description of living circumstances recalls the poem "I Want You Women Up North to Know," but in this instance the situation is evoked through the character's consciousness rather than from the authorial perspective of an outsider. The power of the fictive passage over the earlier poetry lies in the character of Anna. As a consciousness built up from within the narrative, Anna's thought on behalf of her children convinces us of her love and anguish. She becomes the one morally bound with other lives, and her thought offers the representation of their needs and desires. Mazie, too, becomes bound with her mother and the other children in her thought, and when her mother is ill, she is the voice expressing the family's economic and spiritual need.

The very first scene of the novel (written before the poems and essays) suggests this pattern of alternating thought. Mazie awakens to the whistle that announces the mine blowups. Immediately the girl recognizes the sound: "it meant death" to her (9). From this awakening, she views her surroundings: a yellow light, the already "grimy" voice of her mother, "clatter of dishes." Fear of death invades the morning; for example, she thinks of the tinkle of lunch pails as flowers over the "corpse" of the whistle. She overhears her parents discussing a young neighbor who will begin the mines that day.

The mixture of beauty and repugnance in the imagery will be a hallmark of the novel, suggesting both the hope and the severe limitation surrounding these lives. When Mazie falls back to sleep, Anna's consciousness surfaces to continue the story: "Thoughts, like worms, crept within her. Of Marie Kvaternick, of Chris's dreams for the boys, of the paralyzing moment when the iron throat of the whistle shrieked forth its announcement of death, and women poured from every house to run for the tipple. Of her kids—Mazie, Will, Ben, the baby" (10–11). Anna's thought in this opening scene reminds us of the one described earlier in which she thinks of her children. Here her thoughts extend to another family whose circumstances are like her own, reflecting in particular upon the relationship between children and their parents.

Later that day, Mazie lies outside on a single plot of grass. Her imaginative ruminations move to her father and mother:

Men and daddy goin' in like the day, and comin out black. Earth black, and pop's face and hands black, and he spits from his mouth black. . . .

Night be comen and everything becomes like under the ground. . . .
Momma looks all day as if she thinks she's goin to be hearin something.
The whistle blows. Poppa says it is the ghosts laughin 'cause they have
hit a man . . . Chris, that happened too. Chris, who sang those funny
songs [12].

The young girl contemplates her world, in particular the dual
realities of under and above ground. She realizes that the mine
threatens her father's life and remembers Chris Kvaternick, who was
recently killed in a mine accident. The image of her mother
listening for the whistle is prophetic, for later she will see the image
and come running to find that her father has been trapped
underground.

When Mazie meditates, she reflects her mother's pattern of
thought, dwelling upon particular family members and the
community as a whole. Her consciousness provides the primary
consciousness for the first half of the novel.

"One November day the sky . . . packed so thick with clouds,
heavy, gray" (27), Mazie and brother Will attempt to escape the
horror and dread of the mining community by walking to a nearby
grove of woods. Mazie carries the baby with them. The scene is one
of the best in the novel for its portrayal of a child's thought. Falling
on the ground, the young girl looks up to contemplate the sky. Will,
laying his head on her stomach, engages her in conversation about
the wind. Mazie attempts to give answers to things she does not
know. But forgetfulness of home and of her father's dangerous
mining work does not last long. Suddenly Mazie remembers: "The
tightness had come alive again; it strangled around her heart. . . .
Some terror crept upon her. . . . Above the sky were ears. In all their
different shapes they coiled, blurred ears, listening. . . . The face of
her mother, the face of Mis' Connors, the face of Mis' Tikas came
. . . before her eyes" (29). The naming of various women again
reminds us of Olsen's first poem. It will be an often repeated pattern
in the novel, just as the synaesthesia of face, ear, and message
suggests transformations in perception, which Olsen will employ in
later work. These women are not paid workers but are bound with
men who may be killed by their work. The vision Mazie sees is
initiated by the whistle that she actually hears, fulfilling the fear
she has felt from the beginning. A horrible omen, the ears appear
first as vague and spinning images but quickly become the
particular faces of "Mis' Connors," "Mis' Tikas," and her mother.
These ears signify the hearing of disaster, not of human voices.

Running home, the children find the women at the mine and
Mazie's father trapped beneath. The narrative assumes an authorial

voice, speaking on behalf of the community: "Sorrow is tongueless. Apprehension tore it out long ago. No sound, only the whimpering of children, blending so beautifully with the far cry of blown birds. And in the smothered light, carved hard, distinct, against the tipple, they all wait" (31).

Images from Mazie's vision suggested the picture the authorial voice presents. Seeing the ears in the cloud formations and in the grass and finding in the grove the faces of her mother and the neighboring women, Mazie's consciousness offers representation to their anguished lives, the silent listening and waiting for the awful whistle that announces death. In Mazie's eyes and from the authorial perspective, the incident evokes the solidarity of the community. Men, women, and children are bound in the accident. And though the foregoing passage describes their muteness, Mazie's consciousness has read meanings in her environment, giving reflection to the scene of anguish before she sees it. Together the girl and the writer's persona give a voice to the picture, alarming in the reader an emotion equal to the scene: "The shattered dusk, the mountain of culm, the tipple; clear lines, bare beauty—and carved against them, dwarfed by the vastness of night and the towering tipple, these black figures with bowed heads, waiting, waiting" (30).

In this incident, which occurs in Chapter 2 and which was probably written when Olsen was nineteen or twenty, we meet a world of almost unbelievable hardships. We are stunned by the beauty of the language that so carefully, almost lovingly, tells of this despair. Heightening our sense of pain is the writer's style of telling through the girl Mazie. In her youthfully characteristic desire for adventure, for exploration, we recognize our own once-daring selves. Her deep need for room, for affection, and security are also needs we feel a tie with. But when one of the children remarks matter-of-factly, "Ma, I can push my finger in Mazie's skin and it goes in, way deep," we are startled. The comment is almost melodramatic, the writer insisting on the point: these people are poor; these children are not plump and dimpled. Thus are we confronted by a desire we know and by a reality we shrink from.

When the family moves to the Dakota farm, a lyrical voice opens the scene:

Oh Jim's great voice rolling over the land. Oh Anna, moving rigidly from house to barn so that the happiness with which she brims will not jar and spill over. Oh Mazie, hurting herself with beauty. Oh Will, feeling the eggs and radishes gurgle down his throat, tugging the wooly neck of the dog with reckless joy. Oh Ben, feeling smiles around and security [40].

The passage, invoking each character by name, elicits a picture of family contentment and intactness. Gathering the clan together in the text and weaving a blessing over their lives, the narrative voice seems to offer a sense of motherly care.

For a time, the farm does promise a place for everyone, relieving Mazie especially of her burden of contemplating the risks of her father's work and the source of her mother's pain. After the harvest and payment to the land owners, however, Jim finds that they are in debt. The winter that follows is anguishing.

An incident during the late fall expands the pattern of character representation evolving in the novel. "One autumn dusk," Mazie deserts "the smoky kitchen" (47). Running after a star, she finds herself stumbling upon the home of a friendly neighbor, Old Man Caldwell. He is dying. But he and Mazie talk before she leaves, and in the conversation, he pictures Anna's life as an example of courage and true knowledge:

> "Mazie. Live, don't exist. Learn from your mother, who has had everything to grind out life and yet has kept life. Alive, felt what's real, known what's real. People can live their whole life not knowing."
>
> The words were incomprehensible. They parched the fear, but thirstily she still watched his eyes [49].

Mazie's confused listening and the man's longing are expounded by the authorial voice set off from the rest of the text:

> An old man, Elias Caldwell, death already smothering his breast, tries to tell a child something of all he has learned, something of what he would have her live by—and hears only incoherent words come out. Yet the thoughts revolve, revolve and whirl, a scorching nebula in his breast, sending forth flaming suns that only shatter against the walls and return to chaos. How can it be said? [49]

The sense of futility and loss expressed by the writer's persona is actually belied by the passage. The old man grasps at Anna's life as a true representation of knowledge and in the image of her perseverance gives meaning to life's struggle. Her insistence upon hope despite defeats is emblazoned before us as "what's real."

Filtered through Mazie's girlish apprehension and receptivity, the incident before Caldwell's death suggests the human longing to come to meaning as a communal search. The young teach the old and vice versa. The notion of keeping life, attributed to the mother by the old man, discloses both an abiding knowledge of what is really needed in human life and a faith or hope that fans the flames of desire. In Caldwell's monologue we gain the first glimpse, to be developed further in *Yonnondio* and in Olsen's later work, of a mother as one who journeys in hope, yet a hope acquainted with "everything to grind out life." Furthermore, this incident appears to symbolize the very search for voice that the text is working out through the characters, suggesting a universal and beneficent presence or voice binding mother, child, and friend. This medley of figures will find its greatest culmination in Eva, the heroine of "Tell Me a Riddle," when she hears many singing and through their harmonious voice returns to the great truths of life, which give her meaning and sustenance.

Shortly after this incident, another scene repeats the pattern of Mazie's thought for her mother. Out with Will on a spring day, she again sees a maternal image. Escaping the kitchen, the two have wandered to a wood "where hidden wild violets with tears in their eyes carpeted the ground" (55). The imagery of the passage is a confusion of beauty and ugliness; in contrast with the children's thoughts of butterflies in their eyes, the narrator describes "patches of soiled snow," "scabs of old leaves," "swollen breasts of prairie." Mazie's vision is drawn in similar images: "Her mother. Night, sweating bodies. The blood and pain of birth. Nausea groveled. . . . She could feel words swollen big within her, words coming out with pain, bloody, all clothed in red" (55– 56).

In her thought, the daughter uses the image of her mother's pregnancy to understand her own fullness with questions and meanings. Straining for life, her "red" words seem to cost her in blood. Mazie's thought both offers a vision of her mother's condition and of her approaching and painful delivery, and allows the girl a means of understanding her own need to express fears and longings. The vision comes unbidden, and Mazie fights it. But, like her picture of swirling ears listening for the whistle, the images prophesy the incidents to follow.

That night, Anna begins her labor, and Mazie is left alone with her when Jim goes to get help. At last the father returns, and Mazie escapes to the henhouse. Later, she wanders outside; "a strange face, the sky grieved above her, gone suddenly strange like her mother's." It begins to rain, and she goes back inside:

> A shadow of rain. Back in the henhouse, she heard it descend upon the earth, gentle and grieving. Perhaps after a while she slept, a half sleep into which voices came. "Now. Push hard now, Anna. Did you boil the spoon? I have to use it. Hard, Anna."
>
> Then a cry, ecstatic, profound, shattered the night, and a thin wail wove it under. It was dawn [57–58].

Seeking escape from her mother's pain, Mazie cannot escape her thoughts. The sky takes on the aspect of her mother's face, and even in half sleep she hears the sounds and sentences accompanying the birth. As readers, we are with Mazie in the henhouse though the subject of the passage is Anna's delivery. Thus, the representation of the mother's labor is given from the perspective of the girl, and we know what we do of the night's events primarily from Mazie's consciousness, even her semiconsciousness. The authorial voice does not separate. We have only Mazie's eyes and ears.

This introduction to the pain and ecstasy of birth, given in poetic language that surprises us with beauty, leads us further in our recognition of what life is for the Holbrooks, particularly for Anna. Like Mazie, we feel both a tie with the emerging life and a repulsion toward the harsher realities. Because we, like Mazie, are narratively bound with Anna in the birth, however, we cannot escape. Rather, we enter further through Mazie's consciousness into this world.

The second half of the novel takes place in a slaughterhouse neighborhood in a large city. Anna's perspective becomes dominant, though in the crucial event of her miscarriage, Mazie's eyes provide the representation. In a singularly benevolent passage, one which will help us establish transcending experience as essential to Olsen's vision, the mother and daughter together share beauty and intactness given reflection by the narrator's lyrical voice. At the end, Anna's work is the lens through which we are given a picture of the family's circumstance and her last prophetic words suggest her role as the one who hopes for the family.

The images introducing us to the city are infused with evil:

> Myriad and drumming, the feet of sound move always through these crooked streets, trembling the shoddy houses, jerking the skeleton children who scream and laugh so senselessly to uneven rhythms they themselves know not of. Monster trucks shake by, streetcars plunge, machinery rasps and shrieks [60].

The scene is an inferno of noise and machinery, a writhing, eternal dance. The image of skeleton children reflects an extreme dualization in Olsen's early period. Elsewhere in the novel, she refers to the "fat bellies" of capitalists.

The description continues:

> Far underneath thinly quiver the human noises—weeping and scolding and tired words that slip out in monosyllables and are as if never spoken; sighs of lust, and guttural, the sigh of weariness; laughter sometimes, but this sound can scarcely be called human [60].

Human words are smothered by the sounds of machines just as human longings and dreams are smothered by long hours of underpaid work. The binding human voice of presence and hope is gone. This obliteration of voices, then, is the opposite of Olsen's twining voices which evoke learning, knowledge, and "keeping life" as activities truest to human being. To silence human expression is then to deny the divine creative spark in humanity, which is the potential for transformation or redeeming change.

Calling to attention the stench of slaughter, the narrator names the packinghouse ruler of the city. Not animals but the workers "are the streets' lifeblood, nourishing the taverns and brothels and rheumy-eyed stores" (60). The substitution of human blood for money recalls the pattern of substitution in "I Want You Women Up North to Know," in which women's blood becomes thread and cloth. Substitution, which denies individual value, is another kind of silencing. It focuses upon what people can produce for profit but ignores their creative genius, their special talents, and certainly their desires.

In tone and mood, the feeling of the passage is as far removed from the farm as heaven from hell. Again the narrator invokes the characters by name but the lyricism of the farm episodes is exchanged for a throbbing lament:

> A man's face, heavy and sullen . . . moves here awhile and is gone: *Jim*; a woman's face, thinning, skin tightening over the broad cheekbones, the great dark eyes down a terrace of sunken flesh . . . : *Anna*. A child's thin face looks up for a moment, wondering dazed eyes; *Mazie*; a boy's face, scowl over the mouth, eyes hurt with the hurt of not understanding, then insane with anger; *Will*. On this face, half baby's, half child's, the breath of fever glows, closing the sober eyes; a tiny boy running along croons a song that is silenced; a tiny girl's fists beat the air, stiffening, stiffened: *Ben, Jimmie, Baby Bess* [61].

Considering the age of the writer, we must wonder at the depths of her sympathy. The family has grown to five children, but the sense of family blessedness is gone. Each character seems starkly alone and vulnerable. Only Jimmie sings a song, and it is silenced by the noises of the city. The description of the parents recalls the gloomy imagery of the mining town, Anna's "dark eyes down a terrace of sunken flesh" reminding us of a stark geography. The characters seem to be facing a sentence of death, though for what crime, neither they nor we know.

This brokenness of the characters and their alienation from each other points not to individual human failings but to the societal sins of greed and, ultimately, indifference, bringing less advantaged people to spiritual and physical death. Seeing the hope evaporate from the Holbrooks' lives, we become aware that in Tillie Olsen's world, human apathy, carelessness, and neglect are the corporate evils that keep us from our own divine possibilities for re-creation and transcendence. Lost voice is lost hope.

For a while, Mazie refuses to acknowledge the move by pretending she is still at the farm. Anna's unending fight to make a home, to clean, to feed, to clothe, to sustain, becomes our primary avenue for knowing the family's struggle. Dirt is a great antagonist, like the smell of the slaughterhouses, which the children complain of. With so much against her, Anna becomes increasingly weak. The children, in their nearly invincible youth, are miraculous inventors of games and entertainment. But the experience grinds the life out of their mother: "A familiar faintness dizzied her. With Bess still crying and tugging she sank to the bed, thinking: I oughta see what Jimmie's doin . . . And now the gaunt haggard house towered above. Where were the children? MazieWillBen she cried" (68). Anna continues to keep the children in her mind, but with very little energy for dreams and hoping. Her thought, like that of the poverty-stricken and abandoned Eva in Toni Morrison's *Sula*, is simply for keeping them alive. In that novel, a daughter questions her mother's love because she never played with her. Angrily and triumphantly, Eva replies, "I stayed alive for you."[21]

In Olsen's story, the text unfolds from Anna's perspective the fight simply to endure. As she slips into exhaustion, she stops thinking but continues to perform her work: "Remote she fed and clothed the children, scrubbed, gave herself to Jim" (70). "The old Anna of sharp words and bitter exaction, and fierce attempt to make security for her children was gone," the narrator remarks (71). In the image of drowning, we read of Anna's falling into unconsciousness:

> The room swimming, swimming, or was it she? Bess did not seem to be at her breast at all. Soaked, soaked through to the bone, she thought, but her fingers felt no wet. She tried to rise. A great wave of giddiness and illness rose and waited to engulf her; she sank back down. "Them clothes, I guess. Leavin me tired enough not to move for a thousand years" [82].

Like the fracturing and alienation the family feels in the city, the drowning image points to what is evil, because diminishing, in Olsen's fictive world. Evoking amnesia or forgetfulness, Anna's drowning may be understood in Mary Daly's sense as alienation from one's true self. Forced into an existence of extreme poverty and impossible work demands, Anna loses her authentic being, her capacity for hope, and her ability to act in behalf of her dreams. Not to be able to keep her family in her thoughts, to represent them in the world, is like death.

Mazie's refusal of reality takes shape in her feverish running from the cramped and dirty dwelling. But a time comes when Mazie can no longer run. Coming home one evening, she sees death in her mother's face. That night, when Anna experiences a miscarriage, the daughter becomes our eyes again. The scene is more dreadful than Jim's mining accident:

> Running back to the kitchen (so ugly: Momma, all the hair, the blood) running back with water, calling "Poppa" again till he somehow comprehends and comes. How clumsily he lifts Anna and carries her to the bed . . .
>
> What does Bess have to wake up again and cry for? Poppa gone, and I dont know what to do. Dont cry, baby, dont cry. The lamp dancin, dancin. . . . hear the wind in the trees, crying for people that cant cry no more . . .
>
> . . . No, Momma, no, Bess, dont cry, I'll hold ya and love ya, Bess, I'll tell ya a story, see, I'll diaper you and I'll tell you a story, onct upon a time the night was quiet, and the river, a cool river, Bess, was goin along, goin along, talking to itself so happy [92–93].

The scene stays very near the characters' feelings and thoughts, with Mazie as our center of consciousness. The night is sketched from her eyes, thoughts, and words. Alone and afraid, she tries to keep Anna and Bess quiet, offering the younger child her images of wonder: the dancing light and the crying trees. In her young mind, she already understands that people's pain can become inexpressible, so old and habitual a feeling that even tears are impossible.

The girl's lyrical, soothing voice is a triumph of character endurance. Rather than thinking symbolically of her mother as she has in the past, Mazie literally takes her mother's place in relation to the baby. Often before she has diapered and watched, but here Anna's absence is profound and the baby's need absolute. When help arrives, Mazie runs from the scene. In her desperate flight, we sense a longing for relief, for peace and security reflective of Anna's own longing, though Anna can never run.

The transformation from thought to action suggests that in this world, to think or to know symbolically is not enough. One may be called upon to step in for another, to take someone else's place temporarily. It seems cruel, and is, that so young a girl should be called upon to perform such a duty. The effect of the passage, however, is to call from the reader a sense of shared responsibility, a recognition that this should not be. At the same time, Mazie's grace and magnanimity toward her younger sister are reflective of the representative spirit—thinking and acting on behalf of one another—characterizing Olsen's universal vision.

The miscarriage itself clearly metaphorizes the killing nature of the Holbrook's existence, giving the reader a torturous acquaintance with the defeat of Anna's spirit. Our sense of ultimate diminishment in reading the passage comes from our realization that Anna has centered and sustained the family. As readers, we have depended upon her stamina. In her own words, "who's to care about 'em [the children]" if she does not? (107). When Jim holds Mazie at the end of the chapter, we feel with the man and child a deep sense of loss, an unspeakable emptiness generated by our own viewing of Anna's unconscious body. Only the narrator's voice remains, and miraculously, it offers a solacing hope: "And as he sat there in the kitchen with Mazie against his heart, and dawn beat up like a drum, the things in his mind so vast and formless, so terrible and bitter, cannot be spoken, will never be spoken—till the day that hands will find a way to speak this: hands" (95). The image of speaking hands suggests again the idea that speech must become action, just as these people's actions have become Olsen's speech. Truthful language, in Olsen's vision, will elicit moral being, that is, a true symbolization can be literalized and thus remains connected with the physical.[22]

Earlier, Mazie promised Bess a story of pastoral settings, of a river, and of happiness in a place without cities. The story comes to be one day when Anna, with Mazie and the other children, takes a walk in search of dandelion greens. The outing is threaded together from Mazie's and Anna's thoughts. The lyrical narrative voice blends and fuses their experience: "At the end of a cobbly street that had no houses, only high wire fences, they came to a stretch along the river bluff, yellow and green and white with flowers and grass and dandelion glory" (116). The scene that follows is unique in Olsen's early period for its sustained harmonious quality. The freedom and unity achieved by Anna and Mazie on the outing is a touchstone for interpreting Tillie Olsen's world and provides us with a startling revision of transcendence.

In the field, Anna sees a catalpa tree, which reminds her of her childhood. In ecstasy, she calls the children to her, showing them how to suck honey from the flowers. Fearing her mother's strange happiness, Mazie at first fights against Anna's carefree abandonment to the moment. But "a peace and content [begin] to drowse through her" (118). When Anna enfolds Mazie in an embrace, the experience of the two becomes a single experience reflected in the symphonious narrative voice. Paradoxically, the experience of mother/daughter unity is characterized by a profound sense of personal intactness and "selfness":

> Arm in arm, they sat down under the catalpa. . . . [Anna] began stroking Mazie's hair in a kind of languor, a swoon. . . . Her mother sang. A fragile old remembered comfort streamed from the stroking fingers into Mazie, gathered to some shy bliss . . . Young catalpa leaves overhead quivered and glistened, bright reflected light flowed over, 'lumined their faces. . . .
>
> . . . .
> . . . Soft wove the bliss round hurt and fear and want and shame—the old worn fragile bliss, healing, transforming. Up from the grasses, from the earth, from the broad tree trunk at their back, latent life streamed and seeded. The air and self shone boundless [118-119].

The pastoral setting is without hint of corruption. Rather, a beneficence is felt in the omnipresence of "latent life" that infuses and binds each to each. The picture of Anna and Mazie reflects their conjoined perspective and evokes a sense of spiritual connection. Stroking her daughter's hair, the mother's fingers are a source of the energy surging through all of nature, suggesting the harmonious giving and receiving characteristic of an envisioned world of peace and wholeness. The boundaries of self and other, of human and human, are transcended. Even the narrative perspective seems to spring from the earth or to emanate from within the fused and mystical center of being embodied by mother and daughter.

Key to our understanding of the passage is the bodily ("arm in arm") coexistence of mother and child. A striking ontological change has occurred. In the city, Anna and Mazie are physically separate but bound in thought. Here they are physically conjoined but intellectually and emotionally distinct. Their separate beings are bound in the harmonious Being of the universe. The transcending quality of the passage then—its evocation of presences and hopes buoying up the universe—respects the boundaries of self. One does not lose oneself in this harmony; one finds oneself, or one *is* oneself both in separateness and community.

We may read this transcendence as transformation. The text provides the concept and with it the meanings of being healed, made coherent, and free (boundless). In this moment of selfness and togetherness, the characters become as new beings; their truest selves are illuminated. "Up from down under," to use Nelle Morton's image, comes new and blossoming life out of the old.

The scene is fleeting, a singular epiphany in a novel of hurts and losses. But the union of Mazie and Anna and narrator in the lyrical rendering of the moment suggests a fulfillment of the text's struggle to give representation to a vision of the world as it can be, springing miraculously from disdained and unfulfilled lives. The unabashed emotion of the passage, its joy and longing, suggests the human responsibility not merely to make life endurable for "despised people" but to make all lives visionary. Unlike earlier passages in which Mazie or Anna has, of necessity, responded to the other's need or to another member of the family, this scene points to the possibility of moving from survival to true spiritual, that is, authentically creative, being. Out of the thoughts of mother and daughter, Olsen pieces a voice that calls the reader into participation. One does not read this passage and remain untouched. Instead one sits with Anna and Mazie and sees oneself restored with them.

Kathleen McCormack writes in a similar vein about the passage:

Song shines over [Anna's] despair in this scene, making her able not only to reach out to her children, as a true mother, but also, to be her true self. . . . . Transcendence into this true self is not easily sustained in *Yonnondio:* the wind shifts and pac[k]ing house stench plunges Anna and her children back into the "War to Live." But . . . song creates climax by celebrating human connections and by releasing Olsen's characters into a sense of "wingedness, boundlessness" which can transcend pain, decay, and even death itself.[23]

For our reading, the passage suggests a vision of human existence in which one may experience one's and another's well-being conjointly. In such harmony, symbolically echoed by Anna's singing as the two sit, acting out of responsibility for another's needs does not mean a sacrifice of one's own fulfillment and peace. Such an interpretation will find strong echoes in Olsen's last period, especially in *Silences,* where she repeatedly urges readers to understand that one's blossoming should no longer be at the expense of another's. With the catalpa scene as a miniature text within the text, we now have a tentative understanding of a transcending and spiritual presence in Olsen's world by which we may read the rest of her work. In large measure, this scene, written when the writer was moving into motherhood, becomes the context for approaching Olsen's literature as a whole.

The novel closes in the heat of summer. Jim suffers unendurable conditions at work; Mazie is ill; Anna, with Bess on her hip, is performing domestic chores. In a brief interlude from the house, she visits her drought-ridden garden:

> At her feet she sees her garden is dying; . . . "I ain't had time, I'm sorry,"
> she whispered. ". . . *There there Bessie*. I cant stand here and keep being
> shade for you . . ." thinking with bowed head of the dying crops—corn
> and wheat and tomatoes and beans—and farmers' families drooping in
> the miles and miles of baking prairie. "Burning all over, Bessie," she
> said, "Kansas and Dakota and Ioway too" [150].

Though the context is unequivocally stark—the lush vegetation of
the earlier scene replaced by the withering sprigs of dying plants—
Anna reflects the same comprehension of transcending or binding
relationship that her experience with Mazie reflected. She speaks to
the plants as to her daughter, making her body a shade for both. If
Anna is a transcendental being, then transcendence is rooted in such
as water, shade, and food. It comes out of realities that make and
keep life. Her thought of the farmers reminds us of her mental
picturing of the miners' families in the first scene. In this depiction,
she thinks of people in the posture of the plants upon which their
lives depend; both are "drooping in the miles and miles of baking
prairie." Her invocation of the states recalls the numerous passages
in the novel in which people's names are called to our
consciousness, inscribing upon our thought their identity of
desperation and need. The tone of Anna's brief meditation is one of
care, suggesting an extension of her maternal inclinations and habits
to the physical world. In her thinking of her baby, the plants, farms,
and farmers' families in one interconnected sequence, she binds
together the lives of all, offering a prayerful solicitation on their
behalf. Amazingly, this almost benighted woman is still a source of
essential care for others, both in thought and action.

While the children sleep, Anna watches "great columns of dust-
wraiths . . . swirling across the river and down the street" (150– 51).
With Baby Bess, Anna is the lone watcher. Stealthily, she borrows
from the family water to sprinkle a shower of rain over the parched
soil before returning indoors. The action is an indication of her
greater faith in life than in capitulation to death.

In the house, the closing setting of the novel, Anna moves
between the other characters like an angel, sponging Mazie's
feverish brow, singing to the baby, running to help Jim when he
comes in from the sweltering slaughterhouse. Her words to Jim,
collapsed "by the stoop in the evening shadow," are the last of their
story: "Here, I'll help you. The air's changin, Jim. Come in and get
freshened up. I see for it to end tomorrow, at least get tolerable"
(154). The words are a faint assurance; certainly they are not
revolutionary words. They hold us, however, because we, like the
family, have come to respect this woman of uneven graces and slight

resources. Though the family is all around her, Anna's consciousness, aided by the narrative voice, is the singular perspective at the end of the novel. She believes in things getting better, in change. That faith is linked with the sense she has, just before waking Jim, of an urge to be out in the swirling wind and dust. Something in her longs for freedom, expression, and knowledge. She remembers some earlier self, as she did under the catalpa, a self that is an index for true being, for what is in her to be. We are reminded of the song she sang to the children on their outing. She begins it here but is interrupted by Baby Bess:

> I saw a ship a sailing
> A sailing on the sea
> I saw a ship a sailing
> And on that ship was me [119].

The song returns us to the power of thought. As long as Anna can imagine freedom and expansion of her realities, she may be able to hope. And yet, the hope can really be only for her children. Her life has already been written.

Symbolizing the limited situation of the family, the heat and drought point not only to limited food but to limitations upon desire and to the eclipse of Anna's great spirit. The Holbrooks have traveled from bad to worse with only momentary glimpses at a better life. Yet the story, more powerfully than Olsen's essays and poems, evokes in the reader a feeling of solidarity with the working class and a recognition of its longings. In later work, Olsen will expand her writing's representation of vanished working-class lives to a concern with other vanished people.

Beginning with Mazie but building to the perspective of Anna, the text's strength is the strength of the characters' maternal thoughts, especially their imagistic representation in meditation, dream, and daydream of the needs and longing of the family. In particular, the prayerful thoughts of Anna provide the text with a sense of hope, a hope grounded in need and in something intangible in the human spirit, some unquenchable thirst for more, for something greater and larger than what one knows.

Mazie and Anna are not deeply developed psychologically. Rather, they are universal portraits of a woman and a child who struggle in economically difficult circumstances. Their lives are a parable of the working class as Olsen saw it in her youth, a story of limitations that miraculously yields a vision of hope. Olsen knew that experiences of mothers and children had been even more absolutely silenced than those of male and female workers who joined together in the union and the strike. Few newspaper stories mentioned the circumstances of women who labored in working-class homes in the twenties and thirties or voiced their lonely struggles to make a better life and to educate their children.

Yonnondio is largely the writer's struggle to give representation to working-class women and the domestic sphere. But she is not content merely to reflect the exigencies of working-class life even though, given from a woman's perspective, such a description would lend new understandings. Instead, she creates a world out of which dreams arise and depicts a persevering hope that springs from lives we are accustomed to thinking of as devoid of significant insight, longing, and knowledge. Choosing the form of fiction and the evolving consciousness of narrator/daughter/mother, Olsen's early work speaks of the depths of human experience.

Clearly, the novel offers historical understanding of an American period. Of more concern, it offers a vision of ultimacy, an understanding—springing from traditional female experiences—that human lives are bound together and that hope for a better life is an inclusive hope, which begins with the material and spiritual needs of children, the ill and ill-clothed, the sick, hungry, and dying. The understanding we draw from this novel can give meaning to our present experience, if we read ourselves in light of it. To reach for what is in us to be, to carry others with us on the journey, is to be divinely human. To use an awkward phrase, a lateral transcendence is suggested by this world; we journey toward a better future that lies before us. But we are bearing children on the way. We are not solitary searchers. Yonnondio discloses a hope in Olsen's world, which springs from a woman's heart. The narrative voice woven from Mazie's and Anna's thoughts transcends—that is, rises up from—their lives and gives expression to their truest selves. In the speech that is the story, their lives are luminous signs pointing to the profundity of female realities; care for children, "keeping life." From these concerns, the world that is this text is born.

As Olsen's writing matures, she draws her characters' lives less in the dualized images of beauty and ugliness, innocence and evil, and instead seeks to redeem the threatening images that surround her characters. By questioning received notions of degradation and loss, she seeks a new way of viewing histories characterized by both so that lives are renewed and redeemed out of their own pasts. Nothing is lost; instead everything has the potential, in her world's ecology, for re-creation. Perhaps darkness does not always portend death. Perhaps instead, periods of loneliness and scenes of gloom may be transformed into understanding and the beauty of renewed commitment. Moving to a disciplined use of imagery, the second period in Olsen's career invites a more thorough-going reading of the text in terms of metaphorical meaning.

However, we may continue to understand Olsen's comprehension of her writing as a corporate endeavor with her subjects to transcend brokenness through outlining the circumstances of abused and underprivileged life, that is, to elicit a spiritual vision through description. What is true begins in need and pain and reaches for voice and re-creation.

1. "Myriads of human beings—those who did the necessary industrial work in the last century—lived and died and little remains from which to reconstruct their perished (vanished) lives. About them, as about so much else, literature was largely silent, and the charge can be levied: *Nowhere am I in it." Silences,* p. 114.

2. Olsen still speaks with disappointment about the decline of Yiddish when Hebrew became the national language of Israel after World War II. When she was growing up, Yiddish was "the language of the Jews," she says, "the Mother Tongue." (Tillie Olsen, telephone conversation with the author, 1 June 1986.)

3. Olsen, of course, has had other working lives, including "Kelly Girl" and transcriber for a dairy-equipment firm; political activist; mother and houseworker.

4. Giles Gunn writes that in criticism we seek "to reinstate the text in that living dialectic of imaginative possibility and historical actuality which the text explores and is shaped by." "The Moral Imagination in Modern American Criticism," in *Modern American Cultural Criticism: Proceedings of the Conference, March 17–18, 1983,* ed. Mark Johnson (Warrensburg: Central Missouri State University, 1983), p. 37.

5. James, *Theory of Fiction,* ed. James E. Miller, Jr. (Lincoln: University of Nebraska Press, 1972), p. 304.

6. Pells, *Radical Visions* (New York: Harper and Row, 1973), p. 148. Rosenfelt analyzes the ways in which Communist "brotherhood" did not always extend to female partners. See her article "From the Thirties" for a fuller discussion.

7. Baum, Hyman, and Michel, *Jewish Woman in America,* p. 154.

8. Joseph Landis, "Who Needs Yiddish? A Study in Language and Ethics," *Understanding Jewish Theology: Classical Issues and Modern Perspectives,* ed. Jacob Neusner (New York: Ktav Publishing House, 1973), p. 220.

9. The quotation is cited in Rosenfelt's article, "From the Thirties," 404. Others have interpreted Olsen's vision as essentially tragic. See, for example, Clayton, "Grace Paley and Tillie Olsen."

10. Olsen, "I Want You Women Up North to Know." Olsen was nineteen or twenty when she wrote the poem. All of the writing Olsen did in the 30s came out in 1934. She actually wrote the poems after the essays and her first story. I discuss the poems first because they show her struggle for a representative voice.

11. Burkom and Williams offer a reading of the poem in similar terms, in "De-Riddling Olsen's Writing."

12. "There Is a Lesson," originally published in the *Partisan,* was reprinted in Burkom and Williams, "De-Riddling Olsen's Writing," 70.

13. In 1934, a local of the International Longshoremen's Association sought union recognition. When the employers refused, the longshoremen went on strike. On Thursday, 5 July, an attempt to break the strike resulted in the death of two strikers and two others and numerous injuries. On the twelfth, the teamsters, motivated by "Bloody Thursday," struck the entire city of San Francisco. Four days later the first general strike in America since 1919 formally began. Olsen's essay "The Strike" was

published in *Partisan Review* 1 (September–October 1934): 3–9. The essay is reprinted in *Years of Protest: A Collection of American Writings of the 1930s*, ed. Jack Salzman with Barry Wallenstein (New York: Pegasus, 1967). Philip Taft offers a useful discussion of the longshoremen's strike and the general strike that resulted (*Organized Labor in American History* [New York: Harper and Row, 1964]).

14. Olsen helped put out the longshoremen's publication *Waterfront Worker*, sometimes taking her daughter Karla with her to work.

15. Later to become a part of the first chapter of *Yonnondio*, "The Iron Throat" was published as a short story in *Partisan Review*.

16. Tillie Olsen, telephone conversation with the author, 1 June 1986.

17. Cited in Burkom and Williams, "De-Riddling Olsen's Writing," 71.

18. Tillie Olsen, telephone conversation with the author, 1 June 1986.

19. Cuneen suggests an understanding of the reciprocal thought of mother and daughter. "Seldom has the sacrificial aspect of a good mother's life been depicted with such sympathetic reality and awareness of its destroyed potentiality as in this portrait of Anna *seen through the eyes of her daughter* Mazie." "Tillie Olsen," 571 (italics mine).

20. Olsen notes that Smedley was one of the first to show what the life of a working-class mother was.

21. Toni Morrison, *Sula* (New York: Bantam Books, 1975), p. 60.

22. Olsen wrote another scene in which Mazie refused to be comforted by her father but chose this one—"with Mazie against [Jim's] heart," saying she found continuity in Jim's holding Mazie, as Anna holds her beneath the catalpa. These scenes are, as Olsen points out, the only ones in the book in which arms are put around Mazie. The scene between mother and daughter is the only one in which parent and child embrace in leisure and not because of physical suffering. (Tillie Olsen, telephone conversation with the author, 1 June 1986.)

23. McCormack, "Song as Transcendence in the Works of Tillie Olsen," in *Symposium: Tillie Olsen Week.*

IV

The Desire for Time

Transforming Loss into Gain

Wine, water, breath, light, truth, way, vine, door, word,
are essential to human life because without them
people perish.

ELISABETH SCHÜSSLER FIORENZA
In Memory of Her

Ye littles, be more close!
Make me, O Lord, a last, a simple thing
Time cannot overwhelm.
Once I transcended time:
A bud broke to a rose
And I rose from a last diminishing.

THEODORE ROETHKE
"In Evening Air"

All goes onward and outward, nothing collapses.

WALT WHITMAN
"Song of Myself"

The first story of Olsen's second period, "I Stand Here Ironing," presents a mother/daughter relationship that recalls Anna and Mazie in *Yonnondio* and suggests the same desire by a mother that a child's life and future be valued.[1] Remembering Emily's babyhood, the narrator recalls the conflict between the time she worked at a paying job and her desire for her daughter's well-being: "She was a miracle to me, but when she was eight months old I had to leave her daytimes with the woman downstairs to whom she was no miracle at all" (10). The sentence is one of contradiction and decline spoken in terms of time: "She was a miracle to me, but . . . " The child's age is given and the period of separation, "daytimes." The condition of the child's life slips, in the sentence, from the condition of promise and miracle to the condition of ordinariness and inconsequence.

In *Yonnondio*, Olsen depicted characters who were able to think and act on one another's behalf in spite of enormous òdds. In the stories of *Tell Me a Riddle*, characters remember a past of hardships, but they have escaped the extremities of poverty. With more time for reflection they find, amazingly, that even during such struggles, they experienced some beauty, some vital commitment or shared "brotherhood," which offered meaning and transcendence to life. Their hope is to revitalize that part of their pasts that promised hope and human betterment. When their personal lives appear hopeless, it lies with the community within the story and with the community of readers to maintain the hope that once inspired their struggle. Thus, in the second-period stories, we see characters struggling together for more than survival. The worlds we encounter in the *Tell Me a Riddle* collection connect political, material, and spiritual dimensions of life in the characters' journeys toward understanding. In every case we discover that human bonds sustain life and that dreams arising from human experience evoke spiritual, that is, ultimate dimensions of life.

73

What Olsen suggests in this period is not a revolutionary overthrow of existing conditions but a more tedious and historical rebuilding of the world. She finds her way to re-creation, not by a dualization of harmful and beneficent images but by recasting what was once metaphoric of loss and death as a vocabulary of hope.

With a focus upon this world and with an intense interest in this life, Olsen faces the paradox of how—given the apparent indifference of society and economy to personal well-being—it may be possible for the individual and the community to hope for meaning, significance, and harmony. A comprehension of the daughter's life as miraculous, expressed by a mother, requires above all a reevaluation of human time. For Olsen, if the miracle of life is to be sustained, we must first remember what has harmed in the past. Then we can envision those changes that may offer abundance and joy to human existence.

The stories to be examined in this chapter recall past events for the purpose of imagining a different future. The past is recalled, however, not by fixing the immutable histories of the characters, but by making the past active in the present and future. Thus we are led to view history as alive with spiritual presence, which we may rediscover and with which we may learn of our destiny and plot our future. The remembrance of ancestors who fought for freedom, for example, or even of one's own mother's often labored life, makes history a living process through which we move toward fulfillment and wholeness.

Each story focuses on a particular life, which is at the same time every life; for example, subtle allusion in the title story to a Russian Jewish heritage gives the strength of particularity to a universal view of the human predicament of lost potential and forgotten dreams. Evoking a sense of universal human loss, the texts reappraise the situation of the weak. Beckoning the reader to break the bonds of static time, they recast these lives as redeemable. We find our own lives aligned with these through the power of the narrator's sympathetic voice and thus experience in reading a fluid and transcending time, which binds loss with dream and hope. Transcendence is achieved not by forgetting the past but by holding it close.

We might use Paul Tillich's categories for time to illustrate the transformation of histories that occurs in Olsen's work of this period. At first, in "I Stand Here Ironing," the time of the clock, or time as *chronos*, prevails. This is measured or quantitative time, which passes and is lost. *Kairos*, on the other hand, suggests qualitative time, moments of preparedness, abundance, and revelation. Time as kairos is time as full, redeeming, and transcending. In this experience of time, miracles may occur, the dead may come to life, and the lame may walk.[2]

The historic attitude basic to the stories can be traced to Olsen's roots in the Marxist/socialist tradition, in her Jewish ancestry, and in her experience of rearing children. In all of these influences, we notice that a new and redeeming vision of human lifetime is present, but it is born out of the concrete past.

Two related attitudes of Marxist argument inform Olsen's historic vision in a direct manner: capitalist enslavement of the worker's lifetime and the worker's experience of life as fragmentary. Under capitalism, Marxism argues, humanity is essentially split between capitalist and worker. The irony of the individual's existence within this system is that he or she reproduces that split in his/her own existence. Putting oneself into a product that is more valuable than self, people make their own souls salable items.[3] Thus, the human experience of time is loss, not simply of hours, days, and weeks but of one's very spirit.

The lament by the Yiddish poet Morris Rosenfeld, that he sees his son only when he sleeps, exemplifies the fragmentary nature of a turn-of-the-century slum worker's life: "The time-clock drags me off at dawn;/ at night it lets me go./ I hardly know my flesh and blood. . . ."[4] In such a system, the clock is elevated from its simple function as a sign and becomes, depending on one's perspective (capitalist or worker), a symbol of one's power over others or a metaphorical reminder of one's enslavement to the bosses' time, which, quite logically, is indifferent to one's own illnesses and death. There is no opportunity for repair here or for remembrance. One lives, one dies and is forgotten.

Perhaps the fundamental and all-encompassing dehumanization is indifference to the value of life time, either to individual lives or to communal life. What American radicals like Big Bill Haywood were demanding early in this century was not simply more humane hours but respect for workers' lives and for the working class. When an old miner remarked, "Men are cheaper than timber," explaining why inferior pine was used to construct mines, he expressed the pervasive indifference of the powerful toward the lives of the workers.[5] Their time was of no significance *in itself.* Their history, or the *story* of their lives, the remembrance of it, was inconsequential.

Yiddishkeit gives a particular orientation to Jewish historicism. The conditions of life for nineteenth century Eastern European Jews required a division of this-worldly and other-worldly time. Absolutely vulnerable to external attack, shtetl life was a banding together against the outside. In a way, such existence was timeless, not concerned with history as such but with redemption and heaven. The exodus from the shtetl, like the Exodus from Egypt, was a reentry into history, into the experience of one's own lifetime as meaningful and as ultimately sanctified. Yiddishkeit recognized the labored and silenced lives of the past and affirmed the holiness of now. No more should one live as Bontsha the Silent, the Isaac Loeb Peretz character who mutely endured every pain and loss as his religious duty.[6]

An essential correspondence between the Yiddish experience, American socialism, and Tillie Olsen's historical comprehension of life is a fundamental faith in possibility and a desire for change into a more harmonious and life-affirming existence. Time should be felt as the process of human becoming and fruition, not a waiting in slavery and suffering in the hope of appeasing angry gods. Certainly lifetime should not be a slow erosion of all in one that is most sacred and promising: one's talents, one's creativity, one's impulse toward making life. Time must hold beginnings for Olsen, not endings.

In a personal and immediate way, Olsen's experience of mothering gave impetus to her desire for more abundant time. The experience of lost time which she felt as a working mother is an illustration of alienated labor as well as of lost powers, of lost self. In *Silences*, she expresses the anguish of leaving the few months given to writing and returning "to the world of work, someone else's work, nine hours, five days a week"; she refers to the "Time-Master" and although she does not use these words, she means the capitalist system, which requires its workers to deplete their creative energies toward inadequate but essential means (money).[7] But the experience of mothering is not adequately addressed by Marxism, since work in the home, while it has a use value, does not have an exchange value. Domestic work is invisible in an analysis that focuses on an examination of economics. Furthermore, as Olsen records it, mothering is experienced both as an alienation (in that it exhausts one's personal energies toward the reproduction of others' lives) and as a yield (in that Olsen's vision of what human beings can be grew out of caring for her own daughters).

She expresses the paradoxical nature of her experience:

> The habits of a lifetime when everything else had to come before writing are not easily broken, . . . what should take weeks, takes me sometimes months to write; what should take months, takes years.[8]

> One of the yields out of motherhood which could have come to me in no

other way has been a sense of my time, of my world, of my society; a sense of how human beings are lessened, maimed, atrophied, the passion against letting this continue.[9]

In the first excerpt, from *Silences,* Olsen speaks of a harmful pattern of lifetime in which one's needs are always subject to someone else's. The experience of constantly losing one's time and one's self, the dehumanizing cost of mothering, was part of her experience. But under better conditions, mothering instilled in Olsen "a sense of my time"; she indicates by that phrase both a sense of how the world is and a vision of change. The vision requires time as kairos, a right time for new understanding, for re-creation in the light of a new seeing or understanding. Fractured or dualized life as Olsen experienced it, with mothering painfully wedged in the middle—paid work/mothering/creative work—denies the wholeness of one's creative energies. A revision of history (that is, a new interpretation of lifetime) actually revives the past, opening it toward a hoped-for future.

Olsen's narrative strategy itself, beginning in the first story, seeks to dismantle the hold of time and to redirect or reinterpret teleological thinking and understanding of events. Bringing thoughts together and letting them go, the narrative voice denies closure or ending and instead is always opening and reopening. Everything begins in the beginning, in the miracle of life. Everything ends with the same miracle, the same opening. Thus, "I Stand Here Ironing" begins with and ends (or begins again with) the miracle or "more" of Emily's life. In the narratives or stories of this period, there are no final causes, no necessary plots; instead the stories disclose a desire for renewal inspired by the characters' own sacred being. Against the harmful conditions or circumstances of life, the narratives insist on the possibility of more, of openings and rebirth.[10]

"I Stand Here Ironing"

The first story in the collection, "I Stand Here Ironing," is the most perfectly realized of Olsen's stories. It appears to present as its concern a despair over what was and what might have been. It is a story, in religious terms, that cries for redemption (of the mother's and child's loss) and for reconciliation, for a coming back together in terms of original promises. Told in the first person, the story closely parallels Olsen's young adult life and might be said to be her personal avowal of faith, her deepest expression of belief and will. In

the process of recollecting her daughter's life, the story's mother/
narrator hopes that the future may still promise fulfillment for past
longings, that the concern of her life and her daughter's is not only
with what might have been but with what might yet be. This turn
in focus from grief to hope is not a denial or forgetfulness of the past
but a different attitude toward the past, whereby it becomes
transformable through hope. Furthermore, in her contemplation of
the bomb, the mother's thought expands to an international focus,
so that her individual concern gains the transcendence of the shared
longings of the whole earth.

Toward the end, the mother muses in apparent despair:

> I will never total it all. I will never come in to say: She was a child
> seldom smiled at. Her father left me before she was a year old. I had to
> work her first six years when there was work, or I sent her home and to
> his relatives. There were years she had care she hated. She was dark and
> thin and foreign-looking in a world where the prestige went to blondness
> and curly hair and dimples, she was slow where glibness was prized. She
> was a child of anxious, not proud, love. . . . My wisdom came too late.
> She has much to her and probably little will come of it. She is a child of
> her age, of depression, of war, of fear [20].

Yet, in the next—and last—paragraph of the story, the same voice
lets go of the necessity to "total it all," just as she lets go of her
daughter. She begins again without ending, a strategy learned of
necessity: "Let her be. So all that is in her will not bloom—but in
how many does it? There is still enough left to live by. Only help her
to know—help make it so there is cause for her to know—that she is
more than this dress on the ironing board, helpless before the iron"
(20–21). The first sentence, spoken ostensibly to the guidance
counselor whose visit sets off the train of thoughts making the
story, is actually spoken by the mother to herself. She must let go
without totaling. She cannot fix the facts of Emily's life and thereby
explain anything, "There is all that life that has happened outside of
me, beyond me" (9). But she contradicts that recognition, for
throughout she frames episodes of the daughter's life in terms of
their togetherness or separation. As the narrative center of
consciousness, the mother has told Emily's history in relation to
herself.

The second sentence expresses neutrality; it is an attempt to be
reconciled with loss as a condition of being human. But the third
sentence is a sentence of hope. And the last sentence is a prayer
whose audience is the whole human race. Certainly it is not spoken
to the counselor. "Only help her to know" moves beyond the
immediate situation. The sentence expresses the mother's desire

that the daughter may not be overcome by the past but that, understanding the past, she may be strengthened. Emily's life as she continues to write it is still a possibility. If Emily believes she has the power to effect change, her losses may be redeemed. Her sense of her self and her significance will be transformed. If the world receives this mother's plea much more will be possible.

Using the end of the story, which is actually a beginning, we may offer some tentative suggestions concerning the significance and the nature of time in Olsen's stories and then go on to read this first story in light of its end. The core sentence, "she is more," indicates Olsen's attitude toward life story or history as yielding up the possibility of change; it suggests the transcending nature of true human being. In the representation of a life in story, in interpreting history, Olsen seems to suggest that we actually redeem individual and communal loss.

In the quoted passage, an image of abundance and growth is set against an image of uniformity and limitation. A value judgment is implied on the part of the narrator. Surviving is not "enough"; rather, humans need room and time to grow and flourish. Fullness of being is the spiritual and historical hope of the passage. The tension of this story arises between a past lived amid limitations and a desire that its consequences—exhaustion, mundaneness, blight— may yet be recast in the minds of readers, thus gaining the power of sympathy and the possibility of transforming human action.

A central problem of each of the stories of this period is this: How can loss be transformed into knowledge for more abundant living? Or again, what spiritual vision arises from broken and lost lives in the light of which we may experience the promise of new creation?

Unlike *Yonnondio*, narrated by mother and daughter, "I Stand Here Ironing" is sifted through the mother's consciousness. Few stories of mothering have so powerfully and distressingly illuminated a mother's perspective. When women's fiction has depicted mothering, it has, as does Virginia Woolf's *To the Lighthouse* (Mrs. Ramsey), most often concerned women of the middle and upper classes.[11] There is the mother in Agnes Smedley's *Daughter of Earth*, whose portrait is searing in its harsh realities. More recent literature by black women writers like Toni Morrison offers mother characters who can be fruitfully compared with Olsen's mothers.[12] What distinguishes the mother narrator in this story is Olsen's style of building up a world through her sifting moral consciousness. This portrayal of a world through a mother's eyes—her iron-heavy recognition that what she has so painfully birthed (her daughter) may have no future just as she has had so little in her past—may be unsurpassed in American literature. In the story, Olsen contributes something radically new to our arts and letters: life as a struggling mother knows it *and as she wills it to be.* Only her perspective is given here, only her voice. Even Emily's words are spoken in the text through the mother's thought.

The story begins as a response to a school counselor who asks to speak to the mother about Emily: "I wish you could manage the time to come in and talk with me about your daughter" (9). The seemingly innocuous request, ironic because time is the very thing the mother has not been able to manage, leads to the story's reflection. Like the other stories of the collection, this one cannot simply be read from beginning to end. Rather, the reader must constantly reevaluate the story's intention in light of new significances that arise in the narrative and suggest an altered universe. Apparent dualizations are subverted, new associations are made through the mother's consciousness, and out of images first suggestive of death and decay, the vision of valued time emerges, one I would call a maternal vision since it emerges out of a woman's mothering thought.

Roughly speaking, the contrasting images in "I Stand Here Ironing" can be categorized as material and human. The iron, the clock, money, the nursery school, the convalescent home, fixed or formulaic language, and the bomb are negative metaphors pointing to the daughter's alienation from herself and from her mother and the mother's alienation from her mothering work. Smile, creative language, and body motion are more subtle and less frequent images reflective of regained wholeness and reconciliation. The first set of images corresponds with the daughter's illnesses, while the second corresponds with the possibility of health given at her birth and the sacred spark or inherent powers of her humanity. The dualization is overcome when the symbol of a new time—Emily's pantomime—distills the images into fluid motion and sound, thus reclaiming her past as well as her future.

A striking example of the imagistic contrast used in the story is the set of descriptions that dualize Emily and her younger sister, Susan. If machine versus human is the cosmic antagonism of the story, within the family the sisterly contrast mirrors that conflict, suggesting that the laws of competition and a model of scarcity permeate even the family. Emily, without father and often separated from the mother, is "skeleton thin," dark, quiet, slow, and thoughtful. Susan, by contrast, is Shirley Temple blond and curly, chubby and talkative, quick, even glib. Redeeming Emily's past will require a new way of understanding the images that construct a remembrance of her life, not only her physical appearance but the material world: the clock, the iron, the nursery school, and so on. For example, the mother must come to recognize that Emily's "darkness" may reveal gifts as well as hindrances.

Ironing frames the story and interrupts it once: "I stand here ironing, and what you asked me moves tormented back and forth with the iron," the mother begins (9). The prayerful statement "Only help her to know—help make it so there is cause for her to know—that she is more than this dress on the ironing board, helpless before the iron," indicates the mother's turn back to the original promise or miracle of her daughter's life (21). Reflecting at first on the counselor's request for time, she admits that time is beyond her control: "And when is there time to remember, to sift, to weigh, to estimate, to total? I will start and there will be an interruption and I will have to gather it all together again" (9). The mixed metaphors hold a contradiction. Sifting suggests examining but letting go. Gathering and totaling, on the other hand, suggest fixity, staying the memory or putting it firmly in place. The mother's motivation in the statement comes from a learned fear; she must make her language permanent, otherwise all appears lost: time, Emily, her own life. The sifting image, however, subverts her own thought, suggesting that her effort must seek another avenue.

The mother states twice, "She was a beautiful baby," and substantiates the claim with a lyrical passage describing Emily: "She loved motion, loved light, loved color and music and textures. She would lie on the floor in her blue overalls patting the surface so hard in ecstasy her hands and feet would blur" (10). However, in a linear and chronological reading of the story, the beauty is swallowed up by a multitude of remembrances characterized by ugliness and loss. The mother's memory of suckling illustrates this apparent movement from beneficence to pain or sickness. She mentions that she breast-fed Emily. But then she adds that she was governed by the clock: "Though her cries battered me to trembling and my breasts ached to swollenness, I waited til the clock decreed" (10). The passage is the first of many that will draw a parallel between Emily and the imagery of machines.

Naming her own age—nineteen—at Emily's birth and referring frequently to Emily's age, the mother remembers in order three separations from her daughter. In the first instance, Emily goes to live with her absent father's parents because her mother simply cannot support them both. An equation is thus suggested between (the lack of) money and separation. When Emily becomes ill with chicken pox, illness and harm are added to the combination. Returning home, she is pockmarked, her skin yellow, and the beauty gone. The direct effect of the mother's lack of money and her bondage to underpaid work is separation. The metaphoric connection in the imagery surrounding Emily is between illness and separation. A constellation of associations is created: (lack of) money, work, separation, illness, ugliness. Inhabiting the world evoked through this language construct is Emily.

In the second separation, the daughter struggles against the machine:

> She had a new daddy now to learn to love, and I think perhaps it was a better time.
>
> Except when we left her alone nights, telling ourselves she was old enough.
>
> "Can't you go some other time, Mommy, like tomorrow?" she would ask. "Will it be just a little while you'll be gone? Do you promise?"
>
> The time we came back, the front door open, the clock on the floor in the hall. She rigid awake. "It wasn't just a little while. I didn't cry. Three times I called you, just three times, and then I ran downstairs to open the door so you could come faster. The clock talked loud. I threw it away, it scared me what it talked" [12–13].

The clock keeps the time of absence, and its mechanical ticking scares the girl more than the silence. All of Emily's separations are related to her mother's loss of time; thus, her loss of beauty and miracle are an effect of devalued lifetime. Because her mother cannot raise her and work, Emily is sent away the first time. Later, she is sent away because the mother has a new baby and cannot care for Susan and Emily. In the passage just quoted, the mother appears to Emily to be absent simply because the clock is present. If the clock can be destroyed, perhaps the mother will return. The three calls may suggest three betrayals, but more to the point, they correspond with the three separations between Emily and her mother. This middle separation suggests that obliterating or ignoring time will not restore relationship. Rather, the experience of time must be transformed. At present, what the clock tells is the time of the mother/daughter separation, just as the clock in the factory or mill tells the time of workers' loss. Its language is redundancy. What Emily's childlike longing suggests is a desire for time as a condition of union, belonging, and correspondence rather than as alienation, separation, and loss.

In the third separation, the familiar brotherly conflict is rewritten as a sisterly one with the younger child usurping the first child's place. The baby's health is contrasted with Emily's disease. Throughout their childhood years, it will seem that the well-being of the second child requires the diminishment of the first. The convalescent home where Emily is sent to recuperate while Susan blossoms in her baby months is another sign of alienation. Girls and boys are dressed in uniforms; children are not allowed any personal possessions; the food is tasteless; and letters home are set as a requirement. After eight months, Emily comes home, "stiff," "thin," and "dark."

The story, then, concentrates on the time the mother and daughter did not have; that is, it calls to attention the mother's absence and the daughter's alienation. But the mother's still-present sense of connection with Emily and her despair over "what was not" calls into question the necessity of the separations. In turn this questioning creates an attitude of suspicion toward the metaphoric associations made by the mother between the past and Emily: illness, silence, darkness, associated with iron, clock, and lack of money. The mother's contrast between Emily and Susan, described in terms of what Emily "was not"—quick, articulate, chubby, golden—indicates a cultural standard that devalues or ignores the elder daughter. Societal circumstances have made Emily's experience equal with the negatives, not with beauty and creativity.

But the mother retains another vocabulary of images—smile, motion, and creative language—for remembering her daughter. The initial description of Emily seems a stark contrast with what she will later become. As a baby "she blew shining bubbles of sound. . . . loved light, . . . color and music and textures" (10). The language of the passage evokes an almost liquid reality. As a baby, Emily's being corresponded with air, time, and touch. In a much later description, the mother describes Emily when she pantomimes: "when she wants, how fluid. You must have seen it in her pantomimes, you spoke of her rare gift for comedy on the stage that rouses a laughter out of the audience so dear they applaud and applaud and do not want to let her go" (12).

Like Emily's word for comfort, "*shoogily*," passed on to the younger children, her pantomime is a symbol that reexamines the negative imaging of her life. Calling into being an alternate reality, pantomime makes something out of nothing. In the absence of structure, it evokes structures. Absence becomes presence. The movement of pantomime is fluid and uninterrupted by boundaries. The body is not controlled by matter, but the world of pantomime is created by the artist. When the audience laughs and will not let go of the joy, they have glimpsed their own ability to transcend fixity and the death implied by boundaries and ends. The evocation of laughter by Emily's acting is the story's symbolic manifestation of time as fluid and relational. Furthermore, Emily, with the audience, suggests the communal nature of transcendence. She evokes the laughter that is a resounding of her own new sense of having gained an artistic and authentic self.

In another recollection of Emily's gift, the mother thinks, "Then, Was this Emily? The control, the command, the convulsing and deadly clowning, the spell, then the roaring, stamping audience, unwilling to let this rare and precious laughter out of their lives" (19). Her description suggests a surprising blend of attitudes: "control," "command," "deadly" juxtaposed with "clowning," "precious," and "laughter." The combination of seeming opposites implies a rethinking of the images.

Now the silence of her youth is part of her acting. Used creatively, it evokes laughter, not tears. Similarly, her adult control, learned of necessity when she was little, is what makes her a successful comic now. Moreover, she has made connection with her first miraculous self.

The mother notes that her daughter is as alone in her difference as in her earlier anonymity, but Emily seems to defy her mother's despair when she comes home, "run[ning] up the stairs two at a time with her light graceful step" (19). Springing the flippant remark, "In a couple of years when we'll all be atom-dead they [my exams] won't matter a bit," Emily explodes the self-containment of the mother's narration. The casual remark, hurled down the stairs, reminds us of the clock thrown out of doors. Again, the action precipitates deep thinking on the mother's part, but more is at stake now. Suddenly Emily is emblematic of all children, of the next generation, whose universal lifetime may be eclipsed by war. Of course, the daughter's intention in the sentence is not to harm. But her language provokes the mother's breakdown, her seeming loss of hope that parallels her inability to manage time: "I will never total it all." What is most anguishing to the narrator is that Emily "*believes* it," that she appears to have capitulated not only to the losses of the past but to the loss of a future. Without that hope "out in front," Emily will not survive. If she does not believe in future presence, in beginnings latent in her own life, all is lost: past, present, and future.

The miraculous last paragraph of the story offers the sustaining hope of a mother for a child and a world. The effect is our rereading of Emily's life, even her present apathy, as potentially transformable. As a statement of the mother's faith, the closing plea—"Help her to know that she is more"—opens the story again, contradicting endings and death. That the story presents struggle rather than resolution, cutting off in ambiguity rather than triumph, indicates Olsen's historic perspective and her sense of reality as evolving through human relationships. Through juxtaposing a sense of fluid and relational time with static, absent, or fixed histories, the narrator comes to value the daughter's whole lifetime, even the images she first appears to negate. Seeing Emily's pantomime, she recognizes her own power to transform. Rather than viewing her past as lost, the mother reinterprets the contradictions, viewing the whole from the hoped-for promise—symbolized by the laughter evoked by Emily's re-creation of time on the stage—of whole and valued lifetime.

Like the moment beneath the catalpa in *Yonnondio*, Emily's art and the mother's prayer that creation, not death, will remain are moments in the text eliciting spiritual knowledge and response. In "I Stand Here Ironing," the moments are a new kind of conversing. The daughter's silent speech elicits wordless and joyful sound. The mother speaks toward the presence of hope. As in the *Yonnondio* passage, all the promises of the past ask to be restored, and time becomes mutable. The mother's view of time in this story appears to deny that the past is past. Instead, the hoped-for future, reflecting upon the past, regards it in its original promise and claims that the seeds of life present there may yet blossom. We are the mother's audience, and in light of her desire we begin to see that the need of all people for speech and hearing (art and reception) is our own. In this sounding we may find ourselves. In conversation time is converted from competition, which makes less time, to relationship, which makes more.

The mother's story (Olsen's own) seems a profound example of "hearing oneself to truth," to use Nelle Morton's language. With readers as audience, the mother does not "total it all," but she does come to understanding. In turn, we appropriate her truth, and in shared recognition of loss and hope, the transcendence of shared values and struggles is gained.

"Hey Sailor, What Ship?"

"Hey Sailor, What Ship?" is the painful remembrance of the lost dreams and unrealized hopes of Whitey, an aging, alcoholic merchant marine. The four-part narrative tells two stories: the first portrays in realistic detail Whitey's visit to his adoptive family (Lennie, Helen, Jeannie, Carol, and Allie); the second uses another visit, five days later, to limn the whole spectre of Whitey's life: his hope, decline, and loss. Back to back, the two visits begin in the present and then reach into the past. Unlike "I Stand Here Ironing," this story has more to do with loss of faith than with faith's resilience, and thus there is less hope, less opportunity for beginning again. The narrative voice, however, in prizing Whitey's life, gives stature and illumination to what once enlivened him.

Loss of the first-person narration and of the mother's perspective gives this story a more conventional aspect. It tends more toward linear plotting than the first story, despite the use of the juxtaposed visits. Furthermore, Whitey is the least compelling of all of Olsen's protagonists, perhaps because his narrative of loss appears so final. Unlike the mother/narrator in the first story, he does not have the resilience of spirit that arouses the reader on his behalf. What does distinguish the story (and lends it an international context) is the sailor's recitation of the Filipino poem in the last section of the text. Like Emily's pantomime, this text within the text scatters apparent ends and associations and presents momentarily a different reality. One needs to come back to this story after the next two since they develop the same family characters.

In Whitey's story, the alcoholism of the first section points to the deeper disease of isolation and alienation in the second, just as the human embrace between Allie and Whitey in the first is a remembrance of the love and care that once were the foundation of the friendship between Lennie and Whitey. The sailor's story, then, represents the decline of friendship in the context of certain other losses, among them, loss of "brotherhood," the story's word for the human sharing of struggle, circumstance, and opportunity.

On shore leave, Whitey, drunk and almost broke, wrestles with whether or not to go to the family. For years, he has entertained a dream: returning "home," all slicked up, carrying bags of groceries, money in his pockets. But it is a dream pointing to a deeper dream, foggy with forgetfulness, of adventure and brotherhood, of sharing life. He and Lennie had been friends way back; once, in the strike of 1934, Whitey had saved his buddy's life. But that symbol of connection, of one life given for another, has shrunk to a dream of exchanging money and things. This story too attempts to break the hold of simple and static equations (clock/money/lost time and self) by disclosing from within the characters' minds profounder and more affirmative associations.

Recalling the equation of time, money, and clock in "I Stand Here Ironing," Whitey's two opening questions: "Wha time's it anyway?" and "Where'd it all go?" (referring to his pay) suggest an evaluation of time in terms of money. Like the spent salary, the setting elicits a sense of material diminishment: "The grimy light; the congealing smell of cigarettes that had been smoked long ago and of liquor that had been drunk long ago, . . . the greasy feel of the bar as he gropes for his glass" (22). Emerging momentarily from his confusion, Whitey realizes his shipping buddy has slipped out, and the bartender he remembered has also gone. He "lurches through the past" to recollect the lost pay, but he cannot will his body to "feel good." The money has evaporated, and the promised relief of alcohol has turned to sickness.

At Lennie's and Helen's, the same feelings preside: emptiness and illness. Looking at their faces, he sees the reflection of his own age. In a foreshadowing of Eva in "Tell Me a Riddle," the children's exuberance is almost too great for Whitey to bear. He struggles to make connection with the aging parents and the growing children. "Who is real and who is not," he questions. He has "forgotten, how big the living room was. (And is he really here?)" (25–26). The slipping back and forth from narrator's to Whitey's thought gives to the reader the feel of alcoholic illusion and lost sense of time suffered by the sailor. This is not the harmony of the waves but the disequilibrium of a storm. The whole world of the story seems to rock like an unanchored ship. Thus the alcohol both dulls Whitey's memory and signifies to us the hopeless disconnectedness of life when raped of its dreams.

One evening after Whitey's sickness has subsided, the youngest daughter, Allie, comes frightened down the stairs from bed. She was the first to see the new scar on his face. Now she crawls up beside him on the couch. The scene is like an earlier one, painfully remembered in the second story, when Jeannie—the eldest—was four and climbed into his bed: "He starts as if he has been burned, . . . It is destroying, dissolving him utterly, this helpless warmth against him, the feel of a child—lost country to him and unattainable" (29). The "dissolve" of the body-to-body contact reminds the reader both of the fluid movement of Emily's pantomime and, contradictorally, of Whitey's alcoholic loss of perspective, memory, and bearing. "Helpless warmth," like "deadly clowning," reveals the paradoxical character of lives where dreams and time have been largely undervalued and lost. They have been diminished, but they are still human. The feel of human touch so unfamiliar that it burns suggests a situation of isolation and ultimate loneliness. Allie is a small island for Whitey's unanchored ship, but the anchoring is brief. The "lost country" is something like Eva's lost "springs" in "Tell Me a Riddle," an original principle of life now vanished amid the years.

To defend against his exposure, Whitey "strokes, strokes Allie's soft hair as if the strokes would solidify, dense into a protection." In the midst of telling stories of his last voyages out, "a tide of peaceful drowsiness washes over the tumult in him; he . . . strokes, strokes Allie's soft pale hair" (30–31). Between the burn of the initial touch and the self's attempt to defend, to erect a barrier or solidify the embrace, a middle country is gained—a land evoked in the language of "tide," "wash," and "tumult." In the dream country of water, Whitey achieves the peace that the bottle promised and denied.

The remainder of the scene compounds the sense of at-one-ness that Whitey momentarily experiences with Allie. The embrace, like Mazie's and Anna's, offers a moment of transcending love and a symbol of holy communion. When Jeannie walks in, looking to Whitey like her mother, Helen, her cheeks are described as "glistening from the rain" (31). In a language borrowed from the sailor's life, she comments:

> Never saw so many peaceful wrecks in my life. . . . That's what I want to be when I grow up, just a peaceful wreck holding hands with other peaceful wrecks . . .
>
> . . . kneel[ing] down beside Whitey, and using his long ago greeting [she] asks softly, Hey Sailor, what ship? [31]

The scene suggests a generational continuity that transcends the contrast of age and the recognized bonds of blood. "Peaceful wrecks" is another paradoxical phrase suggesting the grace and brokenness of these lives. Len and Helen, who are holding hands, mirror the universal connectedness embodied by Allie's and Whitey's embrace. The scene, of bonding to uphold, seems more than a stoic acceptance of life's vicissitudes. Framed by the rain outside and the stroking of Allie's hair, the passage reads like the lapping of water, gaining the transcendent harmony of connectedness, which Whitey once knew with other sailors in the union. In shared values and concerns there is meaning greater than the parts, purpose that redeems individual loss.

The image closing the scene shadows the one above in the evocation of human relatedness, in the ambiguous coexistence of beneficence and death, and in the discosure of a fluid reality: "And as Len carries Allie up the stairs,the fire leaps up, kindles Len's shadow so that it seems a dozen bent men cradle a child up endless stairs, while the rain traces on the windows, beseechingly, ceaselessly, like seeking fingers of the blind" (32).

Fire and water suggest the writer's determination to hold together the pain and the love that characterize these lives. The text, like the rain, searches for meaning in the apparent contradictions of Whitey's once hopeful life and his present disease. Even nature, personified as the blind seeking fingers of the rain, appears to empathize with the sailor's lonely searching.

Whitey's alcohol, an escape from memory, is also an attempt to break down the barriers that divide. The series of images depicting human to human touch are the text's search for a connectedness that is achieved without the circular and destructive habit of alcohol-induced dream, that "ceaseless . . . searching." The glimpse of right relationship and shared living is given in Whitey's embrace with Allie, twice reflected: once through Jeannie, who is at the same time a youthful Helen, and then through Lennie, who takes Whitey's place, cradling the child up the stairs. The participation of several distinct characters in the imagery of beneficent relating, reminds us of *Yonnondio*. Like actors in a drama, the characters together show the form of human care and sympathy.

Section four of the story begins the second episode, which tells of another visit. Whitey returns in a taxi with groceries, money, and gifts. The realized dream leaves unrealized, however, the deeper dream of brotherhood. On one level, the story embodies the cliché that intimacy cannot be bought. Having returned with gifts, Whitey must face the real and apparently lost dream of human sharing that once directed and illumined his life. When he comes, brassy, handing out money like candy to children, Helen and Len are embarrassed. Carol and Allie are childlike enough to accept gifts, but Jeannie is adamant in her rejection. Unable to express his emotion, Whitey tries to draw from her the memory of his former care:

How's [the] watch I gave you, remember?

(Not what he means to say at all. Remember the love I gave you, the worship offered, the toys I mended and made, the questions answered, the care for you, the pride in you.)

I lost the watch, remember? 'I was too young for such expensive presents.' You keep talking about it because that's the only reason you give presents, to buy people to be nice to you and to yak about the presents when you're drunk [39–40].

The misunderstanding illustrates a failure of language and seems to destroy the picture of their earlier communion. Whitey's words misrepresent his own deep feelings for Jeannie and the history of his care for her. But Jeannie, too, in hearing only the literal question and not the deep question, refuses to bear her part in remembering the past. Both have succumbed to the temptation of equating relationship with money and what it can buy. Both forget the symbolic dimension of gift giving, its pointing to the love that elicits it. In seeking, as Jeannie says, to buy love, Whitey makes his life's work equal to the pay he draws, and in her inability to receive the life that Whitey seeks to give, Jeannie betrays her own unwillingness to bring to light the gift of love being offered.

An interesting reversal has occurred. The first story operates at the literal level of present-tense occurrence. When Allie and Whitey embrace, the imagery points metaphorically to the former time when the relationship between Whitey and his friends was more truly reciprocal and their love more evident. In the second story, which is closer to the symbolic depth of Whitey's life as a universal human story of hope felt and dreams lost, Jeannie and Whitey fail to recognize the spiritual depth of their relationship. No image is evoked by either character to suggest a reality any deeper than the material, which was given and then lost. Without a language to represent it, the once felt love and those earlier times are not recoverable. Unremembered or uninterpreted, time does appear simply to move past us into the dark. We only make history in word, in interpretation of the past, which opens our lives and makes new beginnings.

A family album, brought out by Carol and offered to Whitey, is a second effort by the text to force the characters deeper into the past, to remember the care and love that once permeated the relationship. Moments later, when Whitey recites "Crown 'n Deep," at Carol's request, he gives voice to a vision, disrupting the literal equation of lifetime and money and—through a new pattern of images—reevaluating his own history.[13] Although he cannot consciously appropriate the transformation into his personal life, a different world comprehension is born, acting as a sign for the stories that follow.

The picture Whitey turns from shows, "Under the joyful sun, proud sea, proud ship as background, the proud young man, glistening hair and eyes, joyful body, face open to life, unlined. Sixteen? Seventeen? Close it up, he says, M. Norbert Jacklebaum never saw the guy" (40).

The vocal betrayal "never saw the guy" (himself), is contradicted by his searching fingers touching his now aging and scarred face. As the narrator suggests, it is the same but not the same as the one in the picture. *"Tracing the scars, the pits and lines, the battered nose; seeking to find"* (41). The scars, like Emily's pockmarks, remind us that harsh life experiences leave their mark. In a way, Whitey wears his story on his face. But signs of suffering become, for the reader, indices to understanding.

The recital of "Crown 'n Deep" symbolizes Whitey's recognition of the values that give his own life meaning, even if, by cultural and even personal standards, his future appears valueless. The poem, known as "The Valedictory," was written by Jose Rizal, hero of the Philippines in its fight for independence from Spain. The night before his execution (in 1898), Rizal composed the lines: "El Ultimo Adiós," Whitey was taught them by a fellow shipmate. "Taking the old proud stance," he chants:

Land I adore, farewell. . . .
Our forfeited garden of Eden,
Joyous I yield up for thee my sad life
And were it far brighter,
Young or rose-strewn, still would I give it.

Vision I followed from afar,
Desire that spurred on and consumed me,
Beautiful it is to fall
That the vision may rise to fulfillment.

Little will matter, my country,
That thou shouldst forget me.
I shall be speech in thy ears, fragrance and color,
Light and shout and loved song. . . .

O crown and deep of my sorrows,
I am leaving all with thee, my friends, my love,
Where I go are no tyrants. . . . [41–42]

The promise of the song is especially for those whose lives are spent, for the disinherited of Eden. This lyrical text suggests rereading hurts and losses in the light of a promise, a vision like a guiding star of hope. The songster, now old, promises his life *as if it were young*. The garden motif reflects a universal antagonism: set apart from the original promise, humanity seeks restoration. The second stanza points forward as the narrator follows a future vision. Paradoxically, the spent life brings the vision closer. In further contradiction, the third stanza suggests that the "fall" is not final. Rather, the life is reincarnated as speech, fragrance, color, light, and song.

Remembering the embrace between Allie and Whitey and the intergenerational continuity of that scene, we can reread the country lost and regained as a specific instance of the visionary time and place Whitey evokes in the song. Whereas the fluid water images in the first scene symbolized a more beneficent relating, though paradoxically a relating that included shared suffering, in this instance all of creation's sensual communications are cosmic signs of the given promise: fragrance, color, light, sound harken us to a different reality, to presences and powers that reflect our own inner beauties and possibilities.

In the new context of song, Whitey's scarred life is re-visioned in terms of the dreams that have inspired it. As readers, we begin to understand his life in accordance with his youthful hopes. The title, "Crown n' Deep," signifies the paradoxical vision: suffering and sorrow are both the depth and height of life given for the cause of "brotherhood." Out of these arise hopes, which are the true substance and meaning of life. One can die without having achieved all, but one cannot live without hope.

"Hey Sailor, What Ship?" does not achieve a personal transformation (Whitey's) of the images of death, loss, and sickness. Reflecting the understanding of the other characters, Helen says that Whitey's only power is money. She and Len have lost faith, the narrator tells us, in Whitey's salvation. That the narrator intervenes more and more in the last pages indicates the characters' inability to imagine a way of making life again the life of brotherhood. Whitey's thwarted attempt to represent a fellow sailor suggests that situation and chance have burdened the vision to the breaking point.

In this story, the reader alone is left to supply the historical remembrance that will allow Whitey to live. When Helen and Len ask repeatedly, "What's going to happen with you, Whitey,?" the question comes out of the text and addresses us (45). Leaving the house thirsty for drink, Whitey is clearly descending into the depths. The waters there will not satisfy nor restore the lost time of his once hopeful life. Yet the imagistic clues for a transcending and transforming experience of time are given: Allie's human touch, water that cleanses and renews, and the song of brotherhood. Life lived in hope is true lifetime. Stories of struggle that capture that inspiration reincarnate the lives that embodied it in the past. Thus "all goes onward and outward, nothing collapses."[14]

"O Yes"

In "O Yes" we meet again the family of Lennie, Helen, Jeannie, Carol, and Allie. Yet the story marks a shift in the writing of Olsen's second period. Of the four stories, this one appears to draw least from the history of immigrant life, perhaps because it focuses on the children, who are probably second generation, and the atmosphere of the story has more to do with black/white race relations in the 1950s. Moreover, in telling the story of a black girl and a white girl, the text deals largely with the perspectives of black Americans and of children. In this third story, the imagery of machinery and of illness (iron, clock, alcohol) is not the primary language that reflects the characters' need for transformed understanding. Instead, human images are used to reflect separation and loss, and two girls' personal histories reflect the larger history of their races.

As Virginia Woolf observed, the subject of girls' friendship is rare in literature. Only recently, with novels like Doris Lessing's *The Golden Notebook*, Alice Walker's *The Color Purple*, and Toni Morrison's *Sula*, have we become accustomed to realistic literary portrayals of intimate female peer relationships. In taking on the subject of interracial friendship, Olsen has offered an even rarer portrait.[15]

Within the story, the damaged friendship of Carol and Parialee mirrors a larger societal pattern of segregation. Though these girls actually live in an integrated neighborhood, an antagonistic tide of time appears to be moving them toward separation. In the story, however, we come to see that an understanding of the black American past may offer insight for transforming the girls' future. The black religious faith it depicts depends upon a hope that arises out of black experience. Like Jose Rizal's vision "followed from afar," the hope is both within and in front of them. It is a desire that comes out of historical contexts, out of life, and a light or star that guides. Thus finalizations or end causes are refuted. New being and beginning are always possible in the conversation between past, present, and hoped-for future.

In the first two stories, a transformation in understanding is brought about by symbols suggesting a different experience of time: pantomime, song, and human embrace. Through those human images, the narratives evoke a sense of potentiality and hope capable of redeeming personal and community loss. The message of change is even more pronounced in this story. Tears are transformed through dream into an anointing. By immersion into the reality of prejudice and its destructive power, Carol begins to learn the black rhythms of hope. The way to these transformations is metaphorical. One matrix of meaning, the plot of dissolution and loss, coexists with the text's imagistic evocation of a different time and life experience, in which all will be valued and loved. Through this paradoxical comparison of loss and potential transformation, we glimpse again (remembering the catalpa scene in *Yonnondio*) a relational struggle disclosing the depths and heights of human emotion and thus of our apprehension of ultimacy.

Sorting, the story's metaphor for the broken friendship, evokes the world of industrial production, division, and distribution, which for Olsen reverberates with loss at several levels, especially lost time. As a metaphor for what happens with Carol and Parialee, the sorting metaphor suggests the way humans have structured their alienation from one another. Yet when Alva, Parry's mother, dreams of the convey line, it portends her responsibility for others; thus the negative image is made to serve as the impetus for a new vision of human relationships.

This story, then, like the others, works by posing a plot of descent and loss in language that illuminates a possible transformation in the lives it embodies. If the poem Whitey recites breaks upon the text like waves, coming and receding, the songs in this story come more like a furious rain, drenching the landscape and, in the aftermath, promising renewal to the roots of all living things. From the beginning, song, human movement, and dream subvert the story's plot in terms of its opposite: integration and reconciliation. Thus, in another imagistic description foreshadowing Eva in "Tell Me a Riddle," the story gives "the angle of experience where the dark is distilled into light. . . . It says, in effect, that groaning as we may be, we move in the figure of a dance, and, so moving, we trace the outline of the mystery."[16]

Like "Hey Sailor, What Ship?" the story is composed of two episodes and is told from a limited omniscient point of view. It suffers somewhat from the lack of a central consciousness among the characters; we are not certain whose story this is. The black girl and her mother, Alva, provide the experience from which the narrative voice draws its sense of justice and freedom, but they don't emerge as the protagonists.

The first section of the story pictures Carol's and Helen's visit to Parry's church, where she is to be baptized.[17] Carol, frightened by the unleashed religious emotion of the black congregation, faints and later resists Alva's attempt to help her understand the experience. The second episode provides the background of the girls' friendship and shows the present state of its deterioration. The narrator and the characters are prone to suggest that society makes the present pattern of segregation inevitable, but the closing thought of Helen, Carol's mother, discloses an ethical vision that revises the given of the present and past and makes both transformable. This possibility of change makes even Carol responsible for her future, just as Emily is left in many ways responsible *to believe*, but in change, not destruction. For Olsen, the more one has the means to transform the world, the more one is responsible. And yet, the vision of an ethical universe begins with the situation of the oppressed. Thus Carol must understand what is required by learning from Parry, "the least of these" in this story.

The text opens upon a world in motion. A series of descriptions immediately portrays a feeling of dynamism:

> . . . the crucified Christ embroidered on the starched white curtain leaps in the wind of the sudden singing. And the choirs march in. . . .

> . . . Singing, little Lucinda Phillips fluffs out her many petticoats; singing, little Bubbie bounces up and down on his heels.

> *Any day now I'll reach that land of freedom*
>
> > *Yes, o yes*
>
> *Any day now, know that promised land*

> The youth choir claps and taps to accent the swing of it. Beginning to tap, Carol stiffens. "Parry, look. Somebody from school."

> "Once more once," says Parialee, in the new way she likes to talk now [49].

Only Carol, fearing recognition, steels herself against the movement. Her efforts to "untwine the intertwined voices" (50) is indicative of her reluctance to yield to the emotion that seduces her, not simply because she may be seen, but because the expression itself is foreign to her.

Her resistance takes the form of memory, but while she hopes to lose herself in thought, the images she remembers actually correspond with the present situation, so that her attempt to ignore the present through the past is overturned by the power of the past to interpret the present. She begins the old game of "drumming a rhythm" on Parry's arm. Using the preacher's "voice of drowsiness and dream," she slips back: "As long ago. Parry warm beside her too, as it used to be, there in the classroom at Mann Elementary, and the feel of drenched in the sun and dimness and dream. Smell and sound of the chalk wearing itself away to nothing, rustle of books, drumming tattoo of fingers on her arm: *Guess*" (52). She remembers "the used-to-be play-yard. Tag. Thump of the volley ball. Ecstasy of the jump rope" (52). The images, like the description of the church, are dynamic images of human bodies in relationship. The games are not solitary but communal, not efforts toward escape but expressions of freedom.

The daydreaming offers an insight, which Carol seeks to deny but later comes near to understanding. The church worship and the childhood play correspond in their evocation of relationship and of the human desire for freedom and expression. Carol thinks they are different experiences; furthermore, she thinks of the childhood remembrances as fortresses against the present when, in fact, they lead back into the present, both in form and content. Thus, the text exposes the rift in Carol's and Parry's friendship in terms of contrasting religious and cultural histories. Parry's religion teaches her that a past of suffering is reclaimed by a promise of freedom born within her. She needs that belief in the face of her racial history and even her present situation. Forged out of necessity, the black religious comprehension Olsen represents suggests that time and history must be redeemable through hope. It is in one's soul to be free. Furthermore, if a past of abuse and degradation becomes the lens for envisioning a better future and if one continues to believe, then no struggle is in vain and no death is ultimately final. Helen's hope, spoken to her daughter, "But may be friends again. As Alva and I are" (70), referring to Carol and Parry, is the story's synoptic attitude toward time. It is echoed as well by the preacher, who promises, "All will be returned to you, every dust, every atom" (52).

The story builds in tension, as the more the congregation gives expression to a religious experience of promise, the more Carol resists hearing. Old women and young move into the aisles, "getting happy"; emotion builds as the hymns give way to speaking in tongues, screaming, and even fainting. The preacher's voice, "looping, scalloping," is answered by the choir's thundering: *"Great Day / When the battle's fought / And the victory's won"* (53). The sounds become monstrous for Carol, and the childhood memory seems to be perverted by the events: the "awful thrumming sound . . . like a giant jumping of a rope" (54).

Scream and song, tears and rejoicing are woven together in the service, which evokes a whole range of human responses. The meeting is characterized by voices answering one another, by simultaneity of events, and by the religious eruption of deeply felt desires held communally by the people. The narrator's initial aloofness toward the event seems itself to be transformed into the participation asked of Carol. Even the theology of relationships preached from the pulpit seems to undergo transformation from traditional images—"your mother's rock. Your father's mighty tower"—to the humbler images of the "little baby," "Way maker," "Door opener" (54).

The sermon becomes an invitation to transformation: "I will put my Word in you and it is power." "And I'll wash [your feet] in the well your tears made" (55). Language becomes power; suffering becomes an anointing. In response, the congregation and the entire setting seem metaphorically transformed: "The piano whipping, whipping air to a froth." "The music leaps and prowls. Ladders of screamings. Drumming feet of ushers running" (56–57). When the congregation exults, "*O Yes*," Carol defends with blindness; "No, do not look." But the singing demands more: "*it's time to go higher / Wade wade*," and the people "swaying with it too, moving like in slow waves and singing" (57). At last Carol submits, but it is to the undertow: "Christ spirals on his cross in the window—and she is drowned under the sluice of the slow singing and the sway" (58).

Carol's dream and her fainting, while given in much the same language as the church worship, are strangely different. She tries to make the event controllable, "a record small and round to listen to far and far as if into a seashell" (56). The church is like a great body consuming her, and, understandably, she resists. What comforts and restores some, threatens her. The church service that genuinely expresses the black community's hope alienates the white girl. Carol's response reflects a more decorous spirituality, where music doesn't turn into water, and old women don't shout. Thus the service and Carol's resistance reflect the broader divisions of society as a whole, while the black religious experience, interpreting history as a process of change in the light of hope, points to the story's historical hope for true—that is, chosen—racial integration in America and for economic justice.

Different histories bring different needs and suggest different interpretations. When Carol awakens in the car Alva tries to explain this: "Not everybody feels religion the same way. Some it's in their mouth, but some it's like a hope in their blood, their bones. And they singing songs every word that's real to them, Carol, every word out of they own life. And the preaching finding lodgement in their hearts" (60). Alva suggests that the impetus for the religious expression that Carol fears is the life experience of these Americans themselves. The words are real because they correspond with people's longing, not vice versa. Religion, then, arises from the free expression of one's struggle in the hope that what one feels has real consequence and that one's voice contributes to the divine/human duet. Carol fears the language and the singing as if they are alien to her, although both come directly out of the racial experience of her friend Parry.

In this story, the world is already being transformed, by a black congregation speaking of its experience with the authority and will to claim what is so and what will be. Unwittingly, by refusing to be transformed by Parry's racial perspective, Carol seems to choose segregation. To enter Parry's history would mean, as Helen knows, to feel what it means to live a life in black skin. Thus, a true baptism for Carol would be an awakening to her bondedness with Parry, which transcends difference and the fear we often have of it.

While Parry's baptism is into the church, then, Carol's is into human struggles she does not yet comprehend.

The first episode closes with Alva's dream told to Carol. It is a parabolic witness to the way of change, which Carol must search for. The recollection begins with a brief history of the downward movement of Alva's life: *"When I was carrying Parry and her father left me, and I was fifteen years old, one thousand miles away from home, sin-sick and never really believing, as still I don't believe all, scorning, for what have it done to help, waiting there in the clinic and maybe sleeping, a voice called: Alva, Alva"* (61). Left by husband and father, the shape of her life and that of the child reflect the mother and daughter in "I Stand Here Ironing." "Sin-sick" refers not to individual sin but to the experience of separation from meaningful relations. One feels that it is not in spite of lost faith but because of it that the vision comes:

> *Alva. Fear not, I have loved you from the foundation of the universe. And a little small child tugged on my dress. He was carrying a parade stick, on the end of it a star that outshined the sun. Follow me, he said. And the real sun went down and he hidden his stick. How dark it was, how dark. I could feel the darkness with my hands. And when I could see, I screamed. Dump trucks run, dumping bodies in hell, and a convey line run, never ceasing with souls, weary ones having to stamp and shove them along, and the air like fire. Oh I never want to hear such screaming. Then the little child jumped on a motorbike making a path no bigger than my little finger. But first he greased my feet with the hands of my momma when I was a knee baby. They shined like the sun was on them. Eyes he placed all around my head, and as I journeyed upward after him, it seemed I heard a mourning: "Mama Mama you must help carry the world." The rise and fall of nations I saw. And the voice called again Alva Alva, and I flew into a world of light, multitudes singing, Free, free I am so glad [61].*

The dream takes elements of the church service and of Carol's experience together and integrates them into a narrative that subverts the sorting of races (the story's plot) by subverting the dualism of physical and spiritual realms. It combines personal and religious history into one perspective, telling the story of spiritual encounter in secular imagery. Traditional and Biblical statements— "Fear not," "I have loved you from the foundation of the universe," "Follow me"—are juxtaposed with the almost absurd images of a baby with a parade stick and motorbike and the industrialized Dantesque image of condemned souls.

The story transforms the preacher's apocalyptic vision by bringing it into touch with the sensuous and worldly: "He greased my feet with the hands of my momma . . . They shined like the sun." The child becomes the parent and yet again calls Alva the mother who "must help carry the world." The sentence is a commission that leads to freedom: "I flew into a world of light." The last sentence repeats the Negro song from the service. Thus, Alva is visited by the divine messenger in a secular situation, in an attitude of disbelief, and in a moment of severe personal crisis. And though "as yet" she does not "believe all," she believes in the truth to which the vision points: "You must help carry the world."

Alva's witness to Carol—that what is unconditional and ultimate is one's own life *and* the lives of others whom one may help—is metaphoric of the story's focus upon relationship as the context of morality. True being emerges out of reciprocal acting and caring. Whitey experienced only moments of at-one-ness. He needed to be carried. Amazingly perhaps, the young pregnant Alva, unbeliever and a thousand miles from home, is a carrier, a bearer of others' lives, a black angel who acts and speaks with power.

As in Whitey's story, the second episode returns to the first and, in reflection upon it, expands our understanding. Helen suggests the significance of the church event when she comments to Len, her husband, "Something . . . deep happened" (62). They, with the older sister, Jeannie, try to explain the girls' separation in terms of the school's system of sorting. White children are assumed to be brighter and are put in advanced classes. Negro children learn "jivetalk" and "rhythmandblues." When Len asks Jeannie: "It's that final? . . . Don't you think . . . Carol and Parry can show it doesn't have to be that way," Jeannie is unequivocal: "They can't. They can't. They don't let you" (63).

The key phrase is *"How they sort."* Helen recollects various times in the past when Carol had told of divisive events at school. A certain way of dressing and behaving is appropriate, and that way is consistent with the behavior of those most well-to-do; those who cannot afford to dress "appropriately," or whose ethnic and cultural background leads to alternate ways of acting and speaking, are automatically shunned. Helen begins to understand Carol's dilemma in a system that demands that she choose between being one of the kids (her type) and being friends with Parry.

The impasse is the now recognizable impasse—the riddle— presented in all of Olsen's stories. No solution is possible within the boundaries of a future dictated by an unredeemed past. The narrative cannot proceed toward logical ends. Rather, even the past must be reinvented, structured according to loves and hopes it embodied, in order that separation and ending may be transcended.

The story works its way through the riddle by way of two episodes between Parry and Carol. The first, the family sees from the window:

> In the wind and the shimmering sunset light, half the children of the block are playing down the street. Leaping, bouncing, hallooing, tugging the kites of spring. In the old synchronized understanding, Carol and Parry kick, catch, kick, catch. And now Parry jumps on her pogo stick (the last time), Carol shadowing her, and Bubbie, arching his body in a semicircle of joy, bounding after them, high, higher, higher [65–66].

The scene evokes the sense of movement and rhythm characteristic of the service: "shimmering . . . light," "leaping, bouncing, hallooing, tugging." The language of play is correspondence; bodies give and receive "in the old synchronized understanding," just like the game of tapping a rhythm. The closing abstraction, "high, higher, higher," is reminiscent of the song, *Come on my brethren it's time to go higher.* Witnessed by the family, the scene is given in their silence. Carol's shadowing suggests her deep identity with Parry, while the passage as a whole, set against Jeannie's despair, offers the dynamic feel of a reality in which boundaries are trespassed and the world becomes unhinged. This scene, symbolic of the girls' past, acts as a sign to Carol's later recognition of her true self as the one bonded with Parry.

In seeming despair, the narrative breaks after the scene. Time is speeded by, and the lapse threatens to annul the deep understanding invited by the church experience. The lives are summarized: "And now seldom Parry and Carol walk up the hill together. . . . No more the bending together over the homework." Parry's life is capsulized in language reflective of Emily's mother: "for where is there space or time and what is the sense?" (66).

The second episode brings the sorting back in focus and forces a recognition from Carol that she is culpable. The action is not spectacular: Parry is asked to bring Carol's homework when she is sick; the teacher supposes that Parry's mother works for Carol's and treats her with suspicion and contempt; Parry visits Carol, and the girls make unsuccessful attempts at reconnection. But three actions by Parry, seemingly insignificant, prod Carol toward a transformed understanding.

Parry now reflects the situation of her mother alone in the clinic, mistrusted, but called to be responsible. Parry, too, is the black-child messenger or angel. The signs or actions she performs evolve out of her performance of the role that is her cultural inheritance— straightening the white girl's room. But she transforms what she fixes, and revitalizes the love and identity of her past with Carol. Taking books and binders from the bed to arrange on the dresser, she first marks each one with a lipstick face: "bemused or mocking or amazed—on each paper jacket" (68). Picking up "their year-ago, arm-in-arm graduation picture," she replaces it upside down in the mirror crevice. She sets to movement a mobile she and Carol made of painted eggshells and straws.

Parry leaves her mark. Like the gospel spiritual or the visionary dream, she refuses the authority of a static, nontransformable reality. Setting Carol's room to movement, Parry invites her friend to bring the past into the present and to follow the voice within her, to know herself as the one who must carry the world, one who must go higher. Like Emily's hurled clock, her turning the graduation picture upside down is an act of rebellion against the way things are.

Later, when Carol hears the spiritual on the radio, "*Come on brethren we've got to go higher,*" she finally confesses that she is no longer Parry's friend. The song, the mobile, the turned picture are signs both of the lost friendship and of the possibility that Carol and Parry may be reunited. In tears, the white girl tells her mother that when Parry is hurt, she (Carol) feels "Like I'm her." Wanting to forget, she pleads, "Oh why is it like it is and why do I have to care?" Helen can only think, "*caring asks doing*" (71).

In this closing, Carol and Parry are less individual girls than symbols of their races. Their story is a representation of black and white history in America and of the racial crisis that came to a head in this country in the 1950s. They stand at a moment of cultural decision, a time ripe for new understanding, a kairos.

The black religious experience reflected in the story suggests the interconnection of personal experience and cultural responsibility, of spirituality and politics. "*I have loved you from the foundation of the universe*" is a statement elicited by Alva's (a black woman's) need for help, while the sentence "*You must help carry the world*" makes her (and her race) responsible to live for the sake of others. Jesus' death and resurrection—"*Has risen from the dead . . . / And won't have to die no more*"—suggests a supreme example of care and illustrates the ultimate human need for time: "*We won't have to die no more*" (56). In response, all (black and white) are called "*to go higher.*" Dependence and responsibility are the givens of human existence and only through mutual give and take between the races can transformation occur. We find ourselves not in losing ourselves but *in hearing the deep voices within,* which we all share as human beings.

When Helen thinks, "*It is a long baptism into the seas of*

humankind," she representatively accepts Carol's responsibility for Parry. But Carol, too, must be responsible. The mother, like Alva, believes and doubts: *"Yet how will you sustain?"* (71).

What becomes clear to the reader—like the dawning of moral consciousness in Carol—is that each of these three stories is piloted by a consciousness grappling with the conception of passing or past time. For Emily, Whitey, Carol, and Parry, time cannot simply be regarded as a past sequence of events or a record of unredeemed struggle. If it is, then there is no hope for Emily's losses, the agony of Whitey's life is absolutely unredeemable, and black and white can never share common dreams and struggles.

A different understanding of time, one illumined by the hope that inspires these lives, lends a value greater than mere documentation to the stories. If time is the condition of learning and the context of human struggle toward connection or bondedness, then personal and cultural histories may offer renewed vision to human existence. Knowing Emily's girlhood may lend profounder understandings of life's needs. Participating in Whitey's grief, we learn of the sustaining power of "brotherhood." Carol's initiation into difference is something like our own as readers, since all of these stories ask us to enter worlds we have not often seen in literature and to find our own identity in the context of someone else's pain and hope. Insofar as such learning leaves traces on our consciousness or offers direction to our actions, these lives are dynamically connected with the future. This means that the characters' histories are given new possibilities, and that their losses are not absolute. In our renewed understanding of the past, we may hope not only for the future but for the past, just as the black congregation can hope for their slave ancestors, believing that their lives are not ultimately lost.

The past, as a set of facts or a sequence of events, cannot change, but we can change in light of the past.[18] Our understanding brings with it the very lives that have been sacrificed, and our present struggles reincarnate theirs.

As a metaphor, the song of the church suggests this understanding. For the black congregation, songs have carried the longings of past generations into the present and give voice to the hopes born with each new generation. Long-ago voices are echoed in the words of babes. The singing community, then, remembers the past and draws strength from ancestors. Thus is the community always enlarged and past hopes felt to interact with the present. In this sense, time is always an expansion rather than a loss of possibility and hope. Old notions of time are transcended, and human connections lend a deep sense of power to the people. The community is spiritual and political, believing in worldly change because of a hope drawn out of its deepest sense of self, a sense of justice and of truth. Such a comprehension of human history and ultimate concern finds its fullest expression in the novella "Tell Me a Riddle," where personal and collective identity are deepened in death and re-creation.

"Tell Me a Riddle"

The title story (actually a novella) of the collection is dedicated to *"two* [women] *of that generation / Seevya and Genya* [turn-of-the-century Russian Jews] *Infinite, dauntless, incorruptible"* (125).[19] Through scenes descriptive of her family relationships and remembered fragments of a life, "Tell Me a Riddle" speaks of a woman's death. The characters, Eva and David (parents of Lennie, grandparents of Jeannie, Carol, and Allie), were young activists during the 1905 revolution in Russia. From the story, we learn of a Siberian imprisonment and of escape aboard a steerage ship. What the couple had hoped for, like many socialists and Russian Jews, was a century of freedom and humanism. Instead, as Eva's language reflects, wars flourished, and death camps and bombs extinguished innocent lives. Though their story is last, Eva's and David's are actually the first lives in these interconnecting narratives. We might even say that Eva (Eve) is a first woman or every woman. Read so, her life may be understood to illuminate the history out of which women writers and readers come. In Alice Walker's words, she is one like

> our mothers and grandmothers, some of them, moving to a music not yet written. And they waited.
> They waited for a day when the unknown thing in them would be made known.[20]

In the closing hours of Eva's life, as she whispers fragments of song and rhetoric from her revolutionary youth, she does disclose the music of her truest self. David comes to recognize his collaboration in the loss of their vision. He chose to find comfort in an existence no longer marked by struggle. Shamefully, he feels "the bereavement and betrayal he had sheltered—compounded through the years—hidden even from himself." He reflects upon his "escape . . . to the grandchildren . . . who had never hungered, who lived unravaged by disease in warm houses of many rooms." And he speaks "as if in her harsh voice": *are there no other children in the world?"* (120–21).

From Eva's song and David's reflection come the riddle or paradox of the story: How is it that pain and suffering simultaneously distill hope and faith:

> That world of their youth—dark, ignorant, terrible with hate and disease—how was it that living in it, in the midst of corruption, filth, treachery, degradation, they had not mistrusted man nor themselves; had believed so beautifully, so . . . falsely?

> . . . [He yearns for] *that joyous certainty, that sense of mattering, of moving and being moved, of being one and indivisible with the great of the past, with all that freed, ennobled* [122].

David's questioning accents the riddle that may also be asked of Emily's life: How was it that living in separation, alienated from the feelings, if not the forms of love, in silence and darkness and sterility, she came to trust herself "enough" to try her art and to make others laugh? What crucial human gift was given even in extremity that remained with her and allowed her some blossoming? The question could be rewritten for Alva and Whitey as well as for Steve, the protagonist of "Requa," Olsen's latest novella, still in progress. This dauntless courage and resilience is a hallmark of Olsen's characters, especially her women.

In "Tell Me a Riddle," Olsen continues to use imagery drawn from poverty, disease, and isolation. As indices of Eva's memory, the images yield paradoxical associations that allow a glimpse of the meaningfulness of her life, if not the victory of it. Most striking is the community context out of which this imagery arises. Like the black songs in "O Yes," the imagery of brokenness *and* harmony in this story leads us to understand transcending hope as relational and born out of necessity. Liberation comes through struggling that hears people down to their roots, to their deepest selves.

The story begins with the narrator's description of the couple's quarreling over whether to sell the house and move to the Haven, his lodge's cooperative for the aged. "For forty-seven years they had been married. How deep back the stubborn, gnarled roots of the quarrel reached, no one could say" (72). An organic image of sustenance, roots suggest here a malignancy rather than health. "Old scar tissue ruptured and the wounds festered anew" (75). The extended metaphor—root/disease—foreshadows knowledge of Eva's illness, discovered early in the story, but withheld from her. Set against a description of her solitary caretaking of the garden, "growing things to nurture" and the "old fury of work" when the pears are ready for harvest, is Eva's apprehension of a tumultuous "ravening" within her, "a pull to the bed . . . to succumb" (77–79).

Battle and storm imagery builds upon the images of disease and heightens a sense of foreboding. David is determined to sell, and Eva experiences his insistence as "making of her a *battleground*." "And it came to where every happening *lashed* up a quarrel" (78) (italics mine). The dispute dredges up old memories. Arguing the freedom in the Haven from worry and work, David provokes from Eva the bitter question: "And what else would I do with my empty hands?" (74). When he entices with the promise of time for reading, she retaliates with her memories of early motherhood and her craving for privacy then, which at the time he did not respect. For her, the solitude represented by the house, its room and quiet, is a "reconciled peace" after the battle of caring for many others. Though she would not have chosen this isolation—her best times were in the movement, perhaps even with her children when there was enough time and she was not forced into caring—the peace of her own carved territory is all that she has. It is a kind of identity. Robbed of the vibrant meanings that once gave her purpose, she is left finally with housework and gardening.

The plot's descent into Eva's illness is forecasted in the narrator's second mention of the pear trees: "The birds grew bold that summer and for once pocked the pears undisturbed" (82). A rare image of abundance and health is thus subverted by the prevailing disease that constructs the plot. The pocked pears portend decay and simultaneously point to the characters' past of lost dreams.

Once after a particularly bitter quarrel with David, Eva exiles herself on the screen porch. For a week she is silent, not speaking. During a rain storm one night, however, she awakens David with a fifty-year-old love song from their Russian youth. Her voice, found in the self-imposed solitude, will be her response to the cancer in her body, and to the loss and harm that have largely characterized her life (one year she begged scraps "for the dog" to make soup for her children). Shortly after the episode, the illness is discovered. From Eva's short hospital stay, the plot continues to descend toward her death while geographically the couple moves from place to place, visiting the children and, at the doctor's recommendation, the beach.

The literal or first-level plot of Eva's physical decline is accompanied by another, Eva's spiritual ascension through memory to the transcending beauties and beliefs of her youth. Actually we might read Eva's secular quest (her socialist revolutionary youth) as a metaphor for her present spiritual quest. Carol Christ has analyzed women's spiritual and secular quests in literature, giving attention to the former (though, as she says, she doesn't mean to continue the old dualizations).[21] Our study of Olsen suggests that we might think in more sustained ways of how women's so-called secular lives or concerns disclose spiritual being. For example, Jewish women traditionally found more expression and meaning in the circumscribed arenas of the home than in the synagogue. Many Jewish men may have as well. To discover the values latent in the work of keeping life, we may look at the interface of secular and spiritual. Certainly, Eva's questing invites such an approach. Thus we recognize two apparent paradoxes in the novella. Descent becomes ascent; secular gives rise to spiritual.

The story works by counterposing the directions of life forward and backward, toward death and birth. Similarly, images of decay and transformation, eliciting the contrasting emotions of despair and hope, are juxtaposed. Eva, who travels in both directions, expresses in her last songs and remembrances both her loss of hope and that "joyous certainty . . . of mattering." For women readers, she represents the actual losses of our maternal ancestors and at the same time the power of their faith, displayed in acts of encouraging life.

In a visit with one daughter, Eva angrily portrays her view of history and what has damaged human potential: "Heritage. How have we come from our savage past, how no longer to be savages—this to teach. To look back and learn what humanizes—this to teach. To smash all ghettos that divide us—not to go back, not to go back—this to teach. Learned books in the house, will humankind live or die" (90). Reacting against the rabbi in the hospital and her daughter's Sabbath candles, Eva rejects religious practice as a substitute for life, enlightenment, and wholeness, or as a deterrent to change. Her race is "human," she says, and her religion "none" (89). She declares that her daughter lights the Sabbath candles not "for pleasure . . . [but] for emptiness" (90). In the old country candles were bought instead of bread. Religion stifled, saying, "In Paradise, woman, you will be the footstool of your husband, and in life—poor chosen Jew—ground under, despised, trembling in cellars. And cremated. And cremated" (90).

In czarist Russia, most people had no rights: Jews the least. And women hardly had the hope of heaven. Religion, not only the religion of the state but the religion of the Jews, was an instrument for maintaining things as they were. "God's will" decreed acceptance of suffering. The religion Eva alludes to saw the ghetto as divinely ordained, and "woman's place," too. For her, it is the religion of "savages"; it is "superstition," not truth, hate, not love. But the tension she introduces is crucial to the story's development. At the end, she does "go back" to the vision of her youth, and David will discover that present comforts may have been gained at the cost of past belief. Eva's speech clarifies the tension, for she instructs, "Look back and learn," but not, "Go back." Thus, her philosophy is one of keeping knowledge of the past for the sake of the present and future, in order to act knowledgeably now and to enhance life and truth. Thus a romantic infatuation with the struggles of earlier times is disallowed: what is claimed is the possibility that the past may teach. Eva's understanding of true human being requires a critical questioning of the past for the sake of a better world, a world that sustains and encourages rather than destroys. What connects and integrates, always respecting the seeds of human potential, is to be valued. In other words, liberation *from* oppression and *for* human joys, expressions, and explorations is the political and spiritual truth we glean from Eva's rejection of "religion."

The image of the steerage ship is a striking metaphor for Eva's quest, suggesting a recasting of history for understanding the present. A plane trip elicits the memory of an earlier and more desperate journey:

> There was a steerage ship of memory that shook across a great, circular sea: clustered, ill human beings; and through the thick-stained air, tiny fretting waters in a window round like the airplane's—sun round, moon round. (The round thatched roofs of Olshana.) Eye round— like the smaller window that framed distance the solitary year of exile when only her eyes could travel, . . .
>
> . . . They thought she slept. Still she rode on [92].

Often a symbol of timelessness, the circle in this context evokes a historical passage to America, the steerage ship of infected air below deck where hundreds huddled for days. Further back, the circle brings to focus the childhood village and a year of imprisonment in Siberia. Glimpsed in a moment, the various historical memories suggest Eva's alternate quest—not the journey David believes is necessary: simply to see the children and say good-by—but the quest for meanings that make a life worth living in spite of great contradictions.

The process of Eva's search through images is instructive for us, suggesting that metaphors have the power to limit or to expand, and that in using language faithful to our most meaningful experience, even our losses, we make contact with our whole-souled being. When Eva begins to recite and sing the words from the revolution, she, like Whitey and the black church, calls out of the past meanings that are her own. The words themselves evoke continuity and hope.

The family has held contradictions for Eva. She loved her children passionately, but they took too much. Even in her death, the children's and grandchildren's needs crowd her peace and make demands upon her. In her own journey, she feels a need for solitude, for quiet recollection. Thus, the trip to family, which offers a context for the plot's descent toward death, appears to conflict with Eva's journey of rediscovery. Amid so many other voices, she is not able to hear herself or to remember her language for life.

Searching for the meaning of her youth, she remembers the costs of a life of caring for children:

> On that torrent she had borne them on their own lives, and the riverbed was desert long years now. Not there would she dwell, a memoried wraith. Surely that was not all, *surely there was more*. Still the springs, the springs were in her seeking. Somewhere an older power that beat for life. Somewhere coherence, transport, meaning. If they would but leave her in the air now stilled of clamour, in the reconciled solitude, to journey on [93] [italics mine].

Eva's mothering experience might be fruitfully contrasted with that of other mothers in women's literature. Kate Chopin's character Edna, and Doris Lessing's Martha Quest (from *The Awakening* and *The Four-Gated City*, respectively) are both discussed by Carol Christ. Edna is trapped in motherhood, while Martha chooses at last to mother (someone else's children). For Edna, the choice is self or other, the children or her own coherence and freedom. Martha finds her identity in separation, and then becomes a caregiver. Eva, like Olsen, has felt the costliness *and* the yields or understandings that come with mothering; thus her experience is more ambivalent and more realistic than either Edna's or Martha's. Olsen's determination to show the love and the oppression that characterize mothering in our culture offers complex insights to feminist readers trying to chart the avenues of women's search for meaning.

The passage just quoted offers an example of how Eva's mothering has been fettered with cares and loves. This heroine chooses the imagery of water, a primary symbol of life, to think of her parenting. But the meaning is ambivalent. At first the river is a torrent, a stormy overflow precipitated by the overwhelming needs of many young ones. But with their passage to adulthood, Eva is left a dry riverbed. Once capacities flourished, capacities other than the ability to nurture; too many demands have left her a desert, taking not only her caring instincts but other desires and abilities.

By contrast, Eva remembers "an older power," a source preexistent to the consuming needs of the children. The circumstances of Eva's life have dictated the almost total sacrifice of this power to her powers of caretaking. The result has been a severing of her contact with this fundamental spring. Always consumed with others, she has lost her "older power." Yet still it beats for life; and listening intently, Eva may rediscover it. She believes that even now she may regain "coherence, transport, meaning," transcending her present disease by hearing and speaking the dreams of her youth and the promise of her cherished hope for a new humanity. Thus Eva's spiritual quest is a journey inward, through memory and hearing of her truest self. The transcendence she will achieve will come as she regains her lost self and is able to make a connection between the mother in her and her other deep powers.

Important to our reading is the source of this older power. It is within Eva herself, a power she was born with. The springs appear to be the deep sources in us that female shares with male, the curiosities, hungers, and desires that make us human and lead us into creativity and adventure. The sacrifice of these powers leads to thwarted lives and bitterness, as Eva's disease exemplifies. To cultivate the power in oneself and in others appears to be, for Olsen, the human/divine way.

The complications of Eva's search are given in the mixed imagery of disease, storm, and alienation that began the story. While she seeks an unobstructed path to the recollection of her vision and faith, she finds that her actual history will not allow detachment and separation. No clear division exists between disease and health, decay and transformation. Meditating in silence, she thinks: *How was it that soft reaching tendrils also became blows that knocked?"* (95). The sentence explains Eva's personal sense of the beauties and cruelties of children. They are the "soft reaching tendrils," the miraculous and tender new life. But their needs become "blows that knock," just as their excited and demanding voices diminish the voice within. This organic image, like the image of the pocked pears, reflects both Eva's search for meaning and the deadly cancer that knocks in her frail body. She has, in a way, been eaten; she is herself the pocked pear or the silenced voice. The sentence, then, evokes the contradictory meanings of life and death from a mother's perspective.

In another instance, a grandson's rock collection offers imagistic ponderings on the story's twin themes of life and death, of hope and despair: "Of stones . . . there are three kinds: earth's fire jetting; rock of layered centuries; crucibled new out of the old (*igneous, sedimentary, metamorphic)"* (99). Thinking, Eva extends the application of the images:

> But there was that other—frozen to black glass, never to transform or hold the fossil memory . . . (let not my seed fall on stone). There was an ancient man who fought to heights a great rock that crashed back down eternally—eternal labor, freedom, labor . . . (stone will perish, but the word remain). And you, David, who with a stone slew, screaming: Lord, take my heart of stone and give me flesh (99).

Rock is a product of natural change. Metamorphic, especially, is defined in terms of formal change, and the linguistic relation to the word "metamorphosis" suggests a striking contrast with the meaning that the frozen black rock has for Eva. What cannot change or be transformed is without the "fossil memory" and thus without history. The rock hardened beyond transformation is analogous with the seemingly eternal human struggle to break free of necessity, and thus points to an indifferent time characterized by sameness and amnesia. On the other hand, the condition of transformation suggests freedom from the eternal cycle and our time as consequential, as mattering. Furthermore, the fossiled rock is an actual historical reminder of the way life has come from the beginning. For Eva it means the possibility of learning from the past and creating a new way for the future. Sediment from the once living slowly turns to stone; but even stone may be metamorphized, may begin again. If stone may change, how much more possible should be human conversion to love and humanitarian action?

The stone imagery is revisited at the beach when Eva gathers a fistful of sand, wraps it in a kerchief, and, lying down, presses the bag to her cheek. She "look[s] toward the shore that nurtured life as it first crawled toward consciousness the million of years ago" (103). The fisted sand connects her with the whole sequence of historical and biological growth and change. This brief glimpse of the protagonist provides an imagistic collage of water and earth, liquid and stone. The image is inspiring, but the witness of the scene is dying. Clinging to the sand, she is both the life that ventured from water to land and the life which, by becoming dust again, will replenish the earth.

The constellation of images—stone, sand, desert, water, storm, river, ocean—is provided by the characters' often antagonistic interaction. David's and Eva's relationship in the story is marked by bitterness and years-old anger; Eva's relationship with the children and grandchildren is painfully portrayed. She is sarcastic about the supposed benefits of the beach and is absolutely opposed to the travel agenda that David imposes upon her. Yet, out of these familial struggles, Eva's consciousness interprets the signs of life and death. The cosmic scope of the images connects this life with others and makes relationship the context of human struggle in the face of death. Eva's life, as she sees it through the imagery, becomes a way of understanding the human journey and the final and greatest of life's contradictions, death. Furthermore, her use of organic imagery suggests a maternal identity. She appears to feel a connection with the life-and-death cycle of the universe, which she contemplates in relation to her own biological nurturance, and to mourn the life that dies unheeded. On the beach, she is something like Mazie, who also lay on the ground and pondered life's meanings and contradictions. In our appropriation of both scenes, we begin to see a correlation between a female body, the earth, and the search for identity and understanding. The meanings discovered by both protagonists seem to rise from the foundations of the earth.

The narrator first suggests an organic metaphor for the plot of descent (disease) and thereby introduces the tension between life and death that is the thematic consideration of the story. Collaborating with the narrator, Eva feels the decay of her body and considers her search for renewal in terms of storm and battle. On the other hand, she begins her singing in the rain, and she is reunited with her child self, her true self, at the edge of the ocean. The grandson offers knowledge of rocks, which Eva translates for the meanings she needs to understand the way she must travel: through memory toward understanding and finally death. She charts her own quest, using the airplane window as a connection with Russia and her fervent revolutionary youth.

The memories elicited, like the present family relationships, are both painful and inspiring: memories of imprisonment, betrayal by one whom she respected most, a childhood dance. Recollected in America, Eva's memories are an arching bridge from the old country to the new. While David has abandoned the painful memories, claiming the benefits of a better material life, Eva has remembered. Paradoxically, it is her memory of struggle that keeps her a believer in human possibilities, while David's American comforts have severed his connection with the strength of their youth.

Eva's quest becomes a transcending connection with the lasting experiences of her life. Though her voice cracks and her body is broken, she is able to see her life as meaningful by remembering the struggles of Russian Jews and in communion with the sea, where we were first nurtured to the human heart of learning and consciousness. If the ocean is a great mother whom we must leave to live independently, in this story the human quest for meaning is also a mother's quest.

Two metaphorical images struggle for prominence in Eva's story. Both are images connected with her female life and mothering. On the one hand is the bomb, supreme image of destruction; on the other hand is the song of Eva's youth, newly heard after her life of bearing life, its statement one of belief in the human potential for love and justice. The first suggests the furthest limits of destruction, not merely of the future but of the past, of all human time, struggle, and achievement. We remember the mother of "I Stand Here Ironing," who saw in the bomb the possible death of one she had so painfully birthed. The second image elicits the profoundest human hopes as Olsen imagines them: for fuller, more valued life, for experiences of freedom and creativity, and a sense of connection with or place in history, past and future.

In the airplane, Eva's voice is one with the narrator's as she, looking down at the earth, meditates: "Vulnerable life, that could scar" (92). At the time of writing, Olsen was intentionally concerned with the power of life to destroy itself. The morning after the first atomic bomb was dropped on Japan, Olsen read the headlines with a baby daughter in her arms.[22] She has told her audiences of the reports of light from the irradiated bodies, "a light," she says, "that had never been seen before." And she has commented that it is in that light that she lives and writes. Reading the report, she "knew [she] had to get back to writing."[23]

In the novella, children speak for the danger facing their generation. One of Vivi's youngsters reminds her one morning as Eva listens: "Mother, I *told* you the teacher said we had to bring it back all filled out this morning. Didn't you even ask Daddy? Then tell *me* which plan and I'll check it: evacuate or stay in the city or wait for you to come and take me away (Seeing the look of straining to hear.) It's for Disaster, Grandma. (*Children trust*)" (96). Four characters interact in the brief morning scene; the teacher who does her part in the government's disaster program; the child who is the object of the plan; the mother who must make some choice about her child's future under the outrageous threat against her life posed by the atomic age; and Eva, mother and grandmother, who witnesses the consequences of international violence and hate. Eva's thought intrudes upon the narrative—"*Children trust*"—she thinks, and brings to mind the way that mothers especially are looked to by children to give and restore faith. Thus is the irony of the passage heightened. The antithesis of all faith in human creativity and care, the bomb introduces blankness and annihilation where meaning and community were. Thus, it is an image of ultimate loss, of ahistoricity and severed connections. Looming threateningly in Eva's story, it points to all that has been destructive in her history and introduces the possibility that even her family's future, not only the past, may be lost.

The incident occurs hastily and with seeming inconsequence. The child's strident voice blames Vivi for not making a decision, as though a checkmark beside one option will solve the dilemma. Drawing the incident as an interaction among three generations, Olsen heightens the reader's awareness of the history made by this particular family and the reality of the bomb's potential to erase that history in a moment. The encounter elicits ultimate, if fleeting, questions: What remains in the face of such destruction? What can be hoped for? Is faith possible? Furthermore, set among women and child, the scene causes us to ponder how women have borne generations and have also witnessed destructions. Eva, straining to hear, receives news that mocks the work of her life (keeping life). Thus the bomb threatens the life out of her body and simultaneously suggests the destruction that has already occurred in her, her spiritual fracturing.

Twice, Eva's thought suggests and brings to the story the images of ruin associated with atomic weapons. The first instance has its beginnings in a community sing Eva attends with David and an old friend who is also at the beach because of sickness. Entering the hall, Eva turns off her hearing aid. But she cannot turn off her sight. So she sees, "[o]ne by one [the people] *stream . . . by,*" and they "*imprint . . . on her*" their faces. Miraculously, as in the black worship, materials coalesce, exchange places. The faces become a music she cannot turn off, the "*[s]inging . . . voicelessly soft and distant*" of humanity: "children-chants, mother-croons, singing of the chained love serenades, Beethoven storms, mad Lucia's scream, drunken joy-songs, keens for the dead, work-singing" (106).

In the midst of these voices, unstoppable, entering as if through the pores of her skin, Eva's child self enters. She is a long ago "*bare-footed sore-covered little girl*" dancing "*at a cross-roads village wedding.*" The image is riddled with pain and ecstasy, just as Eva's history is one of struggles and joys. In her resistance, Eva has met the voice she was searching for, though it is soundless. Actually it is the harmony and solidarity of human bodies moving to the rhythms of life and death. In the hall of hundreds, in her own silence, Eva receives the music of her dancing child self.

Later, in the bleak boarding rooms of the friend, Eva recognizes that she is dying at the same time that she mourns humanity's choice, century after century, for destruction.

> Everywhere   unused   the life   And who has meaning?   Century after century   still all in us   not   to grow? . . .
>
> "And when will it end? Oh, *the end.*" *That* nightmare thought, and this time she writhed, crumpled against him, seized his hand (for a moment again the weight, the soft distant roaring of humanity) and on the strangled-for breath, begged: "Man . . . we'll destroy ourselves?"
>
> And looking for her answer—in the helpless pity and fear for her (for *her*) that distorted his face—she understood the last months, and knew that she was dying [108].

The experience recorded here makes the individual life and the life of the universe correspondent. Eva's mourning for the world focuses momentarily upon her own imminent death, and the two are one. She begins and ends with questions: "all in us   not   to grow?" and, begging her husband: "We'll destroy ourselves?" In a parenthesis the narrator alludes to humanity's beginning, the "soft distant roaring" of the seas, the voices she heard in the hall. Though Eva understands the end as her own death, the story offers the heroine the power of song, suggesting not ultimate loss but the possibility of transcendence through shared voice, shared history and struggle. Through pain is pain healed, as in a fever that is at once part of the illness and part of the cure. A voice comes out of silence, the sound of human longing and triumph, of self and community.

> *Even in reality*   (swallow)   *life's lack of it*
> *Slaveships   deathtrains   clubs   eeenough*
> *The bell   summon what enables*
> *78,000 in one minute*   (whisper of a scream)   *78,000*
> *human beings   we'll destroy ourselves?* [118].

The meanings of the fragmented speech are difficult for the reader, as they are for David, who hears them. In the second line, Eva connects a series of violent images and points to historical events of inhumanity: the American slave trade, Nazi camps, police violence against workers. The number—78,000—is a memorial reference to Japanese civilians killed by American bombs. Again, Eva questions in the face of such odds, "[W]e'll destroy ourselves?" She does not make a statement but continues to hope. Her sentence is a question.

Eva's dance and song from her youth are the answers she finally gives to the question she asks. Throughout the story, she has sought to hear in her being what is true and lasting in life through remembered bits of her history. Near the end, she cries to Jeannie, the granddaughter who cares for her at the beach: "The music . . . still it is there and we do not hear; knocks, and our poor human ears too weak. What else, what else we do not hear?" (114). What Eva has not heard for so long is her truest self, that powerful stream *in her* that makes her a transcendental being.

In part, she chants: *"No man one   except through others / Strong   with the not yet   in the now / Dogma dead   war dead   one country"* (118). Her theme is universal humanity and the historical interconnection of past, present, and future. For one to be human, all must be treated as human. Thus true being begins with the lowliest and with the earth. In Eva's vision, dogma is nothing, while the hope of one community, in the interest of all, is a wish both heavenly and worldly. One country—the hope of socialism—is Eva's ideal.

Approaching death, her dream depends upon faith. Coming out of the past, it opens the past and the future. Her idealism is a choice for belief. Given her life of few choices and opportunities, Eva still believes. Her faith is the way she *wills* even now to see the world:

> *Life high banner of reason*   (tatter of an
> orator's voice) *justice   freedom   light*
>
> *Humankind   life worthy   capacities*
>
> *Seeks*   (blur of shudder) *belong   human being* [119].

The words are a patchwork of revolutionary rhetoric, a remembrance of the vision that led Eva and others to revolt and to dream. Earlier she had said to David, *"Humankind   one has to believe,"* and as she dies, she chooses belief in freedom, justice, and light.

Singing the song, "These Things Shall Be," Eva discloses the message of hope by which she has lived in the face of twentieth-century diseases: war, the bomb, violence against those who struggle for freedom:

> *These things shall be, a loftier race*
> *than e'er the world hath known shall rise*
> *with flame of freedom in their souls*
> *and light of knowledge in their eyes*
>
> *They shall be gentle, brave and strong*
> *to spill no drop of blood, but dare*
> *all . . .*

on earth and fire and sea and air . . .
And every life . . . shall
  be a song [120].

When Eva dies, having promised Jeannie she would go back to the moment of dance and song, we, with the granddaughter and David, are witnesses of her faith. "On earth and fire and sea and air," her body like her spirit is one with humanity's, pursuing life and song.

In our reading, Eva's lifetime is itself transformed by the song. She becomes one with all human beings, especially with the mothers of the races, who have lived a life in the light of hope. She is reunited with that first power as her life becomes a force for hope and enlightenment. As witnesses with David and Jeannie, we are illuminated by her life of struggle, by the losses that are perhaps irretrievable, *and* by the desires of her heart, beating still.

Eva's listening was for her own transcendence, for her being. She heard herself, in the story of her death, back to her truth and to connection with presences and powers that still inspire her and give her life. She exists in death as Whitey does, as spirit, as the hope for life, freedom, and harmony that now and always has moved the spheres. A mother of cares and woes, she hovers in our minds as one whose life makes heavy our history of injustice and whose dream may illumine our future, showing us the way.

1. The four stories of the period are "I Stand Here Ironing," "Hey Sailor, What Ship?" "O Yes," and "Tell Me a Riddle."

2. Paul Tillich, *Systematic Theology,* vol. 3 (Chicago: The University of Chicago Press, Phoenix Edition, 1976), pp. 369–72.

3. This analysis is influenced by Fredy Perlman's article, "The Reproduction of Daily Life," in *"All We Are Saying . . . " The Philosophy of the New Left,* ed. Arthur Lothstein (New York: G.P. Putnam's Sons, 1970), pp. 133–54.

4. A section from Morris Rosenfield's "Mayn Yingele" ("My Little Boy") is reprinted in Howe, *World of Our Fathers,* p. 421.

5. Joseph R. Conlin, *Big Bill Haywood and the Radical Union Movement* (Syracuse, N.Y: Syracuse University Press, 1969), p. 17.

6. Isaac Loeb Peretz, "Bontsha the Silent," in *Great Jewish Short Stories,* ed. Saul Bellow (New York: Dell Publishing Co., Laurel Edition, 1966), pp. 128–37.

7. *Silences,* p. 20.

8. Ibid., pp. 38–39.

9. From Olsen's personal journal, quoted in Rosenfelt, "From the Thirties," 377. Rosenfelt says that the time of writing is Olsen's early adolescence.

10. For similar thinking in a book-length treatment, see Rachel Blau DuPlessis, *Writing beyond the Ending: Narrative Strategies of Twentieth Century Women Writers* (Bloomington: Indiana University Press, 1985). Also see Joanne S. Frye's chapter, "Beyond Teleology," in *Living Stories, Telling Lives: Women and the Novel in Contemporary Experience* (Ann Arbor: The University of Michigan Press, 1986).

11. Virginia Woolf, *To the Lighthouse* (1927). Reprint. New York: Harcourt, Brace, Jovanovich, Harvest, 1955.

12. Toni Morrison's novels are *The Bluest Eye* (1970), *Sula* (1973), *Song of Solomon* (1977), and *Tar Baby* (1981).

13. The text explains that the song is "the Valedictory, written the dawn 'fore he was executed by Jose Rizal, national hero of the Philippines" (p. 41). The story itself is dedicated to *"Jack Eggan, Seaman,"* a friend of Olsen's *"killed in the retreat across the Ebro, Spain"* (p. 47).

14. Walt Whitman, "Song of Myself," from *Leaves of Grass*. Reprint. *The American Tradition in Literature*; shorter edition in one volume, ed. George Perkins et al. (New York: Random House, 1985), p. 765.

15. Virginia Woolf, *A Room of One's Own* (1929). Reprint, New York: Harcourt, Brace, Jovanovich, 1957, pp. 85–89. Doris Lessing, *The Golden Notebook* (1962). Reprint, Toronto; Simon and Schuster, Bantam, 1979. Alice Walker, *The Color Purple* (New York: Washington Square Press, 1982). Toni Morrison, *Sula* (New York: Alfred A. Knopf, 1975).

16. Christopher Fry, "Comedy," *Tulane Drama Review* 4 (March 1960): 77.

17. In conversation, Olsen has reminded me that she grew up in an integrated neighborhood and visited the black church until her mother learned of it and punished her. The punishment was for attending church. Olsen also attended socialist Sunday school.

18. This understanding is influenced by the essay on "Time" in *The Encyclopedia of Philosophy*, vols. 7 and 8 (New York: Macmillan and The Free Press, 1967).

19. Genya Gorelick is the better known of the two women. She was a famous leader of the Bund and is written about in some histories.

20. Alice Walker, "In Search of Our Mothers' Gardens," in *In Search of Our Mothers' Gardens: Womanist Prose* (San Diego: Harcourt Brace Jovanovich, 1983), pp. 232–33.

21. See Carol Christ, *Diving Deep and Surfacing: Women Writers on Spiritual Quest* (Boston: Beacon Press, 1980).

22. Tillie Olsen, telephone conversation with the author, Sept. 1984.

23. Tillie Olsen, telephone conversation with the author, 1 June 1986.

New Words for Shalom

Tell me something I need to know—about art, about the
world, about human behavior, about myself.

GAIL GODWIN
The Best American Short Stories 1985

Our deepest sense of bondedness, . . . our most basic
sense of connectedness, . . . is what the Latin term for
religion originally meant.

BEVERLY WILDING HARRISON
Our Right to Choose

Oh, angels.
Keep the windows open
so that I may reach in
and steal each object,
objects that tell me the sea is not dying,
objects that tell me the dirt has a life-wish.

ANNE SEXTON
The Awful Rowing toward God

In 1970, almost ten years after *Tell Me a Riddle* was published, "Requa," the first part of a novella on which Olsen is still working, appeared in the *Iowa Review*. It was reprinted as one of the year's best short stories. As Olsen's latest and most complex fiction, the story illuminates her earlier periods by expanding the themes, motifs, and characterizations that have concerned her from the beginning.[1] Moreover, in evoking a metaphorical pattern of the human journey and search for place (identity), "Requa" is paradigmatic of the evolving vision of redemptive hope that has inspired Olsen's career. The young protagonist negotiates a way through harms and brokenness that we now recognize as Olsen's way.

"Requa," or "Rekwoi," is an Indian name for a holy place, Olsen has said, where dances are performed to keep the floods away.[2] The beauty of the sound is what attracted Olsen to it and the associations it evokes: requiem and reclamation. Both meanings hold important connotations for our discussion.

The story's complex and consistent use of paradox—healing comes through brokenness, wholeness issues from fragmentation, love is achieved as the main character comes face to face with loss and deprivation—is mirrored by the text itself. Sentences are unfinished, words—unconnected—dot the landscape of the page: the story ends without any final punctuation. At times one senses that the writer is at a loss as to *how* to create the feelings of brokenness except in this concrete way. Developing the theme of continuity, Olsen seems to insist rather pointedly that brokenness is the condition that elicits human bondedness. In fact, the story may await not so much Olsen's finishing of it as readers' response.

In a recent article, Blanche Gelfant offers a thematic connection between this and Olsen's second period: "In 'Requa' Stevie continues the quest of the Grandmother in 'Tell Me a Riddle.' Different as they are, the resurrected boy and the dying woman are

121

both searching for a transmittable human past that will give significance to their present struggle."[3]

Gelfant's emphasis on the past in the story is in accord with our reading of the body of Olsen's work. She suggests as well the redemption that evolves through a recollection of history and the story's vision of relatedness. Thus, she suggests but does not fully develop the prophecy of Olsen's story, its pointing beyond itself to a future vision of human wholeness. In connecting not only Eva's and Stevie's quests but also Stevie's and the writer's search for voice, Gelfant provides a glimpse of the story's transcendence, its reflection of longings and hopes that inspire the narrative and lift our reading of it to an attitude of ultimate concern. Though the story dwells in territories of brokenness—the junkyard and the shattered human heart—it springs from the writer's longing for a different way—not, as Gelfant accurately notes, a pastoral past, but for a rebuilding, out of present technological waste, of a humane and creative world in which work and relationship sustain each member of the human community.[4]

The metaphorical resonances that evolve in the narrative suggest a transcending vision of continuity and healing. At the same time, the use of a mother's love as the energy and power that infuses and directs the male characters points to the rootedness of Olsen's universally transforming vision in day-to-day maternal experience.

In the creative essay "The Coming of Lilith," Judith Plaskow proposes "telling a new story within the framework of an old one."[5] Written during Olsen's most consciously feminist period, "Requa" tells the story of daily survival (a theme she has treated primarily in domestic contexts among women and children) in terms of a fourteen-year-old boy and his uncle. The effect is a narrative unique in subject, perspective, and style; I know of no other recent story to which it can be compared. In this last fiction, Olsen transforms male according to female and in so doing universalizes a feminist maternal spirituality, a vision of need and desire springing from the memory of a lost mother, perhaps like Eva, a "first mother, singing mother."[6]

The gender change accomplishes a powerful expansion of Olsen's vision of care and nurture. Making a man responsible for a woman's child, Olsen envisions a conjoined male/female journey to wholeness through the depleting and agonizing realities of illness, waste, and loss. Though the woman is dead, her spirit is the grounding of the story, and her love seems reincarnated in the uncle, in other minor characters, and in the benevolent presence reflected in the narrator's voice.

"Requa" is the only one of Olsen's stories set in the thirties (1932), the years so crucial to her own development as a writer. It builds upon themes from all of her other writing: individual and community loss, impoverishment, and exhaustion; societal waste and destruction; and the indomitable human spirit, source and reflector of faith, hope, and love. As Gelfant notes, the story also continues Olsen's practice of giving voice to unnoted and muted people. These characters are more like the societally marginal Holbrooks than like the more culturally integrated characters of *Tell Me a Riddle*. Sharing the limited omniscient perspective, Steve and Wes, nephew and uncle, recall for us the shared mother/daughter perspective in *Yonnondio*. The narrative situation is the death of the boy's mother, related through flashbacks, and his "adoption" by Wes, his mother's brother but a man he hardly knows. Taken from city to small town, Steve finds healing through working with his uncle in a junkyard.

Very likely, Olsen means for the characterization of this story to mirror the actual destruction brought to families by the Depression. The woman who emerges as Stevie's mother, through his almost incoherent remembrances, is probably in her thirties; she could even have been in her late twenties. What the boy remembers of her life and death is the ultimate exhaustion. In one flashback, he recalls this exchange with her: "(*Are you tired, Ma? Tired to death, love)*" (243). While the brief conversation is extreme, it is not, in Olsen's world, uncommon. People are exhausted "to [spiritual and then physical] death" by overwork, by a world that will not, in any sustained way, aid the poor and the lame.

Embodying the absolute need for human continuity, Stevie's and Wes's relationship is paradigmatic of Olsen's vision of loss and recovery, brokenness and healing, which builds in force and clarity throughout her career.[7] In reading of their experience, we are reminded of earlier characters, the children: Mazie, Emily, Carol, Parry; the men: Jim, Whitey, Lennie, David; and the women: Anna, Olsen herself in "I Stand Here Ironing," Helen, Alva, Eva. The otherness or difference which we have met in these lives—their songs, giving power to the powerless; the miraculous, transforming hope of a mother; the musical sway of a church, which draws the time of redemption out of hearts and declares the day of the Lord— is even more striking in "Requa." The discards of humanity, the wastes of society, the barely reusable, are the sources in this world of redemption and hope. Not a pristine world, but the real world of abused and overlooked possibilities is the source of spiritual reclamation.

Stevie's journey for place and identity recalls journeys portrayed in the earlier work, and his tattered spirit reminds us of the need for healing so characteristic of Olsen's people. Learning of the human bonds that make life possible, the young protagonist glimpses the truth of the human situation as we, the readers, have come to see it in this canon of works. Picturing the boy's healing in terms of discarded objects and their potential remakings, Olsen gives expression to her faith: brokenness will not be the last word.

In "Requa," Olsen continues the strategy of the *Tell Me a Riddle* stories, shifting back and forth between past and present and juxtaposing significant scenes. She experiments even more with interrupting the narrative by introducing countertexts. Earlier, she borrowed poems and songs from other historical contexts. Here, she creates her own poetry out of the story's context. She names machine parts, creating verbs drawn from mechanical work:

> sharping hauling sorting splicing
> burring chipping grinding cutting
> grooving drilling caulking sawing [261].

The collage effect of the writing parallels the reclamation theme, making do out of what is at hand. It also reminds us of Olsen's tendency to deny chronological time and to manipulate the text for the purpose of regaining lost time and opportunity. Even more is effected here, however. The careful aligning of words, chosen for sound as much as for sense, creates a kind of ritualistic chant. Olsen seems to employ these poetic enclosures as a new speech for an old purpose, as new images in a prayer for wholeness. One achievement of the style is its insistence upon the sounds of work as holy or redeeming. Like Jim Holbrook, Wes speaks with his hands.

Stevie undertakes two journeys in the story: the journey to his new home and an evening outing with Wes in search of good times. Beginning the first trip, Stevie feels confused: "He didn't understand how it was that he was sitting up or why he didn't have a bed to lie down in or why or where he was going." But a sign is offered to suggest that even in his alienation, Stevie is being offered a human connection. As uncle and nephew travel in the old truck, Stevie "sag[s] against his uncle who [doesn't] move away" (238–39).

As the boy searches for some sense out of his situation, the narrator describes the annual journey of the salmon: "(*Underneath in the night, yearling salmon slipped through their last fresh waters, making it easy to the salt ocean years*)" (239). Later in the story, when Stevie in springtime joy runs down by the river, the same voice will remind us, "*And still the rippling, glancing, magnifying light. . . . and*

flashing rainbow crescents he does not know are salmon leaping"
(262). The narrator's comprehension of the movement of all life
toward maturation offers to the reader, if not directly to Stevie, a
sense of the beneficent plan and pattern in the universe. The
alliterative sway of the language—"underneath the night," "yearling
salmon slipped," "flashing rainbow crescents"—offers a feeling of
rhythm to the natural quest of all life toward fulfillment. We are
reminded of Eva's "springs" and of Anna's need to be out in the
world, in the wind.

Like theirs, Stevie's journey is undertaken in rupture and
confusion; the human and earthly way of moving toward expression
and fullness has been shattered. The mother's death, even the
conditions of her life, leave the boy stunned and reeling. But the
story's focus is upon the uncle's rescue of the boy and the healing of
Stevie's brokenness. Thus the literal journey to a new home and
work suggests metaphorically the greater spiritual journey toward
wholeness and intactness. Set in a most desperate time in American
history, "Requa" reminds us of the interconnection of physical and
spiritual needs. Body and soul must be salvaged. Here as elsewhere
in Olsen we find political voice disclosing artistic and religious
meaning.

The story begins by depicting the physical disorientation Stevie
feels: "Everything slid, moved, . . . Being places he had never been.
Waiting moving sliding trying" (237). At Wes's place, the boy
transfers the truck's rocking inside his body: "And the round and
round slipping sliding jolting moved to inside him, so he has to
begin to rock his body: rock the cot gently, down and back" (240).
The truck's movement appears hazardous to Stevie's need for
stability and security, yet when he rocks himself, we are reminded of
his youth and his need for the lost mother, for her lap and arms.

Stopping the truck, Wes allows Stevie to rest on their way home.
The boy pulls the tarp "down to [a] . . . stripe of sun" and "curl[s] till
he [gets] all in a ball." When he wakes, he is warm; his uncle sleeps
by the fire, and "across the creek, just like in the movie show or in a
dream, a deer and two baby deers were drinking. When he lifted his
head, they lifted theirs. For a long time he and the doe looked into
each other's eyes. Then swift, beautiful, they were gone—but her
eyes kept looking into his" (238). Eyes become Stevie's link with his
past. His most salient memory is his mother's face in death,
especially her eyes, which he remembers as both "burning" and
"gentle" (241). The deer's eyes are a reflection of the second aspect:
gentle, beautiful, but fleeting. At Wes's in bed his first night, the
other visage appears: "blood dripping from where should be eyes

Out in the hall swathed bodies floating like in bad movies" (241). In understanding the dream and the deer, Stevie likens what he sees to the films of his former city life; they are his texts for interpreting the natural world that now flashes before him. This error in judgment, placing the celluloid world before the real one, suggests Stevie's severing from his natural or whole self.

Fear of the burning eyes keeps Stevie from looking into faces, which are often, for Olsen, maps of the ways people have been. At the landlady's (Mrs. Ed's) table, he will not meet the eyes of those who speak to him. Later, pumping gas at Evans's fix-it shop, he rivets his eyes on the ground and refuses to look into the faces of the customers. But in moments of sympathy with Wes, Stevie's eyes become a means to searching out connection. One day, his uncle, Olsen's most sympathetically drawn workingman, comes home exhausted from work and slumps down in the chair in their room; "for a minute he let go, slept; snored, great sobbing snores." The narrator probes Stevie's sleeping consciousness: "*Something about the light, the radio, not being snapped on; the absence of the usual adopted pleasantries; some rhythm not right, roused the boy* . . . Was that his mother or his uncle sagged there in the weight of weariness" (243). Blurry-eyed from first waking, the boy sees Wes as his mother. In weariness and weight, the bodies are the same, making male and female one. Even when Stevie, fully awake, knows the figure as Wes, he treats him as his mother, urging his uncle to put up his tired feet so Stevie can rub them. Through his own eyes, Stevie makes a connection between former life and new, using the memory of his mother to understand what is needed in the present.

But the memory of the terrible anguish in his mother's face overpowers that first connection, and in fierce determination he shelters himself from the loss she symbolizes, staying shut up in Wes's room, refusing to go to school, and continuing to avoid those who address him. In his helpless sleep, the look of death continues its visitation: "spectral shapes . . . out in the hall, swathed forms floated, wrung their hands" (260).

Stevie cannot choose between the aspects of death and life that characterize his past. He must face both. The deer's face is the mediator. On the second journey with his uncle, to "celebrate," drink, and womanize, Stevie recognizes the deer's eyes. Amid the dancing and drinking and a feeling of sickness mixed with happiness, Stevie looks: "the fire? over the fireplace, branching antlers, sad deer eyes in the fire, branching antlers glowing eyes am going to be sick" (257). The deer head above the fire is recreated in the burning flames. "Branching antlers" and "sad eyes" evoke majesty and utmost loss, a head severed from its body. The male recalls the female and the fawn: a family. Beauty and futility, life and death, are bound in Stevie's encounter with the deer. Human brutality is certainly suggested by the deer so that this more lyrical rendering of rupture and fragmentation recalls the societal sin evoked in the *Yonnondio* passage where machines mutilate, silence, and kill.

Stevie's understanding of death, gained through the deer's "sad" eyes, is followed by his second recognition of family continuity when again, after the long night of drinking, Wes comes home exhausted and despairing. Ordinarily a neat person, the uncle stumbles in, falling onto the bed with muddy shoes. Caring for him, Stevie acts like a mother tucking in a child:

> The blanket ends wouldn't lap to cover. He had to pile on his coat, Wes's mackinaw, and two towels, patting them carefully around the sleeping form. *There now you'll be warm,* he said aloud, *sleep sweet, sweet dreams . . .*
>
> His uncle moaned, whispered something; he leaned down to hear it, looked full on the sleeping face. Face of his mother. *His* face. Family face [259].

Stevie's journey for place, identity, and reclamation begins in his creative response to the pain of death. His quest is to chart a connection between himself and others, which will allow him to interact and to be a part of a community. Like a family of deer, Stevie and Wes are similar. What Stevie understands is their bond, something essentially the same connecting mother, self, and uncle. In his dreams that night, Stevie "hurtle[s] the fall over and over in a maggoty sieve where eyes glowed in rushing underground waters and fire branched antlers, fire needle after shining needle" (260). The dream is a mosaic of earth's elements, suggesting both death and birth, harm and recognition. Whitey too saw fire and water and knew their power to destroy and to cleanse. The young boy, however, has greater opportunity for a new beginning.

Near the end of the story, Steve recognizes Mrs. Ed's face in an old photograph; the incident suggests the triumph of "gentle" eyes in Steve's quest, and of vision that sees similarity and leads to acts of care:

> [Stevie] sees that it is not shadows that hang on the wall around the bow, but Indian things: a feathered headdress, basket hats, shell necklace. Two faces dream in shell frames. One, for all the beard, Mrs. Ed's. *family face* [261].

The arrangement on the wall, a mosaic of human artistry, like Eva's mosaic of songs, stirs connections with the dream. Family pictures of Mrs. Ed's people (of white ancestry) are mixed with "Indian things." Unlike the dream, where death and life mix indiscriminately, and one is helpless before the spectral shapes of fear, this arrangement signifies human choice. Mrs. Ed chooses connection with the Indian past. She, of white descent, intertwines her life with Indian lives. The family face expands beyond mere facial resemblance to human likeness, so that Mrs. Ed's face is a map to the truly human/divine way of integration and bondedness. The difference or otherness of cultural distinctions is bound in the similarity of human need and possibility. Thus the family of humanity is evoked through Stevie's seeing, his recognition of Mrs. Ed in the context of Indian art, a human arrangement aligning race with race.[8]

Stevie's journey is a journey through dream and waking, requiring a transformation of his mother's dying eyes into his own caring eyes. As Gelfant suggests, the way of his journey is similar to Eva's; he must go back through memory, recollecting for his present life the knowledge of love and original promise that can transform brokenness. Near the end, as he works through the past, making connection with the present, the narrator gives this description: "Miming Wes's face Sounding Evans dry ghost cough Gentling his bruised shoulder. Sometimes stopping whatever he is doing, his mouth opening: fixed to the look on her dying face" (261). Miming others, feeling as they do, Stevie's journey weaves a family tapestry of human connections. Like the salmon and the deer, his journey is of death and rebirth, while the emblematic face of his mother is a reminder of pain and of the hope that may heal. Transposing the family order in "I Stand Here Ironing," Olsen creates a child whose life inspirits the dead mother rather than a mother who hopes against the powers of death that threaten her daughter. By this latest story, then, we recognize in Olsen's world the spiraling journey of humanity, from child to parent to child.

Glimpsing the sustaining intergenerational vision that encompasses Olsen's world, we notice, however, that the setting is profoundly "unholy." The junkyard setting seems the most obvious contradiction to growth, beauty, and attainment. Yet, Wes promises Stevie: "I'll help you catch hold, . . . I promise I'll help" (247), suggesting that he will offer Stevie a place to put down roots, to grow, and to blossom. The dump, then, becomes a context for re-creation, for finding wholeness and holiness. Earlier, Wes declared in the presence of Mrs. Ed: "I'll tell you this, though, he's not goin through what me and Sis did: kicked round one place after another, not havin nobody. Nobody" (240). Giving himself to the boy, even at work, in his impatience, Wes creates connection in an apparently hopeless place.

Even before the junkyard is introduced, the truck is an antagonistic setting, forcing the exhausted boy to wakefulness and sickness. Cold and weak, he hopes for a place to lie down and warm himself. But when he can leave the truck to rest, the outside world is a place of discomfort and distrust: "Everything slid, moved" (237). The natural world is not always hospitable. Antagonists loom larger than life: "There might be snakes. The trees stretched up and up so you couldn't see if they had tops, and up there they leaned as if they were going to fall" (237). These threatening places remind the boy of nights of staying up with his mother, afraid to sleep "cause he might . . . not hear her if she needed him" (237). In his isolation, Stevie's world threatens life rather than feeding it. He finds no safe bed between heaven and earth.

Somnambulent, the boy seems suspended between consciousness and death. In his room at the end of a "cave"-like hall, he constructs a fort from the moving boxes. For days he sleeps, hardly getting out of bed, fighting desperately against Wes's prodding. When the uncle opens the door, he jumps from the bed to close it: *"Keep away you rememorings slipping slidings having to hold up my head Keep away you trying to get me's . . . I work so hard for this safety Let me a while Let me"* (245).

On his first visit to the junkyard, the world rises up around Stevie, threatening him like the giant trees of the forest: "Too close: scaly, rapid river; too close: dwarfing, encircling: dark massive forest rise" (250). But Wes's promise and his insistent caring begin to get through to the boy, and movement begins in Stevie's uneasy slumbering.

Having unpacked and distributed most of the belongings from Stevie's former life, Wes comes home one day and demands that they unpack "her" things. The box includes an array of cheap objects: "tiny Indian brass slipper ash tray," "Happy Joss/ Hollywood California painted fringed pillow cover/ kewpie doll green glass vase, cracked" (245). Stevie cannot endure the exposure of his woundedness and the next day refuses to wake. But almost miraculously, he is up for the first time when Wes comes home that evening. "I did everything like you told," he offers (248), but when Wes tries to send him to school for the second time, he still refuses.

At work with Wes after begging for the chance, Stevie is at first only slightly more alert than at home. He does not listen: "Your ears need reaming?" Wes asks (250). Deaf and mute, Stevie shivers in fear and cold, hardly noticing Wes's careful instructions for sorting. Reverting to his former behavior of turning inward and fending off the world, the boy wraps himself in an old quilt, rocks himself, and sleeps. His behavior is like Eva's, though less self-conscious. He must turn off the outer sounds and sights to hear and see himself. First there is movement inward, then outward, though paradoxically his reconnections are also dependent upon the proddings of Wes and others' needs, to which Stevie slowly awakens.

The junkyard, like the earlier settings and like Whitey's bar, is at first only a place for Stevie to carve a moment of aloneness. But the sheer size and complexity of it insists upon the boy's attention. In moments of self-forgetfulness, Stevie meets the world, and remembrances—hunger, the excitement of doing something with hands, even the feeling of the bruise on his shoulder—bring awakening. The germinal feelings of warmth and anticipation slowly work in him, and he begins to respond to Wes's friendship, the job, and the coming spring:

> Afternoons, if the strong northwest winds of May have cleared the sky an hour or two, the coat distills, stores the sun about him as he moves through mound-sheltered warmth in and out of the blowing cold; or sits with Wes, poncho over the muddy ground, eating their boloney and bread lunch in the sun-hive the back of the scrapiron pile makes.
>
> Weeds, the yellow wild mustard and rank cow parsnip, are already waist high, blow between him and the river. Blue jays shrill, swoop for crumbs; chipmunks hover. Wes gabs, plays his harmonica. The boy lies face down in his pool of warmth. In him something keeps trembling out in the wind with the torn whirled papers, the bending weeds, the high tossed gulls [253–54].

A blossoming world is suggested, brought by the spring weather. The comfort and promise of rebirth, warmth, and beauty touch Stevie, calling him to join the celebration of returning life. Lying on the ground, he is like a seed close to the surface, lured from his slumber. He is called by the wind and Wes's music to break the boundary of isolation and join the living universe.

The body struggles to life; more difficult is sustaining and enhancing the boy's spirit. The outing with Wes is the context for Stevie's understanding of what nurturing is and how necessary for humans. The incident suggests that seeing life's beneficence in nature, Stevie may find his own way of blossoming.

Waiting for his uncle, who has left him in the woods when he goes to buy love from a prostitute, Stevie is outside when a rain comes up. He has never seen the rain in the country where it falls to the receptive earth. But he remembers another rain that caught him outside. Something about this rain and that memory culminates in Stevie's spiritual unfolding:

> Slap. On his face. Another slap. Great drops. *Rain*. Move, you dummy. Pushing himself up against a tree, giant umbrella in the mottled dark. Throb, sound in and around him (his own excited blood beat?) Rain, hushing, lapping

> City boy, he had only known rain striking hard on unyielding surface, . . . not this soft murmurous receiving: leaves, trees, earth. In wonder he lay and listened, . . .

> . . . .

> Far down where Wes was, a branch shook silver into the light. Rain. *His mothers quick shiver as the rain traced her cheek. C'mon baby, we've got to run for it.*

> Laughing, one of her laughing times. . . . Tickling him, keeping him laughing while she dried his face [258].

The rain serves to move the passage from Wes's abandonment of Stevie to a remembered moment of joy. Stevie will "twist . . . away from the pain" of the memory, but the episode ultimately leads to Stevie's recognition of his uncle *as his mother*. Thus, in back-and-forth movement—toward memory and away from it—Stevie learns, from the rain and the receptive earth, something about human connection.

The meeting of earth and water is new to the boy, and he is intrigued. But unlike nature, Stevie needs a mediator, not only nutriment but *someone* to nurture him. Water is a symbol of sustenance; the mother is a symbol of sustainer.

Stevie's learning and healing become evident when he actively demonstrates his understanding at home. The text suggests that Stevie's blossoming, metaphorically germinated by the rain passage, is discernible in his learning to care for his uncle, whom he sees as a reflection of his mother. Reaching out to reciprocate the attention he has received, he begins to unfold, subverting the notion that the poor or the young cannot be nurturers or have little to give.

Thus the story portrays human caring as an act of beauty and as a fulfillment. Stevie's blossoming in "Requa" is precisely his learning to reach out to those around him and to recognize human likenesses. The lilting good-night wish: *"sleep sweet, sweet dreams"* suggests Olsen's poetic sense of small but essential deeds of care. Looking for a way to cover his uncle's ungainly body, Stevie fits together various garments and clothes. His actions suggest the human penchant to mime and mimic, to discover new ways of acting and responding, but for a significant purpose, to attend to someone's needs. Stevie's care of Wes symbolizes two central and interrelated human characteristics: human creativity—the ability to make, change, direct, connect, and discover; and human caring. The first makes the second possible, while the second is always the moral legislator of the first. Human wholeness and holiness are born in creative acts, moral and artistic, binding self's and other's identity and destiny. One's own creativity satisfies the self, who serves the other. In her latest story, Olsen portrays most successfully the absolute interrelatedness of morality and creativity by showing that it is when Stevie reaches beyond himself to others that his potential is tapped. Like her first communal "I," the voice of the people, Olsen uses Stevie's eyes as the eyes of the world, seeing need and hope as one. Thus, the perspective of the lowliest is the mirror, inner and outer, for knowing the truth and understanding the human heart.

If Stevie's journey for a vision of connectedness and his blossoming are shown in terms of his ability to care for someone else, the salvaging of junk is Olsen's metaphor for personal and universal integration and restoration. People, like the earth and her materials, are broken, used, discarded, and wasted. In sorting and fitting together—junkyard work—Olsen, who once worked in a junkyard herself,[9] gives imagistic vision to a congruent and valued existence, where persons manipulate materials creatively and find a place for their contribution.

The piecing of spare parts is metaphoric of the human piecing or fitting together that takes place in the story at two levels. Stevie, the sickly protagonist, must piece together fragmented memories from his past in order to understand that his mother's love continues in the present. But Stevie's recovery happens communally. The nurture and care of the expanded family—Wes, Mrs. Ed, Yee (the cook), and Evans (his new boss)—make the story's theme of reconstruction a communal possibility. No one in the story, certainly not Stevie or Wes, is completely whole or self-sufficient. In fact, one becomes almost weary of the writer's insistence upon Stevie's sickliness; once he is described as "blowing out the biggest bubble of snot you ever saw" (265).

The characters live in near poverty, with the uneasy knowledge that "half the grown men in the country's not working" (249). Wes is an imperfect parent, and Steve's near wellness at the end is tentative. But a community develops among the "family," composed of three races (Native American, Oriental, white).[10] One cooks, one works a job, one remembers the dead. Working together, they create a holy, that is, a life-giving community of sojourners. We remember the intactness and bliss of the Holbrooks, for example, when they journeyed to the farm.

Stevie's brokenness is symbolized by the "broken" text, which lends to the reader a pictorial representation of the shifting and moving that the boy feels. The fragmentation of his only known world is represented by the distribution of his mother's worldly goods: "That one on top: left over groceries. Into the kitchen, Yee. . . . Bedding stuff, Bo; up to the attic. Pots and kitchen things, High. . . . (Lowered voice) Just her clothes, Mrs. Ed, you know anybody? Mrs. Ed's room. Lamps and little rugs, . . . Anyone for a lamp?" (240). Afterward, Stevie thinks, "I don't know where anything is" (241). The text suggests an association between the mother's death and material fragmentation. The boy wants to bury the possessions and the hurt: *"Put it back," "all of it dead bury buried"* (246). Like the mother in "I Stand Here Ironing," he first attempts to stay or fix the memory.

At work, Stevie's job is to sort, to find a place for each thing, and to put it there so that when a customer comes, the sought piece can be found. Though he cannot face his mother's "junk," this sorting work is the means of the boy's personal recovery. Like the deer, it mediates the mother's presence. Discarded pieces from other homes remind him of some forgotten memory or feeling: "Wheat wreathes enamelled on a breadbox he is tipping to empty of rain Remembered pattern; forgotten hunger peanut butter, sour french bread Remembered face, hand, wavering through his face, reflected in the rusty agitated water" (253). He destroys the breadbox, but the memories are too many and eventually, in the human reflected image—Wes/his mother—Stevie begins to let the past live. This reconnaissance in the junkyard is a striking and certainly "other" imagining for twentieth-century understandings. Olsen seems to point to the masses of broken and unheeded human lives, not to traditionally sacred texts and symbols and not to the glitter and polish of high technology, as harboring the divine promises of life for the future. If we read the story as disclosing political and spiritual truth, then we must consider the possibility that the historically abused are the source, and not simply the means, of the earth's renewal and hoped-for future.

The narrative voice has foreshadowed Stevie's recovery from brokenness:

But the known is reaching to him, stealthily, secretly, reclaiming.

Sharp wind breath, fresh from the sea. Skies that are all seasons in one day. Fog rain. *Known weather of his former life.*

Disorder twining with order. The discarded, the broken, the torn from the whole: weathereaten weatherbeaten: mouldering, or waiting for use-need. *Broken existences that yet continue* [252].

The pieces of junk pass through Stevie's hands, "hard, defined, enduring," linking his new life to the city of his former existence. He uses the discards metaphorically to accomplish his own reclamation of body and spirit.

Wes offers a pattern for Stevie's work: "Singing—unconscious, forceful—to match the motor hum as he machines a new edge, rethreads a pipe. Capable, fumbling; exasperated, patient; demanding, easy; uncomprehending, quick; harsh, gentle; *concerned* with [Stevie]" (252). Teaching the boy a skill, Wes illustrates his care for his nephew's whole self. The man's response to the child mirrors his work at the junkyard; in both he seeks to make something useful, functional, vital.

In Wes's work, Stevie sees *"the recognizable human bond"* (252) reflected:

accurately threaded, reamed and chamfered
Shim Imperial flared

cutters benders grinders beaders
shapers notchers splicers reamers

how many shapes and sizes,
how various, how cunning in

application [260].

The narrative summary: "How many shapes and sizes, / how various, how cunning in / application" might describe humans, and the names of the parts might be human names.[11] Olsen respects machinery, but only as a means: humanity is the beginning and the reason for its existence. Wes sees the parts of a whole, is able to break apart the useless old, and redeem it by reconstruction. The work itself is a bond, something man and boy do together. Yet this particular work of reclamation elicits the "more" of Stevie's personal healing and makes the bond between uncle and nephew a bond of spiritual redemption.

A brief closing scene takes place in a cemetery. On Memorial Day, Stevie acccompanies Mrs. Ed to the graves of soldiers and of Indians.[12] The boy separates himself, stumbling on an old jar, and coming upon the grave of an infant. He sits down by a small stone lamb: "How warm it felt down there in the weeds where nobody could see him and the wind didn't reach. The lamb was sun warm too. He put his arm around its stone neck and rested. Red ants threaded in and out; the smell was sweet like before they set the burn pile; even the crackling flags sounded far away" (264). A sense of beneficence infuses Stevie's meditation and isolation. This solitude will be germinal, as Stevie, amid the disparate objects—the lamb, the weeds, the industrious ants, the crackling flags—is given a sense of safety and wholeness, the well-being he has sought since his mother's illness. Ultimately, Stevie's salvage comes from the grave, a human "junkyard." The mother's loss of her child is the obverse of Stevie's loss of his mother. Two halves remain. Together, Wes and Mrs. Ed can be the lost loved one (a mother) if Stevie (a child) will live and join them.[13]

Like "I Stand Here Ironing," "Requa" closes on the edge of its beginning. Unlike the earlier story, however, this one is unfinished. Olsen intends more. One of the great paradoxes of Olsen's texts is the sympathy their incompleteness evokes in her readers. Considering her small canon, the never completed novel, and "Requa" (now over a decade since it was published as a work still in progress), one marvels at the way Olsen's vision seems to hover on the brink of expression. It is almost as if her art is a new form, as though she waits for an answer or echo. Even if "Requa" is completed, we can say that Olsen's words to us are brief, her style fragmentary, almost hesitant, her writing like a voice searching for itself and listening as much as—even more than—speaking.

Stevie's muteness, Eva's darkness, Carol's hibernation, Anna's inner ponderings, Jim's silent hands: these may be read as signs of desire for a new speech, a speech (as Nelle Morton says) that we must hear deeply to understand. Olsen's fictive vocabulary, concluding for now with an orphan whose life appears as tentative and unheeded as a dandelion, is both image and form. The images come primarily from maternal realities and hopes; they are of stooped mothers, of children in tears and laughter, of tables, beds, and wreaths of flowers. The form is listening, speaking, and waiting.

Olsen spent years listening, often against her will. Like the mother of "I Stand Here Ironing," and like Eva, she almost lost her voice. But miraculously she regained enough to give us these few stories. She ends them asking for beginnings, and the hope that is in them is her own waiting for an answer, for the echo of readers' voices. Thus is virtue made of necessity, as spirit rises from matter. The image of Stevie crouching in the cemetery is a word before words, a message whose form creates meaning. The unholy child ascends in our reading and meets the unholiness (the brokenness, loss, weariness) in ourselves. In our compassion for him, in our own crouching, we ourselves are cleansed and made new.

1. Olsen is presently completing the novella. For ease of reading, I shall refer to the story as "Requa," though in its present form the story is only the first part of the novella Olsen is still writing.

2. Tillie Olsen, telephone conversation with the author, Fall, 1984.

3. "After Long Silence," *Studies in American Fiction* 12:1 (1984): 61–69.

4. Ibid.

5. Judith Plaskow, "The Coming of Lilith," in *Womanspirit Rising*, p. 205.

7. In personal notes from the seventies or early eighties, Olsen writes of the divisions of the world:

Sometimes already in the cradle, the inequality of
    the world,
the separation . . .

the infant that was all of us at birth
the human baby that was all of us before we were
    separated
misshapen into a sex, a skin color, an economic
    class, a nationality
a religion . . .
before the divisions of the warring world misshape
    and lessen us.

8. The imagery of the passage suggests Olsen's tendency to mix nature and manufactured goods, here the human face and the Indian art, thus evoking the whole of human life: both the givens of nature and the re-creations of human ingenuity.

9. I owe knowledge of this fact to Gelfant's article, "After Long Silence."

10. In the twenties, Waldo Frank wrote novels and travel books concerned with " 'overcoming the false individualism that is the essence of our capitalistic order,' and of supplanting it with the collective spirit that animated Spanish, American Indian, and Russian cultures" (Daniel Aaron, *Writers on the Left* [New York: Harcourt, Brace, and World, 1961], p. 193). Olsen's work is influenced by all three cultures. In finishing the novella, she has said, more emphasis will be given to the American Indian element.

11. The "naming" recalls *Yonnondio*; the style of piecing words and fragments recalls "Tell Me a Riddle."

12. Gelfant says in her article that Olsen has told her that in the expansion of the story into a novella, Mrs. Ed will play a larger role.

13. The power of the mother and the child's need for a rebirth through others who take up the mother's role but do not replace her is beautifully reflected in Tony Talbot's paragraphs appearing in *Mother to Daughter: Daughter to Mother*, pp. 234–35:

I knew a beautiful woman once. And she was my mother. I knew a tenderness once. And it was my mother's. Oh, how happy I was to be loved.

And now I mourn her. I mourn that cornerstone. I mourn her caring. I mourn the one who always hoped for me. I mourn her lost image of me. The lost infant in myself. My lost happiness. I mourn my own eventual death. My life now is only mine . . .

Every blade, every leaf, every seed in my portion of the world has shifted. Your presence hovers everywhere, over house, over garden, over dreams, over silence. You are within me. I'll not lose you.

Once I was born. Can I be born again? Oh, wean me from pain to love. Help me to use your love and strength in my own life. Help me to carry the world.

The last sentence recalls Olsen's character Alva, in "O Yes," who realizes she must help carry the world. The transformation in these paragraphs from loss to expansive love as well as the mother's presence in the world of nature is very close to Olsen's reflection of love and caring and her comprehension of beneficent powers embodied in humanity.

CHAPTER

VI

When the Angel Gains a Voice

Silence and Encouragement

I stand here ironing and what you asked me moves
tormented back and forth with the iron.

TILLIE OLSEN
"I Stand Here Ironing"

But perhaps it is my task in these dark times to keep
alive at least the desire to sing with everyone, including
the dead, including the cosmos.

DOROTHEE SOELLE
The Strength of the Weak

And my mouth was opened like a cloud of dew,
And my heart gushed forth (like) a gusher of
    righteousness.

And my approach was in peace,
And I was established in the Spirit of Providence
The Odes of Solomon

P
ublished in 1978, Olsen's prose essays, collected and
expanded in the book *Silences* ("garnered over fifty years"),
recalls the motivation of her early career, the conviction
that working-class experience should be reflected in
literature.[1] But as a book that draws from and reflects years of
experience—in literary, domestic, and working worlds—it is larger
than its beginnings, offering the writer's vision of human struggle
through the lens of artistic silence and fulfillment. Like Olsen's
fiction, the prose includes frankly autobiographical passages,
suggesting a conjoined story of the artist and the people she
represents. The guiding desire throughout the book is not for a
writer's utopia. There are too many contradictions in the various
silences Olsen names for her to imagine change simply as escape
from struggle. Rather, the desire that elicits the essays is for the
experience of tapped potentialities, for the experience in a lifetime
of affirmation, expression, of being heard (by oneself and others), and
of knowing oneself in harmony with the voices that call one out.

Silences must be read with Olsen's fiction or one may simplify
the imaginative voice that undergirds it.[2] At the most literal level,
the essays say that freedom from chores, daily maintenance of
children, and other paying work is the necessary condition for
fullest creation. This is an over-easy summing up of the work,
however; Olsen knows the yields of productive work and the insight
gleaned from a life with children when conditions are not extreme.
True human being is always struggling: if not for bread, for truth.
And truth may be found in the difficult interplay of relationship and
freedom. Life lived expressively both is grounded and soars. We can
neither conclude that freedom from all interruption is fullness of
life nor that bondage to pains and losses will miraculously yield
knowledge, understanding, and redemption. Somewhere between
the extremes, humanity may live responsibly and creatively,
transcending silence in the encouraging community of other

songsters and poets. Where Olsen suggests less than this—and at times in the essays she does seem to be arguing simply for special circumstances for creation—she is not consistent with the sustained paradoxical vision of her stories. Where she chooses to remain in the contradictions, as in the autobiographical sections, the essays are more provocative.

Like the fiction, *Silences* offers realistic and detailed descriptions of the conditions of working life, here, of the working writer's life (a writer who must work at another job) and the working-mother/ writer's life (Olsen's life: a writer who is a parenting mother also working at a paying job). In the characteristic method of her other writing, Olsen grounds her vision of creative and fulfilling life in the circumstances of historical experience. Yet the metaphorical title— silences—offers the prophetic impulse that evokes another reality, a hoped-for future of voice. In this book, more diffuse in many respects than the stories, Olsen develops paradigms for her paradoxical and transformative vision of harm and healing, loss and wholeness. For her, silence is metaphoric of unredeemed loss, while voice, regardless of how feeble, inarticulate, and unheeded, symbolizes the hope of recovery and the promise of signification. In the first essay, she describes her own rebirth as a writer when she was given time: "and it was in those months I made the mysterious turn and became a writing writer" (20). The sentence suggests the conjoined realities of material and spiritual being. The mysterious capacities of spirit require bread and sustenance, perhaps begin in such fertilization.

One can quickly scan the fiction for glimpses of the developing metaphor of silence. Mazie's and Anna's thoughts need the authorial consciousness because so much of what they feel they do not have words for. Emily, the girl in "I Stand Here Ironing," finds her talent for pantomime, an art form in which the actor is mute. In Whitey's and Parry's stories, community held texts (poem and song) reflect personal struggle for voice. Though he stumbles in articulating his personal anguish, Whitey's recitation—like the singing of the black congregation—reunites him with the power of "our words."

Stevie's and Eva's voices are broken. He stumbles in the vast silences of death, like a "dummy." She has forgotten her own visionary tongue in the years of caring for others' everyday needs. When she remembers it, in song and rhetoric, the voice is cracked. Her pieced-together words are an odd quilt of meaning: anguish over the loss, and yet renewed faith in human potential.

In *Silences*, Olsen continues the struggle of her fiction to draw out of literary and historical silences the voices and the art forms of people who have been largely ignored. Like the medley of art forms in "Tell Me a Riddle," where Eva uses folk art and song as well as political rhetoric and the music of the "acknowledged great" (Olsen's phrase in *Silences*), the essays spring from Olsen's conviction that disadvantaged people have still expressed their creativity. We might say that for Olsen spirit and creation are one. The creative spark born in every child is the redeeming spirit in which she believes.

Thus the book is more than Olsen's representation of the conditions in life that have silenced many, including herself. In its compassion for the subject—silence and the silenced—and in its faith in another way—voice and understanding—*Silences* represents genuine encouragement, calling readers to respond by finding their own voices and redeeming the losses of many whose words have been forgotten or never heard. One meaning of silence, as we learned with Eva, is quiet that allows hearing. Thus *Silences* is, among other things, a hearing.

Recalling the fiction, the prose enlarges it in the writer's focused and prophetic effort to elicit voice and truth. It is a practice of Olsen's faith in possibility as well as a demonstration of her abiding love for her medium and for the people she comes from.

Parts of *Silences* were first published as essays in 1965 and 1972. In Olsen's words, her purpose is "to re-dedicate and encourage" the writer who struggles against the discouraging circumstances of sex, race, and class. In particular, the work is dedicated to

> our silenced people, century after century their beings consumed in the hard, everyday essential work of maintaining human life. Their art, which still they made—as their other contributions—anonymous; refused respect, recognition; lost.
>
> For those of us . . . their kin and descendants, who begin to emerge into more flowered and rewarded use of ourselves . . . and by our achievement bearing witness to what was (and still is) being lost, silenced.[3]

Thus, the challenge is twofold: to make more flowered being possible in the present and to remember and reinterpret the ways in which people have expressed their being or spirit even in the most discouraging circumstances. The great human expressions (and necessities) of food, clothing, art, ritual, and religion give witness to fundamental desires for being that are inherent in humanity. We desire more than survival, and we celebrate what resounds most deeply the voices and directions within us.

The thesis of the book—the human birthright to a whole, that is, expressive, life—clearly reflects the impulse of Olsen's fiction. In her stories, she shows the artistry of everyday work. In *Silences*, she suggests an understanding of the labor of art and the excruciating toll it exacts from the individual. In both we glimpse the larger vision—pointed to metaphorically—of spiritual fulfillment, of expression as the process of being in harmony with the sacred, or of expression as holy Being.

In an untitled foreword, Olsen defines the silences of which she speaks, recalling the organic metaphor developed in her fiction, as well as echoing language often employed in speaking of spiritual becoming:

> *These are not natural silences, that necessary time for renewal, lying fallow, gestation, in the natural cycle of creation. The silences I speak of here are unnatural; the unnatural thwarting of what struggles to come into being, but cannot. In the old, the obvious parallels: when the seed strikes stone; the soil will not sustain; the spring is false; the time is drought or blight or infestation; the frost comes premature.*

The explicit use of the plant metaphor reminds us of the prophetic strain in the fiction, the sense conveyed through Olsen's stories that what the writer points to is a different way of life in which blossoming, not thwarting, is the rule. In *Silences*, she quotes Rebecca Harding Davis, who said of nineteenth-century steelworkers' lives, "Wrong, all wrong," and who wrote of the poor and unfulfilled, imagining them "as they might be."[4]

Part One of the book is composed of three essays. The first, "Silences," defines types of silence, referring often to the "great" of literary history. It was originally "an unwritten talk, spoken from notes at the Radcliffe Institute in 1962" (foreword to the essay) and was first published in 1965. The second, narrowed to a focus on women writers, entitled "One out of Twelve: Women Who Are Writers in Our Time—1971," was delivered as a talk at the Modern Language Association. Only the last, an essay on Rebecca Harding Davis, was originally written in essay form. It was prepared "as an afterword for the Feminist Press 1972 reprint of the 1861 *Life in the Iron Mills; or The Korl Woman* by Rebecca Harding Davis" (foreword to the essay). Part Two is a deepening of the inquiries of the first half of the book by way of other writers: excerpts from their lives, pieces of poems, stories, diaries, and letters, facts about circumstances, brief conclusions by Olsen not always written in sentences.

Topically, the book "is concerned with the relationship of circumstances—including class, color, sex; the times, climate into which one is born—to the creation of literature" (foreword). Olsen draws from the experiences of writers like Hopkins, Conrad, Kafka, Melville, Fitzgerald, Blake, Dreiser, Rilke, and Hardy. But in the second half of Parts One and Two, the book focuses upon women whose femaleness is added to class and race distinctions, making it even more difficult for the artist to garner the essential means, conditions, and faith for a sustained literary career. The result, Olsen shows, is that for every twelve writers "of recognized achievement" who are men, we find one writer who is a woman.

Throughout *Silences*, Olsen deliberates upon the individual and communal search for "truth." "The writer's question," she says, must be "is this true? is this all? if indeed gargoyled, then what misshaped," adding later, "is this true in my own experience and life-knowledge?" (250, 253). In "One out of Twelve," she calls "the writer's deepest questions" questions of meaning: "What is happening here, what does this mean?" (61). She quotes Davis's questions, a reflection of the writer's own anguished search for truth: "Is this the End? . . . nothing beyond?—no more?" (282–83) One's truth is the spiritual dimension of a writer's work, the "more" that binds and sustains, but only if it gains audience, a resounding or affirmation. By the end of *Silences*, Olsen's search for truth adopts a specific framework: how to conjoin truths, to integrate in literature (as a reflection and expansion of life) what one knows and feels as deepest and most valuable from the disparate experiences of one's life, and in so doing to encourage others toward more fulfilling life. It is a method similar to Alice Walker's in her essay "In Search of Our Mothers' Gardens," where she seeks in her matrilineal heritage clues to spiritual, literary, and political expansiveness and integration. Her mother's flower gardens, brilliantly planted in circumscribed environments, are akin to Olsen's truth: Here is this beauty, she and Walker imply, but might there be more? In Walker's words, where do we go from here, being faithful to that "respect for the possibilities"?[5]

Olsen's effort in these essays is to tell the truth about silences, the breaks, absences, and discontinuities in literature and history, where a person's or a community's experience is not allowed or encouraged written formation and reflection.[6] That certain experiences have not been recorded does not mean that they did not exist or that they were not valuable. Rather, the silence tells something of the circumstances of life where people spend ten, twelve, or fourteen hours a day at work or where a parent's, usually a mother's, writing is interrupted by children and the day-to-day realities of domestic chores. Olsen is concerned with the truthful depiction of such lives in order that political and cultural change occur, which in turn will elicit a fuller vision of human struggles, needs, and dreams.

In her examination of the subject, both in her own language and in the language of the writers she invokes, Olsen develops extended metaphorical descriptions of silence: blight, aridity, disease, imprisonment, exile, breakdown, fragmentation, thwarting, blankness. Of these, fragmentation and disease are particularly suggestive of the moral vision inherent in all of Olsen's work. Clearly, the first recalls Stevie's brokenness, while the imagistic description of loss and constriction in terms of illness reminds us of Anna, Emily, Whitey, and Eva. Thus it appears that in *Silences* Olsen extends and expands the metaphorical lens of her fiction to an examination of artists' lives. That is, the stories seem to provide the sustaining images culminating in the paradigmatic metaphor of silence.

Using the metaphor of fragmentation (and, conversely, totality, which I read as wholeness/holiness), Olsen describes the silence that occurs when one cannot integrate the parts of one's life. She suggests the frequency of this silence among women writers. Like spiritual brokenness, the metaphor implies loss of coherence and will. The silence that results is not natural silence (waiting for voice) but an "unnatural thwarting of what struggles to come into being but cannot" (6). Artistic eclipse denies being, thus making humans less than they can be.

In the title essay, "Silences," Olsen invokes "the accomplished great" concerning what is needed for creation. The answer—from Balzac, James, Rilke, Conrad, and others—is totality of self, abundance of time, wholeness of vision. From their answers, Olsen is moved to ask: "But what if there is not that fullness of time, let alone totality of self?" (13). Focusing upon women, whose voices have entered literature in substantial numbers only in the last 150 years, she notes the inbred contradiction in their lives between creation and gender roles: "Wholly surrendered and dedicated lives; time as needed for work; totality of self. But women are traditionally trained to place others' needs first, to feel these needs as their own . . . their sphere, their satisfaction to be in making it possible for others to use their abilities." (17).[7] If being and expression are synonymous, if spirit and creation are one, then what are the religious implications of silencing? Is denial of voice equal to denial of spirit and holiness? What does this say about religious as well as literary traditions that silence?

Asking after her own kind—the worker/mother/writer—Olsen

observes that this writer cannot put writing first.[8] In her work, writing "can have at best, only part self, part time." For Olsen and those like her, "it is distraction, not meditation, that becomes habitual; interruption, not continuity; spasmodic, not constant toil." Loss of harmony is a fracturing of spirit and thus a loss of one's essential self. "Almost no mothers—as almost no part-time, part-self persons," she concludes, "have created enduring literature . . . so far" (18–19). The description of her own circumstances reflects the circumstances of Olsen's characters and suggests the sustained metaphorical use of fragmentation in her writing. Eva, the young revolutionary, found her vision eclipsed when, as a mother, she had neither time nor place to express and develop it. Her deep sense of call to a universal struggle for humanism was almost entirely silenced by the urgent needs of her own family. Even in the end, she is not able to integrate the two halves of her self—her visionary spirit and her nurturing mother self—though she knows the yields of both.

Olsen's analysis of Rebecca Harding Davis's characters and of Davis herself illustrates the partiality and eclipse suffered by these people, which Olsen understands as a silencing and which we are coming to see as a spiritual deprivation. Analyzing Davis's "The Wife's Story,"[9] Olsen describes it as "the working of woman's 'conflict' in the insoluble situation of commitment to the real needs of other human beings and the real need to carry on one's other serious work as well" (90). Hetty, the protagonist, is a musician, but she has chosen the family life of mother and wife. The two are contradictory in her experience, and each determination toward creativity is followed by a renewal of sensitivity to her family's needs. At last, in a passage quoted in *Silences,* Hetty thinks: "I got it [the score of an opera] out now by stealth, at night, putting my pen to it here and there, with the controlled fever with which a man might lay his hand on a dear dead face, if he knew the touch would bring it back to life. Was there any waking that dead life of mine?" (93).

The woman's language reveals a feeling of physical division, even death. By day she is mother and wife; by night and in secret, a musician. Her tone is doubtful, expressing her fear that in her forgetfulness of them, her powers have died. Her art, like her children, demands nurture, but the music is more like an abandoned child. When she lives as a mother, her artistic body atrophies and is "silenced." Revival may be impossible; integration of her roles into a harmonious voice seems out of the question.

Olsen describes what she imagines about Davis, whose work was interrupted by mothering and family duties: "Probably to the end of her days, a creature unknown to those around her lived on in Rebecca, a secret creature still hungry to know" (111). Clearly Olsen values this secret being as Davis's deepest self. The statement implies the fragmentation true of Davis's female characters and sounds like Olsen's Anna: their gifts, like their truest selves, silenced by circumstances that fragment the artistic and the domestic selves, in Anna's case, deny the artistic to such a degree that she is hardly aware of her own possibilities. Rebecca's sense of the inadequacy of her art, recorded by Olsen, communicates her intuition of partiality and incompleteness in her work, which was born out of interruption, a fragmented center, a consciousness whose self-understanding had to remain largely in the dark.[10]

Though Olsen sees fracturing as a silence abundantly characteristic of women, the metaphor extends to all experiences of life where one's circumstances require a partial existence. For Olsen, partiality is a significant silence that robs persons and communities of the opportunity for searching, creating, and expressing selfness, which is the distinguishing mark of humanity. Thus Davis's characters, as well as Davis and Olsen as artists, represent the condition of all persons whose deep longings have been partially or entirely denied. Totality of self is not freedom from all harms but the freedom to experience physical and spiritual being, as one who nurtures others and one's self, as worker and artist. In dualized life experience where work competes with creation, fragmentation can seldom be overcome by an expressed vision through which one may be reconnected with one's calling, one's deepest sense of truth. What one may hear in one's soul will most likely remain silent in the world and may even be silenced in one's own experience if one has no occasion or means for relating it. Thus is one denied, in Olsen's words, "*this endowment to live the whole of human life*" (43). Thus do we live chronologically, always losing ourselves to the past.

Fragmentation and partiality do not merely lessen wholeness, but infect it. Unlike the metaphor of fragmentation, which points to a break in consciousness and a forgetfulness of one's capacities (Mary Daly's loss of authentic being), Olsen's use of disease imagery portends a physical paralysis, leaving the victim conscious of the vision she is unable to fulfill. The anguish is over thwarted capacities, which one still feels. This image is closely connected with the imagery of exile since it suggests *separation from* one's truth and identity but not loss of memory. It may point to a more anguishing experience.

Organic imagery is the basis of Olsen's use of the disease

metaphor in *Silences,* as it is in "Tell Me a Riddle." "When the time is drought or blight of infestation," the human search for meaning is diseased. Developing the metaphors of fragmentation and disease together, Olsen writes of Franz Kafka: "[His diaries] testify . . . unbearably to the driven strategems for time, the work lost (to us), the damage to the creative powers (and the body) of having to deny, interrupt, postpone, put aside, let work die" (14). Enumerating the causes of fragmentation, Olsen connects harm to the creative process with harm to the body, suggesting the interconnection of partiality, loss, and disease.

Excerpting from the diaries, Olsen records Kafka's own description of his loss and impending silence: "Distractedness, weak memory, stupidity. Days pass in futility; powers wasted away." Without time, spending energy in the mere but necessary drive to overcome the fragmentation of lost opportunity, Kafka's "powers wasted." In the end, he was "eaten into tuberculosis," writes Olsen, suggesting the physical manifestation of the spiritual disease of unfulfilled mental powers and vision (15).

Blight, atrophy, malformation, crippling are Olsen's images for diseased literary work—writing accomplished, if at all, under constriction rather than in the fullness of time when vision asks to be realized. Such work results primarily from circumstances "where the claims of creation cannot be primary," or where the writer's truth is denied or scorned by culture and convention. By contrast, health occurs where subterranean forces are "passionately fed," where there is time for nurture, and where one's work is received. Feeding and sustaining elicit health, while starvation (for time, energy, vision, audience) results finally in death to the soul and, perhaps, as with Kafka, to the body. Olsen's organic understanding of creation's needs suggests a cyclical pattern: "only the removal and development of the material frees the forces for further work," as with the planted field, where one year's harvest must come in before another can be prepared for, plowed, and planted. Untended and unharvested, mind, like land, grows cluttered and is overburdened (13–14).

In the essay "Silences," Olsen uses a cluster of disease images to describe herself at times when writing could not be primary in her life: "This was the time of festering and congestion. . . . Always roused by the writing, always denied. . . . 'It convulsed and died in me.'" When she had time, she "could manage only the feeblest, shallowest growth on that devastated soil" (19–21). In the personal testimony, it becomes clear that the disease in terms of which Olsen imagines wasted human creativity is generally not born from within

but more often is generated from harmful conditions outside. Not
malformations of the individual human soul but poor soil and
"devastated" circumstances lead to festering and congestion. Where
people live and how makes a crucial difference in health and
productivity.

Olsen uses Gerard Manley Hopkins to reflect the
interconnection of body and spirit and poor health: in his words,
"disappointment and humiliations embitter the heart and make an
aching in the very bones" (129). A great part of the writer's
fulfillment comes in the reception of his or her work. The vision is
only complete if it is shared. Thus, as Olsen clearly remarks, "Not
to have an audience is a kind of death" (44). One's work, like one's
spirit, may suffer crippling and paralysis if readers reject one's truth
or if it is ignored.

Giving evidence of the power of culture to thwart and disease
human potential in the "acknowledged great" writers, Olsen regards
the greater harm to women who write and to writers of working
peoples' lives. By denying range in women and refusing to recognize
the forms of art among the working class, those with literary power
have discouraged the artistic spirit in many. Olsen reminds the
reader of *Silences:*

> Remember that "eclipsing, devaluation, are the result of critical
> judgments, a predominantly male domain. The most damaging, and
> still prevalent, critical attitude remains 'that women's experience, and
> literature written by women are, by definition, minor'" [232].

Early in her discussion of Davis, she quotes a character from *Life in
the Iron Mills,* a mill owner: "If I had the making of men, these men
who do the lowest part of the world's work should be machines,—
nothing more,—hands. It would be kindness. . . . What are taste,
reason, to creatures who must live such lives?" (49).

Denial and devaluation by culture thwart individual talent and
condemn a class and a sex to lives in which artistic development is,
at best, secondary. By definition, a sense of ultimate value is denied
to "women's topics" and "women's experience," while the working
class is denied the search for ultimate meaning and expression, in
that time and means for reflection and creation are excluded from
their lives.

"One out of Twelve" suggests that women's self-consciousness is
infected by prevalent attitudes that ask them to deny and
undervalue their truths, among them:

> Ways in which innate human drives and capacities . . . denied
> development and scope, nevertheless struggle to express themselves and

function; what goes on in jobs; penalties for aging; the profound experience of children—and the agonizing having to raise them in a world not yet fit for human life; what it is to live as a single woman; having to raise children alone; going on; causes besides the accepted psychiatric ones, of breakdown in women [43].

If women accept male strictures and values in writing, Olsen implies, they must malform their own experience to fit within the limits before them.

In Olsen's view, the self-doubt that characterizes the woman writer symbolizes the draining loss of confidence and aspiration of many in our culture who find that their own experience and deepest truth are not valued. Eva exemplifies the person who once dreamed of great harmonies and sharing, but who finds that the world of her experience in the home has been little recognized and that many have forgotten the dreams that have directed her life. For Olsen, the dying human *spirit*, or loss of belief, is the greatest tragedy, and it follows largely from silencing.

In summarizing the literary situation of women, Olsen expands her subject to offer an understanding of the interconnection between literature and wholeness in life: "Not to be able to come to one's truth or not to use it in one's writing, even in telling the truth having to 'tell it slant,' robs one of drive, of conviction; limits potential stature; results in loss to literature and the comprehension we seek in it" (44). The absence of one's truth, in the forms of culture, whether one is male or female, child or adult, is the profoundest silence. Where there is no answer to one's query, no interest in one's perceptions, no affirmation of one's voice, we meet the void, unredeemable loss. Olsen's vision is based on her conviction that human experience yields ultimate truth, not final but life-giving truth. Yet most, she suggests, are denied the human privilege of testing ideas and searching for understanding in their own voices, out of their own experience.

Throughout the essays, Olsen portrays the agony of the unfulfilled. Silence is a kind of death. In terms of her own metaphors, what is diseased by undervaluation or fragmented by lack of freedom and choice is turned from vision and voice to forgetfulness and death. For those people whose experience has never been recorded, the silence is profound. Without memory of ancestors and without a reflection in literature of the struggles of one's people, one is left homeless in a formless landscape.

The world comprehension of *Silences* is consistent with Olsen's fiction, distilled in terms of muteness and voice.[11] For Tillie Olsen, silence signifies attrition, denial, restriction, isolation, and extinction in any of life's significant endeavors. The book itself is an emblem of loss, a tangential reminder of death to the human spirit. Yet Olsen's paradoxical transformation of silence into voice reveals a human story. Neither irretrievable loss and agony nor the apparent success of the traditionally great is the central interest of the book. Rather, the "uncircumstanced" life, often unfulfilled, yet still searching for meaning and coherence, is the human story evolving in *Silences*. It is Tillie Olsen's own life. She first saw such a life reflected in literature in Rebecca Harding Davis's *Life in the Iron Mills*, and she brings it to our attention in *Silences*. Hugh Wolfe, the steel worker with a hunger for beauty, sculpts a giant figure of a woman from the korl. Ungainly and crouching with arms outstretched, she is, he says, asking for "summat to make her live" (49).

Tillie Olsen imagines the search for meaning—something to make one live—as evolving in the creative process. The work of literature is her subject but the process of creating is similar in any human endeavor. Attending to literature, she does not view it simply as a reflection of reality, an embodiment of an understanding already fully formed in the artist's imagination. Rather, in creating, a person comes to spiritual understanding and expression. "Subterranean forces" and powers within, mysteriously garnered in conscious effort, and given necessary time and encouraging circumstances, produce a rendering of life. In so giving form and dignity to one's experience, one may find sustenance. Thus, for Olsen, the opportunity for creativity is essential to human well-being, and a story of one's own (by which I mean an understanding of one's life) is an essential human need. Becoming fully human means "coming to one's own truth,"[12] ascending toward the voice that is both inner and outer, grounded in self and calling from the mystery of creation larger than oneself.

In *Silences*, then, we begin to feel the full measure of Olsen's vision. The claims on which her writing is grounded can only be described as radical. Olsen appears to believe what most of culture and history deny: that every life is a miracle, that a human world is possible, that with faith in life's promises we may heal the divisions that engender alienation, pain, and death. Placing her belief first, she writes upon it like one who builds a bridge in the air and crosses over. In theological language, it is not an omnipotent God but Spirit indwelling the people that is the liberating presence in the world. Always, readers must remember that this faith comes out of personal struggle and loss, not comfort and security, and that if Olsen's beliefs appear overly optimistic, her vision is hard won and engaged. If one views the world as Olsen does, in terms of children's wonder, beauty, and sympathy, is it so hard to believe that with learned patterns of sharing and encouragement we might create the time of promise and renewal?

Olsen's concern with silence, then, is a concern with her own understanding of ultimacy and truth. To be circumstantially and historically denied the opportunity to create is a denial of sacred being. Yet, paradoxically, those like Davis's Hugh Wolfe and Olsen, whose searches have been restricted and whose efforts toward creating beauty and coming to meaning have been imperfect and marred, still lend to us—if we break the silence of forgetfulness and ignoring—a story that may renew our search for wholeness. Despite great odds, Olsen's life and literature testify: "THE TREE DID—DOES—BEAR FRUIT" (259).

Through an examination of her past, refracted through others' stories of similar struggle, Olsen offers a vision of the human situation as the struggle to fulfill powers and truths—what she calls "subterranean forces"—latent in each one's deepest self. Her desire is for more rewarded and flowered use of ourselves, for life that knows the holiness of growth, and the grace of expression and re-creation. Journeys toward shalom are individual and communal, personal and spiritual. In the old language, the particular yields the universal.

To my mind, the stirring visionary questions raised through *Silences* might be thus paraphrased:

Can there be any reconciliation for all that is lost of vision, totality, wholeness, expectancy, fruition, in those lives whose creativity and fulfillment were circumscribed? What human act, sentence, or memory can redeem fragmented human lives that are, in history, refused fulfillment in voice, expression, and in the search for their own truth?

If the search for meaning and understanding is the human quest, what lends humanity and dignity to those occupied with "necessary work," who dream dreams but are diseased by circumstances that thwart and cripple their art?

Without the assurance "of a compassionate God to save us,"[13] Olsen seeks answers in the vast powers of the human spirit. In *Silences*, a model of encouragement is elicited, pointing toward a way of being human that will enable greater blossoming and more holy, because more whole, existence.

In reading Olsen's work, we have met "encouragers," people who act as catalysts of grace and enhancement in others' experience. Throughout *Silences*, as in her fiction, Olsen prophetically suggests that encouragement calls forth grace or "fortune." Whether in terms of opportunity and opened doors (as with Olsen's own grants and fellowships) or in terms of essential love and self-esteem offered by a parent to a child, only generous nurture makes possible the blossoming and creativity humans are capable of. Olsen's vision of encouragement is embodied in her preface to *Silences*. Furthermore, she proposes that encouragement should be a universal principle, when, in her discussion of "The Literary Situation (1976)," she records her "long ago and still instinctive response: What's wrong with the world then, that it doesn't ask—and make it possible—for people to raise and contribute the best that is in them" (172).

The actual working out of the paradigm of encouragement comes through Olsen's critical examination of the imperfect forms of nurturing that we have practiced in our culture. The vision of a transformed humanity, arising from a reevaluation of the human need for care and grounded in a recognition of women's traditional roles in providing nurture, suggests the reconstructionist attitude of Olsen's writing. Refusing to choose between the boundless human desire for creativity and the human necessities of care and nurture, Olsen forges a different way: "No one's fullness of being [should be] at the cost of another's" (258).

Olsen's most imaginative use of Virginia Woolf, whom she cites often, may be in her recalling of Woolf's "angel in the house." For Woolf, "the angel" is the ideal feminine, who empties herself for the sake of others, one who "must charm . . . sympathize . . . flatter . . . conciliate . . . be extremely sensitive to the moods and wishes of others before her own." Woolf claimed to have the killed the angel in herself "or she would have plucked out my heart as a writer" (34). But in her analysis of Woolf, Olsen writes: "[She] never killed that aspect of the angel 'extremely sensitive to the needs and moods and wishes of others': [that angel] remained—an essential part of [Woolf's] equipment as a writer." Olsen cites Woolf's description of her work: "I think writing, my kind of writing, is a species of mediumship; I become the person" (213). The character of one sensitive to the needs, moods, and wishes of others is one that Olsen deems valuable for the creation of true caring between human beings. She suggests that sympathy is an emotion often elicited in literature by women: "Indeed, one of the most characteristic strains in literature written by women . . . *is* conscience, concern with wrongs to human beings in their time" (42).

From her experience and knowledge, Olsen defines "the essential angel," the female (mother, wife, daughter, or sister) "who must assume the physical responsibilities for daily living, for the maintenance of life" (34). This angel has little freedom or choice. To abandon her role, to kill the angel in herself, might mean the actual death of children and other dependents. Like Gerty Nevels in Harriette Arnow's *The Dollmaker*, she is the actual, not symbolic, sustainer of many young lives.

Both angels have been essential in making it possible for some men to write. Olsen reminds the reader that Rilke, in his words, had one "like a sister who would run the house like a friendly climate, there or not there as one wished." Conrad expressed his own freedom to wrestle with his creativity, "never aware of the even flow of daily life made easy and noiseless . . . by a silent, watchful, tireless affection." Yet both angels, Olsen observes, are "curiously absent . . . from the actual contents of most men's books, except perhaps on the dedication page" (34–35).

Whether the angel emerges of necessity or by convention, Olsen finds value in the sensitivity learned by each. In describing her constriction to work and raising children for twenty years, she writes: "[I] could not kill the essential angel (there was no one else to do her work); would not—if I could—have killed the caring part of the Woolf angel" (38). Just as the mother/protagonist must redeem the apparently negative characteristics of her eldest daughter in "I Stand Here Ironing," so Olsen, in reviewing her life, given more in energy and time to care for others than to her art, is compelled to redeem that work and time in order to come to an integrated sense of her life. Having been the essential angel and having found profound "maintenance-of-life" satisfactions as well as centuries-old injustices and restrictions in inherited mothering work, Olsen looks for the "caring part" of the angel, and her writing implies that from a reconstruction of that character, another model—the encourager—may spring.[14]

Woolf's understanding of her own work suggests the concept of representation, taking another's place to give voice to overlooked or undervalued experience. Representation in human relationships is necessary because many are hurt and silenced, and they depend upon those who have voice for any speech at all. Thus one like Olsen writes for many. But the model of the encourager is more reciprocal and prophetic. It is a model for an equitable world in which all humans are capable not only of receiving but of returning care and encouragement. In such a world, all would have voice. From her description of the essential angel in *Silences* (a representative *"so lowly as to be invisible"*), we can trace in her fiction Olsen's attempt to transform sacrifice into mutually encouraging human relationships (34). The impulse of the transformation is Olsen's profoundest dream, that *"every life shall be a song."* While this vision is built out of what already exists, it is radical rather than revisionist in implication. To believe that accomplishment, fulfillment, and the most profound human experience arise from shared life-maintainance work and from equitable sources of encouragement negates the far more prevalent Western models of competition, scarcity, and individual quest.

In the novel *Yonnondio,* Old Man Caldwell and Anna are split halves of the mother/encourager. Together, their characters represent Olsen's first attempt at transforming sacrificial love into mutual love. Anna, bound by poverty to house and children, is too exhausted to encourage her children's education. She wants them to learn but can hardly afford school clothes for them, much less offer them the daily reinforcement, discipline, and tutelage they need. It is Caldwell, not the mother, who has had the circumstances that allow some self-reflection and who can encourage Mazie with books and in stirring language: "Keep that wondering, Mazie, but try to *know.* . . . Live, don't exist. Learn from your mother, who . . . has kept life" (49).

Olsen uses the neighbor's understanding to point to the almost miraculous spirit of the mother, who has maintained a vision of beauty and hope for her children in spite of their poverty. Caldwell brings to light the losses in Anna's own life and encourages the daughter through the mother's hope toward a more fulfilled life. His voice for her and for Mazie connects mother and daughter, thus binding together the hopes of each.

In "I Stand Here Ironing," the mother has been an encourager, but her powers for sustaining the daughter's artistic expression are limited. Unlike Anna, she has overcome extreme poverty; her children go to school. And she can say, though only "once": "Why don't you do something . . . in the school amateur show?" (18–19). A muted, even silent theme in this story, particularly significant given its autobiographical nature, is the issue of the mother's own desire and need to be creative. The counselor spurs the mother's reflection on her daughter's life and on all that has been lost in it. Yet the story must be read as a double mirror, since Olsen's life has been the story of struggle for her own artistic becoming. The anguish that the persona feels over the counselor's questions is not only anguish over her daughter's thwarted potential but agony over her own. The loss and the sacrifice multiply in negative numbers. Not having become herself all that she longed to become, she must now mourn the loss of her daughter's potential. And yet, since the story is a metaphorical reflection of daughter/mother, the daughter's newly found art is also a sign of encouragement for the mother. Writing the

story of her loss (reflected in her daughter), Olsen begins to
transform the sacrificial angel in herself. Thus the loss of years to
other work is redeemed in the story Olsen makes out of it. This
does not mean that the lost time vanishes or is forgotten, but that
the voice garnered in the story gives reconciling grace to the
mother's loss by voicing her transcending hope.

The grandmother in "Tell Me a Riddle" stills the caring angel in
herself while her granddaughter, Jeannie, "mothers" both
grandparents, bringing food, consoling, providing counseling and
encouragement. Only with Jeannie can Eva be herself, and Jeannie
performs the function of hearing her beloved "Granny." Thus, Eva
finds her voice with her granddaughter, lamenting her own losses as
well as the losses to humanity in her century. Again, though the loss
must not be forgotten, the granddaughter's care, her relative
independence, and her education suggest that her own life may
embody and engender mutual love among persons. The actual
historical and political realization of humanitarian change reflected
in Jeannie encourages the life of the dying one who has seen so
much more of destruction. The reciprocity we see between Jeannie
and Eva suggests that we are faithful to our parents and to our
children as we make ways (are way-makers) for human expression
and flowering.

Paradoxically, in "Requa," where the mother is already dead, the
most complete transformation occurs: the memory of Stevie's
mother, mysteriously present in his awakening, leads uncle and
nephew into a way of relating in which each nourishes the other.
Though at first Stevie seems a "dummy," he responds to the uncle's
need and comes alive himself in the actual performance of caring
actions. Covering his uncle's body and speaking graceful words of
assurance, the boy reciprocates love. The angelic posture of the
sickly child brings beauty to the uncle's life and recognition of
relationship to the nephew. He and his uncle are the same body. A
source of mystery and joy to the uncle, the promise of Stevie's
healing symbolizes their mutual giving, transforming the mother's
sacrificial love, which visits the characters throughout.

Olsen's "truth" emerges as an advocacy that all learn the
necessary human art of caring and encouraging. The vision is almost
mathematical. If part of humanity offers all of the "essential" care—
whether that part be the half who are women or the more than half
who are working class—those people are denied their human
creativity in other areas. On the other hand, to live without offering
to someone else "essential" care and encouragement may be, in
Olsen's view, a greater poverty.

"Dream-Vision," Olsen's short essay about her mother's death, published in *Mother to Daughter: Daughter to Mother* (1984), performs a second transformation of the essential angel (261–64). Throughout the fiction, we recognize the writer's desire for her mothering characters, that they might be freed of patterns of complete self-sacrifice toward relationships inviting mutual fulfillment. The losses of her "essential angels," like Anna and Eva, point to the more wholly beneficent model of "the encourager." But in this brief essay, recounting her mother's dream, Olsen suggests that the world, not only working women and mothers, needs transforming according to the alternate vision and the differing sense of values of the caring angel: men become women and economic poverty becomes spiritual knowledge. The mother's dream, like her life, bequeaths encouragement to the daughter even though the life was one beset by uncountable discouragements.

In her dream, the mother is visited by three wise men, magnificently dressed in "jewelled robes of crimson, of gold, of royal blue." Since she is not a religious person, she suspects that they have lost their way. But the men insist that they have come to talk to her "of whys, of wisdom." Welcoming them, the woman sees that *"they were not men, but women"*: *"That they were not dressed in jewelled robes, but in the coarse everyday shifts and shawls of the old country women of her childhood, their feet wrapped round and round with rags for lack of boots; . . . That their speech was not highflown but homilies: their bodies not lordly in bearing, magnificent, but stunted, misshapen"* (262). From three wise men to three old-country women, the visitors are transformed into many women. They begin to sing a lullaby—Olsen's mother included—around a universal infant, taking turns to cradle it.

The essay is a revisioning of wisdom and value. In this instance the truth manifest in the infant lies not with those of lordly bearing but with humanity's "essential angels." The mother names the child "joy, the reason to believe." The description itself of the women's bent bodies is transforming, making beautiful the old shawls and the rags in the atmosphere of music and worship. The essay transforms present into past and future, recalling the old country and the youth of the women, their own hope for vitality and vigor. Death itself is transformed—through the melody, the swaying bodies, the raised voices—into faith. Though the mother dies, her vision lives with her daughter:

> She, who had no worldly goods to leave, yet left to me an
> inexhaustible legacy. Inherent in it, this heritage of summoning

resources to make—out of song, food, warmth, expressions of human love—courage, hope, resistance, belief; this vision of universality, before the lessenings, harms, divisions of the world are visited upon us.

She sheltered and carried that belief, that wisdom—as she sheltered and carried us [162–64].

The summary suggests the communal nature of encouragement and the miraculous transformation in human lives when many together elicit from their resources the best of human expressions: love, hope, courage, belief. The daughter/narrator draws a parallel between the vision and the mother's essential caring for her children, though in her own life the care of others and the fulfillment of her own talents could not be integrated. Thus the dream, as Olsen tells it, points to a past of injustices but recognizes essential truths and values present in the face of "hardship, limitation, longing."

Like *Silences*, the essay reflects the wisdom of essential angels, of workers—men and women—who know the value of life. Their understanding of what is needed for a wholesome world is the basis of Olsen's vision. She seeks to give voice to the knowledge of her mother for the sake of transforming the world. In a miraculous way, the essay encourages the dead mother, making her presence felt by offering linguistic commemoration to her struggle. The beneficence Olsen depicts is the grace of human relatedness. The mother lives, as the daughter remembers her and seeks to actualize her dream. The human bond of encouragement transcends death and transforms loss if, Olsen suggests, we are faithful.

Olsen's vision is one of mutuality and plurality rather than of sacrifice and singularity. It denies either/or thinking (either spirit or body; either my child's well-being or my own; either work or relationship) and believes instead that a harmonizing of needs yields the truthful expression of holiness. Care and encouragement, given and received, liberate people toward their fullest being. Since some still talk about God, we may say that divinity is grounded in our world and comes into full Being with us in our own hearing and speaking. We deny sacred Being when we deny the Being in ourselves and others. We experience the process of Being Becoming in the encouragement of all humanity toward self-discovery and celebration. In such a vision, the community of the saints is all people. One may even imagine the world (flesh) as an original word calling forth hearing and response, initiation and integration. The human infant, so important to Olsen's thinking, is a new word spoken to humanity daily. Encouragement is another word, our response. When we are silent—discouraged or discouraging—the earth and holiness are diminished; when we speak on behalf of each other, the whole world and God are expanded.

The transformative agent in the essays is the encouragement, the affirmation of human spirit, which they embody. Though Olsen shuns hasty conclusions about her own life as a model for others, *Silences* is an illustration of the encouragement Olsen's fiction pleads for. In offering the grace of remembrance and esteem to many who have been forgotten and in advocating the right of all people to a full life of creativity and care, she transforms her own life of many sacrifices into a life of encouragement. She overcomes silence as she encourages the same hope for others. In the mutual quest (for self and for others) toward fulfillment as a writer and as a human being, Tillie Olsen's presence in her writing is a model of encouragement that is mutual rather than sacrificial.

She writes, she says, "to re-dedicate and encourage." In "One out of Twelve," she urges others to encourage in their readership and teaching:

> You who teach, read writers who are women. There is a whole literature to be re-estimated, revalued. . . .
> Read, listen to, living women writers; our new as well as our established, often neglected ones. Not to have an audience is a kind of death.
> Read the compass of women writers in our infinite variety. . . .
> Teach women's lives through the lives of the women who wrote the books, as well as through the books themselves; . . . Because most literature concerns itself with the lives of the few, know and teach the few books closer to the lives of the many. . . .
> . . . .
> Help create writers, perhaps among them yourselves [44–45].

The passage reads as a commission. Encouragement is suggested as an activity that leads to understanding, which will actually elicit creativity, even one's own best expression. The impulse of the plea is egalitarian rather than elitist: "Know and teach the few books closer to the lives of the many."

In "Silences in Literature II," Olsen uses Rilke's voice to present the absolute human need for encouragement: "I look for some person," he writes, "who will understand my need without taking me for a beggar." "It is clear to me that I need help in order to continue on my way" (164). Rilke's statements point to the empowering agency of an encourager. One who encourages or "helps" actually provides the power or energy for the one who falters. Implied is the special need of encouragement in a time of crisis. Olsen suggests, in harmony with Rilke's confession, that encouragement should be brought into alignment with need. Strengthened and healed, the writer, or any person enabled to be creative and fruitful, will regain a sense of autonomy, though people always need relationships of encouragement for giving and receiving.

The radical announcement in *Silences* is that all humans need encouragement because all are gifted. In a postscript to the book, "Creativity; Potentiality. First Generation," Olsen writes: "Not many would accede to creativity as an enormous and *universal* human capacity (let alone recognize its extinction as the question of the age). I am one of those who, in almost unbearable, based conviction, believe that it is so" (261). Because Olsen's faith is in human capacity, her vision rests on the possibility that humans may elicit beauty and love from each other. Written achievement is only "one area of recognized human achievement" (262). Olsen's fiction testifies that in her estimation, all acts of beauty, all sentences of encouragement, all creations of use and benefit, all moments of hope, all witnesses to truth, are achievements.

The image of the essential angel is Olsen's "word" for the need that grounds experience. The "word" exemplifies the great Olsen riddle or paradox. It is a word we speak because we have heard and seen, not because we understand. The essentials are bodily and spiritual: food, clothing, place, tenderness, community, voice, belief, hope. The angel is likewise a presence that arises from need and struggle. She is way-maker, life keeper, one acquainted with sorrows and grief. In the economy of Olsen's world, she is in need of respite. Other encouragers must help carry the world.

We may say that for Tillie Olsen truth is whatever understanding or insight leads to a more inclusive, more coherent, more fruitful way of living. Because the same life that is fraught with exclusion, fragmentation, and blight holds the potential for beauty, care, nurture, and wholeness, she suggests that the path to truth is the dialectical no/yes. All experience—what hurts as well as what heals—must be "read," must come to critical consciousness, in order that we, as individuals in relationship, can say "no" to whatever thwarts creativity and wholesome relating and "yes" to whatever expands, enhances, and connects. Olsen expresses the search for truth metaphorically in terms of bondage and liberation:

There is also—love. The need to love and be loved.

It has never yet been a world right for love, for those we love, for ourselves, for flowered human life.

The oppression of women is like no other form of oppression (class, color—though these have parallels). It is an oppression entangled through with human love, human need, genuine (core) human satisfactions, identifications, fulfillments.

How to separate out the chains from the bonds, the harms from the value, the truth from the lies [258].

Truth is liberating. It is, in Olsen's vision, the understanding that allows one to choose, to say "no" and "yes." The ultimacy or religious dimension of her writing rests in its comprehension of truth. If one is not allowed—in reflection, creation, and memory—to understand one's experience, one is alienated from one's truth because one has no choice. One's sacred spark, and thus Divine Being, is diminshed. Freedom and the search for truth are inextricably linked. Truest being is life that comes to self-consciousness comprehending one's past and making a choice for life in terms of one's own discovered values. However, freedom, in Olsen's literature, is ethically bound; it is freedom to choose relationships and ways of encouragement, not freedom from relationships, nurture, and care.

Religiously speaking, Olsen understands as sacred and holy the wisdom and courage of ancestors and the historical powers of renewal, creativity, and transformation manifest in the human infant. Past, present, and future are linked in the human struggle to know what has gone before and what is yet possible. Holiness is born in human relationships that tap the infinite and mysterious energies and talents for creation, sustenance, and beauty latent in all human lives. In song and poem we revive the dead and give beginning to our own spiritual journeys.

Paradoxically, those who have been denied fullness of being and whose exhausting work eclipses the expansiveness and time needed for reflection, for writing, for remembering, have still given expression to the human longing to know, to reflect, and to create. Where the special needs and circumstances of their lives yield new comprehensions of human struggle, our vision of the human situation and of human dreams is expanded. Where they create forms of art and expressions of beauty, bearing their fruit against all odds, our comprehension of the sanctity of the human drive to express, to make, to reflect, is infinitely enhanced. The miraculous straining toward fulfillment in the lives of the poor and oppressed suggests the fundamental impulse of humanity toward righteousness. *Silences* is emblematic of such a journey, where many muted voices raised in concert reveal the transformation of silence into voice. The reader of this, like the reader of any of Olsen's writing, receives an ethical vision vitally linked with the world of experience.

Olsen keeps faith by affirming life. She invites the reader to share the responsibility for actualization. Insofar as readers respond, her hope—transcending all harms, partialities, sicknesses, deaths, separations, and losses—may blossom in our time. Encouragement will redeem us from brokenness, binding Human to Spirit in love.

What *Silences* evokes is part of the Olsen message. The deeper and broader vision her body of work illuminates may be understood as the reference of her words here. The process of hearing and speaking, of learning identity and moving into expression, is the coveted life promise pointed to by Olsen's metaphorical silences. *Silences* inspires us to imagine new worlds, new Being.

1. References to *Silences* are given in the text of the chapter.

2. Much of the negative criticism *Silences* received when it was first published (reviews were polarized) stemmed from readers' oversimplification of Olsen's thesis. Some found Olsen's suggestions in the book contradictory, failing to understand that Olsen's point is to deal with the contradictions. I read *Silences* not as concluding but as opening for discussion the question of what is needed for creativity. See Abigail Martin's *Tillie Olsen* for a survey of the criticism, pp. 11–17.

3. From the dedication page and untitled foreword of *Silences*. A crucial aspect of Olsen's prose is her examination of the economic factor in determining what becomes of talent, desire, and dreams, especially in the lives of working-class people. In *Silences*, Olsen observes that most literature has been written by men or by women who have had special situations. It could be observed that most recent studies in black and feminist theology as well as in women's studies have been written by people who have come from or found economic privilege in the course of their lives. As one whose experience is working class, Olsen offers a world vision from the perspective of the less fortunate in culture. At the same time, Olsen is herself an exception, since the great majority of the economically underprivileged do not "come to writing" or recognized achievement at all.

4. See, for example, her use of these phrases on pp. 49 and 63. Though Davis is inspirational for the study as a whole, Olsen has said that the theme came from Blake's sentence, "Blight never does good to a tree"; see *Silences*, p. 177.

5. Alice Walker, *In Search of Our Mothers' Gardens* (San Diego: Harcourt Brace Jovanovich, 1983), p. 242.

6. Other scholars have built upon Olsen's method of reconstructing from silences a picture of what life has been like for the historical losers. A notable example is Elisabeth Schüssler Fiorenza's *In Memory of Her: A Feminist Theological Reconstruction of Early Christian Origins* (New York: Crossroads, 1983).

7. Olsen's research testifies that until very recently, only unmarried women or women without children, who have also had the advantages of servants and economic means (in other words, women who were able to live, like most accomplished male writers, apart from the personal care of others or the necessary work of making a living) have been able to sustain writing careers (see p. 16 of *Silences*). Olsen is aware of the limitations placed upon male artists who must work for a living. She makes

this distinction between men and women: "Compared to men writers of like distinction and years of life, few women writers have had lives of unbroken productivity, or leave behind a 'body of work'" (*Silences*, p. 38). She also writes, "Where the gifted among women (*and men*) have remained mute, or have never attained full capacity, it is because of circumstances, inner and outer, which oppose the needs of creation" (*Silences*, p. 17).

8. Olsen calls the worker/mother/writer the rarest of writers (*Silences*, p. 262).

9. "The Wife's Story" was first published in *Atlantic*, July 1864. Olsen discusses the story on pp. 89–94 of *Silences*.

10. Davis herself wrote to C. E. Norton (an editor and Harvard professor) on a presentation note that Olsen discovered one hundred years later in the pages of a library copy of one of her books: "judge me—not by what I have done, but by what I have hoped to do" (*Silences*, p. 114). Like her characters, Davis suggests a desire for wholeness of self reflected and expanded in artistic expression. Instead, in the words of Katherine Anne Porter (and quoted by Olsen), she illustrates "the dispersion of the self in many small bits" (*Silences*, p. 216).

11. For an excellent review article of *Silences*, which comments upon it as a distillation of Olsen's other work, see Alix Kates Shulman, "Overcoming Silence: Teaching Writing for Women," *Harvard Educational Review* 49:4 (November 1979): 527–33.

12. Various recent studies in a number of areas have focused upon the importance of story to self-understanding and to the human community. In addition to Carol Christ and Michael Goldberg, see Elaine Showalter, *A Literature of Their Own: British Women Novelists from Bronte to Lessing* (Princeton, N.J.: Princeton University Press, 1971). A book whose explanations for the lack of women's writing is near to Olsen's is Virginia Woolf's classic, *A Room of One's Own* (New York: Harcourt Brace Jovanovich, 1957).

13. Phyllis Trible, *Texts of Terror: Literary Feminist Readings of Biblical Narratives* (Philadelphia: Fortress Press, 1984), p. 4.

14. Olsen's attempt to integrate the values of traditional women's experience with the feminist experience of liberation from habits, conventions, and beliefs that inhibit fullest growth is a significant contribution to all areas of women's studies. For another and similar approach, see Alice Walker, "A Writer Because of, Not in Spite of, Her Children," in her *In Search of Our Mothers' Gardens*, pp. 66–70.

A Feminist Spiritual Vision

I am serious about the images I make.

MIRIAM SCHAPIRO
"Notes from a Conversation
on Art, Feminism, and Work"

The last step in this process is to leave God. I take this to mean, in religious terms, that we have to leave the Lord in order to find God in our brothers and sisters. We have to give up obedience to find solidarity. We have to give up relationships of domination, even if our role in them is the servant's role. We have to overcome the master-servant relationship and become one with our brothers and sisters. . . .

That would be a major step in the direction we have to travel. I think what we need in order to take that step is a new language, and feminists (both male and female) are working hard today to develop a language that says more clearly what it amounts to and means to leave God for God's sake.

And so . . . I ask God to make me quit of God for God's sake. And with that I would like to close.

DOROTHEE SOELLE
The Strength of the Weak

I f spiritual Being begins in life experience, we are in the process
of disclosing the truth, the light, and the way. Human beings
are then responsible for all that is in us to be. We leave the God
of dominion, power, and priority, for divinity that is on the
journey, among the people. Dorothee Soelle, German feminist
theologian, says we can no longer use sentences like "Christ is the
Son of God" as a departure for theology. She suggests that sentences
derived from human experience, like "Mrs. Schmidt has been
waiting for seventeen months for an 8-by-12 foot room in a nursing
home," are more promising beginnings for religious understandings.
Such a sentence, she says, "can lead us somewhere" in
contemplating the nature of God.[1]

Tillie Olsen's narrative and poetic texts "can lead us
somewhere" in our search for truth, light, and way. Moments within
the texts (words, images, metaphors) and the span of the stories
themselves confront us with news of a world in which people
struggle for identity and purpose. Emerging language patterns (like
life/miracle/flower) are the writer's means of evoking in readers a
comprehension like her own. The otherness we confront in Olsen is
the depth of her longing and faith arising from abused and despised
life. For readers instilled with a theological sense of our helplessness
and God's supreme power, the notion that human care and
community may be the locus for the world's and divine's recreation
is alien indeed.

Reading Olsen with a religious interest, we come to ask why it is
that for so long we have needed God to be separate from us. Why
have we needed to deny change and to fear a humane world? Why do
we prefer destruction, and why do we use God as a reason for it? In a
vision of life that supposes the expansion of Being in human
becoming, we begin to wonder why it has been assumed that
divinity is diminished in human contexts. In other words, reading a
woman writer like Tillie Olsen religiously accomplishes a major

task in the present work of feminist theologians. It allows us to make "the mysterious turn" to an entirely different way of thinking about holiness and redemption, about beauty and salvation. Olsen's body of work is a source of new thinking about what matters in the intertwined realms of physical and spiritual life, about what efforts are lasting.

A Metaphorical Rendering

From the perspective of Olsen's latest period, we can fruitfully reflect upon a metaphorical pattern that has developed through her writing, communicating a vision of human transformation.[2] It is telling that the metaphors are mixed, drawn from nature and human manufacture. Using the *journey* or quest motif, Olsen pictures the human search for a viable place to be, an environment or home in which one may grow and *blossom*. Inheriting an abused and broken world, people search the past and their environment to discover what inheritances may nurture life. The yields of the search, like the members of the community, are *threads of a whole* to be woven or *pieced* together in a pattern of humane coexistence. Thus, full human being, like a quilt or a mosaic, is envisioned as a coherent and patterned search for truths faithful to human needs and visions and leading to actions that elicit mutual well-being and wholeness. Like Nelle Morton, who writes in a different mode, Tillie Olsen shows that "the journey is home."[3] Not ends but beginnings and makings are the goal. The way is the negotiated, not pure way of being faithful in relationship. Movements toward human unfolding and being cast light on the journey, disclosing what is essential and true "for human beings in our time."[4] Faithfulness to one's own time and circumstance, not allegiance to distant worlds, is the calling echoed in Olsen's literature.

JOURNEYING

To journey at one's will is an expression of freedom. At the same time, journeying may be a quest for freedom. The literary use of journeying as a leitmotif for human dreams and visions is standard. As reflected in a contemporary anthology such as *Myths and Motifs in Literature*, the journey or quest motif in Western literature has largely been concerned with the individual (almost always male) and "his hopes to find the Self" through "a slow process forward to a final goal (heaven) along a linear movement of time."[5]

Recently, feminist scholars have begun to identify trends and patterns in the female quest, as reflected in literature by women. One such study is Carol Christ's *Diving Deep and Surfacing: Women Writers on Spiritual Quest*.[6] Christ suggests the often communal nature of women's quests and the grounding of women's struggle in the historical reality of their traditional voicelessness. The pattern she discovers in women's texts, however, is by and large a radical break with the past and a mystical, futuristic naming of a new reality.

Houston A. Baker's *The Journey Back: Issues in Black Literature and Criticism* may offer a better parallel for understanding Olsen's use of the metaphor: "The black writer, having attempted the journey, preserves details of his voyage in that most manifest and coherent of all cultural systems—language. Through his [sic] work we are allowed to witness, if not the trip itself, at least a representation of the voyage that provides some view of our emergence."[7] For Baker, the writer makes an "effort at return," which then leads to emergence. Journeys in a literature like Olsen's are the re-presentation of historical quests, which in turn spark new worlds and imaginative voyages. Out of people's past comes the way of journeying in the present. Language, then, is a kind of map, a rendering of valleys and highways, of crossroads and destinations.

A book like Nelle Morton's *The Journey Is Home* is a language map for feminist scholars. It records the way women have come in recent years (to self and other understanding and truth) and charts paths for their continued journeying. In the process of Morton's own use of the image in relation to women's lives, new or different meanings emerge. While we journey politically, historically, and geographically, we also journey spiritually. In a note at the end of her book, she writes, "Maybe 'journey' is not so much a journey ahead, or a journey into space, but a journey into presence. The farthest place on earth is a journey into the presence of the nearest person to you."[8] These sentences are evocative for literary criticism. The reading journey is one into presence, into the presence of characters and of their world, where we learn as much about ourselves as about the peopled text.

Olsen's reconstructionist vision shares a basic impulse expressed by Carol Christ in the conclusion to her book, the impulse toward integration. Olsen's use of journeying expands the possibilities for understanding the human quest by an integration of past and future, self and other, male and female. Depicting in her first fiction the quest for a better life, in later stories Olsen uses the journey to illuminate her characters' communal struggles for understanding and for a sense of meaningful participation in life.

A journey bridges the first two settings of *Yonnondio*. Though there are other brief episodes of happiness in the novel, this scene (Chapter 3) is uniquely joyful, marked by singing and bodies in relationship: "Willie slumbered against Mazie's shoulder. Ben drowsily had his head in her lap, staring into the depthless transparent green above. . . . 'Roses love nightwinds, violets love dew, angels in heaven, know I love you.' Their voices were slow curving rhythms, slow curving sounds. Voices, rising and twining, beauty curving on rainbows of quiet sound" (38). Throughout the chapter, the emphasis is less on the passage from place to place than on the community created by the travel. The family's bodily support of one another is imagized in the twining voices. The passage suggests an understanding of human bondedness and the possibility of human cooperation.

Mazie is infused with feelings of expansion: "[She] stood up, her hands on the wagon seat, screaming with delight. The wind came over her body with a great rush of freedom" (35). A range of nature images—snow, wind, rainbow, sunshine—points to the characters' anticipation and wonder as they travel. The girl, in particular, senses the flow of life's energies and intuits her connection with the vast possibilities of the new geography.

Joyous, exhilarating, the journey is portrayed from Mazie's perspective as a wondrous moment; for Anna it is a hallmark of the future: "with bright eyes [she] folded and unfolded memories of past years—plans for the years to come" (38). The family's search is for work, home, schooling, for identity and connection. In their moving, the Holbrooks express their dearest hopes: "A new life . . . in the spring" (38). Thus the journey is metaphoric of the desire for opportunity and renewal. They hope not merely for survival, but for beginning and building: "lovely things to keep, brass lamps, bright tablecloths, vines over the doors, and roses twining" (38). Things of material beauty suggest a sense of permanence and belonging, where children can ponder questions and invite their souls to wander, where relationships that offer sustenance for life can be fostered.

In the Holbrooks' journeying, two human quests are metaphorically intertwined: one, the necessary quest for sustaining work, a living wage, and the other, the desire to begin anew, to find a life of meaning characterized by mutual caring and abundant yields. As the journey for work is described, certain characteristics of the human quest for meaning are suggested. Mazie experiences release, boundlessness, and contentment as they travel. Furthermore, the journey is characterized by solidarity, by human community and interdependence. Mazie helps her father when the wheels are stuck, and Anna shelters the children bodily when it snows.

In the story of Whitey, the journeying metaphor reflects the hopes of the past. The sailor once felt connected to others in his work because they shared "the brotherhood." What was good for one was good for all. Now that the camaraderie has disintegrated, he struggles to sustain meaning in his life. He is like a wrecked vessel, no longer able to make himself "feel good" because the adventure and community his travels once embodied are no longer intact. Without the community he once knew, the journeying of his present is empty.

The steerage ship of Eva's story connects her past journey for political freedom with her present quest for self-identity. A former embarkment, made in desperation, now signifies the way Eva must travel to gain a sense of herself and of the belief that has given her life meaning. What she discovers is an unshakable faith in human beings. Though her present journey is singular, it gains its meaning from the movement of thousands toward freedom and dignity. We might understand the journey's conclusion to signify Olsen's own faith. Searching for meaning, Eva finds that the quester (herself) finds meaning by sharing with others the same struggle for freedom. She (and Olsen) embody the truth that the "purpose of freedom is to create it for others."9 Thus, Eva's spiritual search suggests that to understand the journey of one's life is to see it in the context of movements larger than oneself.

As readers, we journey into Eva's world. Reading fosters journeying into another's presence. In "Tell Me a Riddle," we are invited into Eva's human heart, to learn of her understandings, pains, and hopes. The result is an expansion of our own journeying. Meeting another on her way, we have made a detour on our own. Thus we might say that reading fictive worlds teaches sympathy born out of interruption. Practicing a willed suspension of our own world, we enter the otherness of a new world, thinking and feeling as another. Journeys are thus intertwined, and we carry in our minds the crossed paths of self and other.

While Eva's personal hope is symbolized by the socialist dream, Stevie's journey begins at the personal level and expands toward a vision of universal quest through imagistic association with animal and plant worlds and the significant relations of this life. The longer light of spring, accompanying the boy's quest for a place and for the knowledge that he is connected with others by love, points to the metaphysical depth of the story. Through the settings of junkyard and cemetery, journeying becomes a metaphor not only for the living but for the hopes of the dead, whose memory sparks the present search for meaning and for a feeling of continuity.

The journeys of Olsen's characters are marked by struggle and community. Employing the quest as a leitmotif of American literature, the writer revitalizes its metaphoric potential by offering an unlikely set of vehicles: the poor, minorities, women, and children. The incoherent chantings of an old Jewish immigrant woman; the vision of an eight-year-old girl or a fourteen-year-old boy; the desires of a poverty-stricken woman, balancing a baby on her hip; a union sailor, reeling drunk, whose quest he no longer understands: these are the people whose journeying Olsen depicts as the essential human quest for freedom, place, and meaning. She makes us feel the desire "for mattering" from their perspectives and shows the springs of hope flowing, almost miraculously, from their lives. These questers come in groups, struggling together as family: mother/daughter, husband/wife, friend/friend. The black church in "O Yes" is emblematic of communal journeying, where everyone is brought along: the old, the sick, the infant.

In her notes, Olsen has written, "In the human being is an irrepressible desire for freedom that breaks out century after century."[10] In her fiction she shows that desire to be not merely for freedom *from* want, hunger, and fear, but freedom *for* fulfillment, expression, and community. Using women's, children's, and working-class perspectives, Olsen transforms the vision of human longing from solitary to community questing. Through the lens of domestic needs, limitations, and promises, Olsen suggests that the movement toward freedom is most genuine and realistically promising as an inclusive journey that begins where people are the weakest and least fortunate.

In *Silences*, Olsen writes of "the unnatural thwarting of what struggles to come into being, but cannot" (6), suggesting that the human quest is the journey into Being, into authentic and expressive selfhood. When she writes of the desire for "spaciousness that puts no limit to vision" (102), she evokes for us an image of creativity in geographical terms. Imaginative work needs room without a roof. The journeys inward and outward reflect similar truths. Movement, change, and possibility are core human needs that are also liberations. In the modern world, many take for granted the sense of expansiveness gained in travel. But in sympathy with people who are denied journeying, as today black South Africans (and others) are and as Olsen's people are, we may remember the power of the journey to express the human movement into holiness.

BLOSSOMING

The flower—witness Emerson's rhodora—is a symbol of beauty and fulfillment as well as vulnerability, the time of blossoming the apex of the plant's development and the glory of its existence. To speak of human blossoming is to suggest the natural beauty of our selves, even more, abundance and future fruition. Olsen's use of the image is prophetic, suggesting the condition of life as it should be, not as it is. In the world of her characters, the hope of blossoming is slim; parents witness the atrophy of children's talents because the world garden denies them the nourishment that might help them grow and flourish. For now, "the time is drought or blight or infestation."[11] But if the "subterranean forces" are fed, if the "rootlets of reconnaissance" are showered, "the mysterious turn" may occur, and a time of blossoming be ushered in.[12] Like other organic images literarily employed, blossoming suggests cycles of growth, bounty, and return, pointing to the interrelationships of seed, soil, and flower, of child, environment, and future yield. While the metaphor has often been used, Olsen's employment of it in contexts of depletion, exhaustion, and death offers new insights.

Alice Walker's use of organic imagery may be used as an interpretive grid for Olsen. Writing about art and women, Walker uses the imagery of seed and flower: "And so our mothers and grandmothers have, more often than not anonymously, handed on the creative spark, the seed of the flower they themselves never hoped to see."[13] In the next paragraphs she offers her mother's gardens as the source of the imagery:

> Whatever she planted grew as if by magic, and her fame as a grower of flowers spread over three counties. Because of her creativity with her flowers, even my memories of poverty are seen through a screen of blooms . . .
>
> I notice that it is only when my mother is working in her flowers that she is radiant, . . . involved in work her soul must have.[14]

The connection Walker makes between her mother's work and her soul, between art and deep human need, suggests an understanding of the organic/spiritual connection as more than a literary device. The connection is rooted in human being. The work of hands feeds the spirit, blending body and soul in radiance.

The singular moment of repose experienced by Mazie and Anna in *Yonnondio* follows their discovery of catalpa blossoms "scattered in the green." The flowers' fragrance and beauty transport Anna back to her childhood, making it possible for her to abandon the worried present and feel for a moment with her daughter the wonder of the universe: "Up from the grasses, from the earth, from the broad tree trunk at their back, latent life streamed and seeded. The air and self shone boundless. Absently, her mother stroked; stroked unfolding, wingedness, boundlessness" (119). The description combines images drawn from flower and butterfly. Petals and wing "unfold," flowers "seed," and the butterfly's compass is "boundless." The girl, like the budded flower, contains within the capacity to come to fruition. Here and elsewhere in Olsen's writing, blossoming signifies the potential for wholeness and holiness in human beings.

At the close of the story "I Stand Here Ironing," the blossoming metaphor is the mother's way of expressing her daughter's capacity. Reflecting her hopes and fears, the protagonist pleads, "Let her be. So all that is in her will not bloom—but in how many does it?" (20–21). Earlier she thought of the girl's gift for pantomime as too often "clogged and clotted," not "used and growing" (19). In this story, the association of flower and girl yields ambivalent meanings. She may not grow at all; she may grow but never come to fulfillment; or she may blossom fully, like Anna's catalpa.

The mother's fear and her negative expression of the metaphor— "so all that is in her will not bloom"—is reflected in Olsen's essay about her mother's death. Describing her mother's life, Olsen writes of "that common everyday nightmare of hardship, limitation, longing; of baffling struggle to raise six children in a world hostile to human unfolding."[15] The allusion to the metaphor is slight but recognizable: human unfolding is an image drawn from nature. It is the normal condition in favorable circumstances where, like flowers, children may grow and blossom. But because our world unnaturally limits potential in children by preferring war and destruction to creativity, the blossoms of humanity wither prematurely or never come to flower at all. Some may be skeptical of the seemingly romantic view that most children are born with vast creative potential. From Olsen's perspective, what is unbelievable is the bomb, mass indifference, wholesale destruction. In a deep hearing of her literary voice, we perceive how twisted is the "truth" of greed, competition, and slaughter that directs so much human behavior.

Reading a passage from the last pages of *Yonnondio*, cognizant of Olsen's continued use of the metaphor in later work, we are able to see blossoming and its denial as a metaphorical lens for human potential and what threatens it:

Bang!

Bess who has been fingering a fruit-jar lid—absently, heedlessly drops it—aimlessly groping across the table, reclaims it again. Lightning in her brain. She releases, grabs, releases, grabs. I can do. Bang! I did that. I can

do. I! . . . That noise! In triumphant, astounded joy she clashes the lid
down. Bang, slam, whack. . . . human ecstasy of achievement; . . . *I can
do, I use my powers; I! I!* Wilder, madder, happier the bangs [153].

Against the family's poverty and the story's preoccupation with
losses and limitations, the brief episode of unfolding human
potential is a reminder of the latent powers in human life. Like the
unfolding of one petal, the first lesson is only the beginning of the
blossom. But in her environment, will Bess continue to flower?
Coming back to the story from Olsen's later fiction and the probing
question of the unnamed mother in "I Stand Here Ironing," the
reader is undoubtedly led to ask the question.

When in later addresses or talks, Olsen refers to "fullness of
life," "thwarting of the human," or "the sense of one's *unused
powers*," the blossoming metaphor from her first fiction is evoked.[16]
Expression, creativity, and purposeful action are the human values
to which Olsen gives imagistic expression in terms of the flower's
full maturation and glory. In "Tell Me a Riddle," Eva's speech evokes
the metaphor when she, dying, pleads with David: "So strong for
what? To rot not grow?" (108).

Olsen gives interpretation to her metaphors in many of her
unpublished texts. In personal notes, she writes of "[t]he
irrepressible little ones in whom all the art qualities are . . .
germinal." But experience has taught her that often family
circumstances, more than potential, determine what one will
become. In children, she sees "the passion for language, for
imitation, make-believe acting, deft use of the body, love of rhythm,
music."[17] As a seed whose germination and growth depend almost
entirely on favorable conditions, the child whose potential is
miraculously given at birth, depends on a world of encouragement
and means if he or she is to grow in health. The "word" of the
human infant spoken into the world is an act of divine faith. Our
faithfulness or unfaithfulness lies in our human response to that
word.

In language reflective of Eva's, Olsen uses the organic image for
cosmic questioning: "Has it always been this: this world of winter,
only breaking on the new life toward the longer light, the warmth,
the blossoming"?[18] If the world is a great seed, then light is the
morality of valuing each human being, and warmth, the sustenance
of human caring.

The miraculous rebirth of dead objects in "Requa" makes it
possible to believe in the resurrection of human potentials. Even dirt
has a life wish, and junk desires the holiness of being made useful.

Through Stevie's eyes, we see beauty in rust patterns and the mystery of decay. All about are living clues to the cycles of death and rebirth that turn the universe. Seeing his own worth reflected in his uncle's face, Steve learns a central lesson of life: others need caring for, too. Reciprocating Wes's attention reflects Stevie's most difficult journey into another's presence; his blossoming is intimated by his unfolding from isolation and reaching out to others. Thus his story expands our sense of the religious dimension of human flowering, since the moral principles of shared responsibility and mutual enhancement are the truths that elicit Stevie's own resurrection.

In portraits of human struggle, Olsen shows some, like Eva and Whitey, who know the feelings of waste and untapped potential. Others, like Emily, Carol, Jeannie, and Steve, seem to span our lives and pose a question that waits for the reader's reply. How might those whose lives are still before them bring their gifts to bear on the world and find their paths of righteousness?

PIECING

Repairing, patching, and sewing, work that women have traditionally performed in the home, are all piecing activities. Piece goods are materials purchased by the yard to be patterned, cut, and sewn, especially into garments. But any creativity that combines parts into a whole may be understood metaphorically as piecing. Olsen's use of the image brings a historically female sphere of work to consciousness as a perspective for viewing human activity and values. The metaphor implies *re*construction, since in Olsen's world, the characters seldom piece new goods but rather sort through discards and make something new from something old.

The quilt is a most salient work of piecing. Colorful and patterned, it symbolizes not only the human ingenuity that creates something of use out of something old, but as a finished product, it suggests an eye for the beauty and harmonious design that characterize human creativity. While all of these meanings are suggested in Olsen's employment of the metaphor, more dramatically, she suggests a morality of reappropriation: choosing from the past usable patterns for life in the modern present.

Miriam Schapiro, a contemporary artist, expresses a similar morality and evokes the imagery of piecing in describing her own movement to feminist consciousness in her work: "The new work was different from anything I had done before. I worked on canvas, using fabric. I wanted to explore and express a part of my life which I had always dismissed—my homemaking, my nesting. I wanted to validate the traditional activities of women, to connect myself with the unknown women artists who made quilts, who had done the invisible 'women's work' of civilization."[19] Schapiro's collage style is drawn from the historical work of foremothers (including their quilting) and seeks to integrate the values of their traditional lives with her current feminist perspectives. Using more than one medium and fabrics and objects out of women's traditional contexts, Schapiro's "piecing" on canvas is like Olsen's in word.

Olsen warns against the danger of glorifying one aspect of women's work (homemaking) or overemphasizing one creative expression of women (like needlework), while not encouraging women in different ways of making art. Schapiro's use of a piecing style seems important, however, in that it gives her a female tradition and allows her to claim a part of herself that she had not expressed before (the caring angel). Olsen's use of the metaphor in word and image appears, as it does with Schapiro, to grow out of her experience in female contexts, though she expands it in her universal vision.

In the second chapter of *Yonnondio*, as the family works desperately to gain the necessary money for moving, we are given this narrative depiction of Anna's participation: "Somehow to skimp off of everything that had long ago been skimped on, somehow to find more necessities the body can do easiest without. The old quilt will make coats for Mazie and Ben, Will can wear Mazie's old one. This poverty's arithmetic for Anna" (26). The gift Anna brings to a limited situation is her ability to create something of use out of what she has, to divide and multiply fragments. The quilt, already something made of fragments and leftovers, can be remade as two coats; a girl's coat can be converted into a boy's.

Children, like their parents, learn the art of making something out of scraps and leftovers:

> On the dump there is Jinella's tent, Jinella's mansion, Jinella's roadhouse, Jinella's pagan island, Jinella's palace, whatever Jinella wills it to be that day. Flattened tin cans, the labels torn off to show the flashing silver, are strung between beads and buttons to make the shimmering, showy entrance curtains. Here sometimes, . . . Mazie is admitted—*if* she brings something for the gunny sack. The gunny sack . . . stuffed with "properties": blond wood-shaving curls, moldering hats, raggy teddies, torn lace curtains (for trains and wedding dresses), fringes, tassels, stubs of lipstick, wrecks of high-heeled shoes and boots, lavish jewelry [127].

Like an artist or a "bricoleur," Jinella determines the name of what she creates, as she strings tin cans, beads, and buttons to form a chain curtain, brings together the worn old toy and lady's lipstick stub to form her treasure, or turns a bit of lace into a bride's veil.[20] She is a namer of her world—mansion, palace, roadhouse—and by naming creates her reality. Through Jinella's cunning, if desperate, imagining, Olsen points to the unique human ability to make and create. Furthermore, the writer uses the girl's piecing to reflect the value of cast-off junk, still recognizable to the discerning eye.

The piecing imagery of the *Yonnondio* passages is evoked in "O Yes" by a description of voices raised together in song. The passage reminds us of the Holbrooks' intertwined voices as they journeyed to the farm. In "O Yes," the young protagonist ponders: "If it were a record she would play it over and over, . . . to untwine the intertwined voices, to search how the many rhythms rock apart and yet are one glad rhythm" (50). Twining is an action of lapping and turning, yet it brings separate, even disparate, pieces together and suggests the intention of combining. The pieces intertwined may be characteristically the same, as a rope or chain, or they may, as voices, be different. What is pieced together in "O Yes," through song, sermon, and scripture, is a message, a plea by the black community for ultimate justice on earth as well as in heaven.

The "spinning" preacher's voice elicits in Carol's mind a tapestry of childhood games: "Tag. Thump of the volleyball. Ecstasy of the jump rope" (52). In Carol's thought, words and images are combined that will in the end remind her of her allegiances and responsibilities. The twining voices, singing of justice and humanity, metaphorize Carol's moral situation: she must choose from the past what will direct her future. Similarly, Alva's dream is drawn from pieces or fragments of experience: her own pregnancy, loneliness and poverty; the diminutive guide who leads her to paradise with parade stick and motorcycle; the convey line and the damned souls. Furthermore, in an interview Olsen has remarked that her writing of the passage came about as a combination of stories she had heard from black women.[21] Thus, the writer's method reflects her characters', and vice versa: choosing images and thoughts from the past and weaving them into a coherent, if also paradoxical, narrative for understanding life.

In "Tell Me A Riddle," we are told of Eva's "one social duty . . . the boxes of old clothes left with her, as with the life-practiced eye for finding what is still wearable within the worn . . . she scans and sorts—this for rag or rummage, that for mending and cleaning, and this for sending away" (77). Eva's sorting is reminiscent of Anna's piecing, looking for what can be remade or used again. Looking through the old clothes, Eva's sorting reflects not only the artistry of Anna's novel use of an older object, but also a sense of human interconnectedness. When she looks through the clothes for what can still be used, she reflects the human moral choice to bring need into alignment with resource. From this perspective, we conclude politically and religiously that an imbalance or nonalignment of goods and people is evil, and that in regaining the original holiness/wholeness and promise of the universe, we are responsible to right such imbalance.

Stevie's rebirth is elicited by sustained use of piecing imagery. Acts leading to wholeness—bringing parts together, teaching a skill, meeting human needs—are the seeds of holiness. Because individual human wholeness cannot be fully and timelessly achieved, the human community must impart wholeness, offering the individual a place in the pattern of life. Moving from the domestic sphere to the contexts of industry and technological waste, Olsen universalizes the metaphor, making clear her vision of redemption as the historical and material reconstruction of beauty and health out of waste and brokenness.

The metaphor of piecing contributes to the moral vision Olsen describes in her interviews and talks. Her first sentence is structurally parallel with Anna's thought (what can be saved, what cannot) in these remarks: "Our situation . . . is: what do we keep, what do we discard. What is going backward, what narrows us, limits us, makes us too liable to hatreds, bigotries, closing off, not recognizing what the central enemy is, where our allies lie, where our common humanity lies."[22]

Olsen's view of intergenerational responsibility may also be interpreted in terms of "piecing." She understands that the dreams and struggles of revolutionaries form the basis, indeed are the beginnings, of our present struggle, knowledge, and hope.[23] Like Will's coat converted from Mazie's, such an attitude suggests that we inherit possibilities and hopes from the previous generation. Our task is to sort, discard, and piece, to find what is fitting for a life of commitment to human unfolding, and out of our inheritance, to weave a garment for today.

Women have long been needleworkers. They have designed their art for beauty and warmth. Piecing images, Olsen is a word worker, a designer of life in fiction, poetry, and report. Like earlier women workers, she starts with what is needed. Her vision of truth and beauty begins with the essentials: voice, place, affirmation, warmth, light, way.

A MOSAIC OF MEANINGS

Journeying, blossoming, and piecing together suggest the vision evoked by Olsen's writing. Each elicits a matrix of meanings that can be used effectively as an interpretive grid for reading Olsen's stories. Viewed together, their meanings offer a way of understanding three central and interwoven concepts in Olsen's writing, and "lead us somewhere" in religious ponderings: journeying suggests the struggle for place, identity, and community engaging all humanity, while blossoming reflects the hope for each individual—and for the whole earth—to attain fulfillment and to become whole. The piecing metaphor points to a new spirituality wherein individual and community gain grace and freedom through patterns of life that are mutually enhancing. Faithfully sorting from the past what is usable for a new earth, a new humanity, and a new sense of divinity, we gain the transcendence of Spirit as the miraculous power that makes things new.

Together, the metaphors evoke a set of meanings. All point to human desires for coherence, pattern, continuity, fullness, and connection. All suggest a sense of intergenerational responsibility. The roots of future generations are planted today, and the direction and resources of the present generation were yielded from the past. Human responsibility flows both ways—toward root and blossom— past and future. The dead are not lost as long as we struggle in their name, and bondage to time is overcome in faithful telling of the dreams that inspirit us.

The metaphors imply moving, direction, and purpose. They are historical images connecting resource and yield, nature and creativity. Earth and human, ancestor and grandchild, material and intellect, male and female are bound in imagistic visions. And in each, the desire for "more" compels human action. Olsen's metaphors reflect her own representative hope for her characters and suggest the ultimate vision inspiring her fiction: a universe in which we act as though human quests are the very matter of truth and where no person, no hope, is ultimately lost.

Wholeness is holiness; the words describe an existence in which no part is broken, impaired, injured, or useless. Rather, every element, resource, action, decision, person is remembered and integrated.

The vision offered by the metaphors sustains the actual and often despairing struggles of the characters and thus is a lens for a liberation theology, which begins where people today struggle for bread, civil rights, and freedom of expression. To integrate the seeming conflict between vision and historical reality, Olsen draws her images as a paradox: beauty is created from seeming ugliness, the hope for a new life is born out of degradation and despair, the "pieces" that may mold a better world come from fragmented lives of hurt and disease, even from the graves of our ancestors.

Conclusion

The miraculous is not, for Olsen, the extraordinary, but the ordinary: birth, small acts of kindness forged in darkness and loss, learning, art, songs of faith, moments of meditation, creativity in all of its forms. Everyday life is the miracle she limns and celebrates.

The morality her writing elicits transcends all human-made divisions and depends upon the possibility that people can become essentially caring. Olsen's stories and prose offer an understanding of what is right as what enhances human growth and potential. Thus, her vision points to experience and need as the legislators of morality. In our reading, we have called the powers of life and sustenance (in traditional language, God) the encouraging presence of love evolving with humanity in the quest for fulfillment and beauty. Human responsibility, then, is for nothing less than the co-creation of the world. In such a vision of possibility, all actions have ultimate potential because they make us who we are; they give us identity and purpose.

It is only a step from Olsen's moral understanding to her prophetic vision. Mutual love and care will not only make possible more abundant living individually but will redeem the struggles of generations before who have striven for a more humane and beneficent universe, transforming all human losses into an expansive pattern of living, which we continue with our own lives. Thus are we participants in the ongoing struggle of humanity *and of God* to be free and committed, independent and yet bound in relation to those things that concern Being most deeply.

Critical to the religious awareness Olsen's writing offers are the characters, settings, dilemmas, themes, and metaphors drawn from and reflecting historical female experience in domestic spheres. For example, while socialist Jewish men often broke radically with traditional religious practice and the sacred spaces and texts of orthodox religious understanding, Jewish women were never full participants in that religious life. Like most American women of the same period, turn-of-the-century Jewish women attracted to new ideologies still largely maintained their life activities in the spheres of action and with the values they had traditionally inhabited and sustained. The sacred space of Olsen's foremothers, like the stories they wrote with their lives, were primarily, though never exclusively, domestic.

Bringing to light the essential values and ethics of women's caretaking as well as the hindrances, encumbrances, and silences of mothering, Olsen's fiction—insofar as we interpret its implications for understanding the depth dimension of human life—gives critical voice to a religious consciousness arising out of women's historical experience. Its criticism of religion is a criticism of traditional, male-dominated religions, and its prophetic vision of blossoming life reveals a spiritual understanding that has long undergirded and empowered women: the belief that making life possible is a holy activity. The feminist bent of Olsen's world attitude simply extends that belief to women's own lives. It is also holy to nurture oneself and to ask for encouragement from others that one may experience one's own fulfillment.

We may, as Olsen's writing imagines, hear the voices of truth, like Mazie, in the wind, or, as Alva does, receive a divine message from a child. Some still need another to speak for them because they cannot yet speak for themselves. But Tillie Olsen's vision is for a world in which we ourselves—men and women—are born in our own voices, as we search for truths that may redeem us in our own stories of faith.

Olsen is one writer who has told her truth. Other women writers—voices out of Africa, Latin America, Eastern Europe, and elsewhere—are telling their stories. We have much to learn from them of truth, journey, spirit, and way. In the past we have feared this plentitude, preferring instead one text, one truth, one way (all male authored in our Western Jewish and Christian traditions). It is time to read new stories and old stories newly told. It is time for the truth in women's lives to find hearing and voice. Why do we fear expansiveness, Tillie Olsen's literature asks. What small God binds our hands and mouths, fearing human talents? Mysteries remain; Olsen's world offers no new idols. Instead her vision frees us to imagine our lives as if our living mattered, as if our care leads to care and our hope to hope. Every life is a potential text for understanding the depths of human longing and possibility, and human actions undertaken in the Spirit of Holiness are the hope of our salvation.

1. Dorothee Soelle, *The Strength of the Weak: Toward a Christian Feminist Identity*, trans. Robert and Rita Kimber (Philadelphia: Philadelphia Press, 1984), p. 91.

2. Page references to Olsen's books given in the remainder of the chapter are to the editions noted in the Bibliography.

3. The phrase is the title of Morton's recent book.

4. Olsen's phrase.

5. *Myths and Motifs in Literature*, ed. David J. Burrows, Frederick R. Lapides, and John T. Showcross (New York: The Free Press, 1973), p. 135.

6. Christ does not suggest a monolithic understanding of women's questing but carefully asserts that she is describing "*a* common pattern" in women's literature.

7. Houston A. Baker, *The Journey Back: Issues in Black Literature and Criticism* (Chicago: University of Chicago Press, 1980), p. 1.

8. Nelle Morton, *The Journey Is Home* (Boston: Beacon Press, 1985), p. 227.

9. Bernard Malamud, *The Fixer*, quoted in James Cone, *God of the Oppressed* (New York: The Seabury Press, 1975), p. 147.

10. From Olsen's personal files, written in the seventies or early eighties.

11. Olsen, *Silences*, p. 6.

12. Olsen's phrases, used in the first chapter of *Silences*, where she speaks of her own experience.

13. Alice Walker, *In Search of Our Mothers' Gardens* (San Diego: Harcourt Brace Jovanovich, Publishers, 1983), p. 240.

14. Ibid., p. 241.

15. Olsen, "Dream-Vision," p. 261.

16. These phrases come from notes or transcriptions of talks in Olsen's personal files.

17. From Olsen's personal files.

18. From Olsen's personal files.

19. Miriam Schapiro, "Notes from a Conversation on Art, Feminism, and Work," in *Working It Out*, ed. Sara Ruddick and Pamela Daniels (New York: Pantheon Books, 1977), p. 296.

20. In French, a "bricoleur" is a Jack of all trades, a professional do-it-yourself person. Claude Levi-Strauss uses the concept of "bricolage" to describe the human process of creativity and coming to knowledge that is practiced by one who, with limited resources, puts things together in novel ways. See "The Science of the Concrete" in *The Savage Mind* (Chicago: The University of Chicago Press, 1966), pp. 16–33.

21. Tillie Olsen, telephone interview with the author, July 1984.

22. Tillie Olsen. Quoted by Rubin in "Riddle of History."

23. Rubin makes this point in her summary introduction of Olsen in "Riddle of History."

Selected Bibliography

I. TILLIE OLSEN'S PUBLICATIONS

"Baptism." *Prairie Schooner* 31 (Spring 1957): 70–80. Reprinted as "O Yes" in *Tell Me a Riddle.*

"A Biographical Interpretation." Afterword to *Life in the Iron Mills* by Rebecca Harding Davis. New York: Feminist Press, 1972, pp. 69–174. Reprinted in revised form in *Silences.*

"Dream-Vision." *Mother to Daughter: Daughter to Mother: A Feminist Press Daybook and Reader,* ed. Tillie Olsen. New York: The Feminist Press, 1984. Reprinted in *Ms.,* December 1984, p. 136.

Foreword to *Black Women Writers at Work,* ed. Claudia Tate. New York: Continuum, 1983.

"Help Her to Believe." *Pacific Spectator* 10 (Winter 1956): 55–63. Reprinted in *Stanford Short Stories,* ed. W. Stegner and R. Scowcroft. Stanford: Stanford University Press, 1956, pp. 34-42. Reprinted as "I Stand Here Ironing" in *Best American Short Stories,* ed. Martha Foley. Boston: Houghton Mifflin Company, 1957, pp. 264-71. Reprinted as "I Stand Here Ironing" in *Tell Me a Riddle.* Throughout, references are to *Tell Me a Riddle.*

"Hey Sailor, What Ship?" *New Campus Writing No. 2,* ed. Nowland Miller. New York: G. P. Putnam's Sons, 1957, pp. 199–213. Reprinted in *Stanford Short Stories,* ed. Stegner and Scowcroft. Stanford: Stanford University Press, 1957, pp. 1–21. Reprinted in *Tell Me a Riddle.* Throughout, references are to *Tell Me a Riddle.*

"I Stand Here Ironing." *See* "Help Her to Believe."

"I Want You Women Up North to Know" (by Tillie Lerner). *Partisan* 1 (March 1934):4. Reprinted in *Feminist Studies* 7 (Fall 1981):367–69.

"The Iron Throat" (by Tillie Lerner). *Partisan Review* 1 (April-May 1934):3–9.

"O Yes." *See* "Baptism."

185

"Requa." *Iowa Review* 1 (Summer 1970):54–75. Reprinted as "Requa-I." *Best American Short Stories*, ed. Foley and Burnett. Boston: Houghton Mifflin Company, 1971, pp. 237–65. Throughout, references are to *Best American Short Stories*.

Silences. New York: Delacorte Press/Seymour Lawrence, 1978. Reprint. New York: Dell Publishing Co., 1980. Throughout, references are to the reprint edition.

"Silences: When Writers Don't Write." *Harper's* 231 (October 1965):153–61. Reprinted in *Silences*.

"The Strike" (by Tillie Lerner). *Partisan Review* 1 (September-October 1934):3–9. Reprinted in *Years of Protest: A Collection of American Writings of the 1930s*, ed. Jack Salzman. New York: Pegasus, 1967, pp. 138–44.

"Tell Me a Riddle." *New World Writing 16*, ed. Stewart Richardson and Corlies M. Smith. Philadelphia: J. B. Lippincott, 1960, pp. 11–57. Reprinted in *Stanford Short Stories*, ed. Stegner and Scowcroft. Stanford: Stanford University Press, 1960, pp. 82–122. Reprinted in *Tell Me a Riddle*. Throughout, references are to *Tell Me a Riddle*.

Tell Me a Riddle. Philadelphia: J. B. Lippincott, 1962. Reprint. New York: Delacorte Press/Seymour Lawrence, 1979. Reprinted, Laurel paperback ed. New York: Dell Publishing Co. 1981. Throughout, references are to the paperback reprint edition.

"There Is a Lesson" (by Tillie Lerner). *Partisan* 1 (April 1934):4. Reprinted in *San Jose Studies* 2 (1976):70.

"Thousand Dollar Vagrant" (by Tillie Lerner). *New Republic* 80 (29 August 1934):67–69.

"Women Who are Writers in Our Century: One Out of Twelve." *College English* 34 (October 1972):6–17. Reprinted in *Silences*.

Yonnondio: From the Thirties. New York: Delacorte Press/Seymour Lawrence, 1974. Reprinted, Laurel paperback ed. New York: Dell Publishing Co., 1981. Throughout, references are to the reprint edition.

II. ARTICLES AND REVIEWS ON TILLIE OLSEN'S WRITING

Adams, Barbara. "Tillie Olsen: Wings of Life." *Ithaca Times*, 24–30 April 1980, p. 13.

Atwood, Margaret. "Obstacle Course." *New York Times Book Review*, 30 July 1978, pp. 1, 27.

Avant, J. A. Review of *Yonnondio. New Republic*, 30 March 1974, p. 28.

Baro, Gene. Review of *Tell Me a Riddle. New York Tribune Books*, 17 December 1961, p. 8.

Bellows, S. B. Review of *Tell Me a Riddle. Christian Science Monitor*, 9 November 1961, p. 7.

Boucher, Sally. "Tillie Olsen: The Weight of Things Unsaid." *Ms.*, September 1974, pp. 26–30.

Burkom, Selma, and Margaret Williams. "De-Riddling Tillie Olsen's Writing." *San Jose Studies* 2 (1976): 65–83.

Cantwell, Robert. "Literary Life in California." *New Republic*, 22 August 1934, p. 49.

Clayton, John. "Grace Paley and Tillie Olsen: Radical Jewish Humanists." *Response: A Contemporary Jewish Review* 46 (1984): 37–52.

Coles, Robert. "Reconsideration: *Tell Me a Riddle.*" *New Republic* 6 (December 1975): 29–30.

Cuneen, Sally. "Tillie Olsen: Storyteller of Working America." *Christian Century* (21 May 1980): 570–73.

Duncan, Erika. "Coming of Age in the Thirties: A Portrait of Tillie Olsen." *Book Forum* 4:2 (1982): 207–22.

Fisher, Elizabeth. "The Passion of Tillie Olsen." *Nation* 10 (April 1972): 473–74.

Frye, Joann A. "'I Stand Here Ironing': Motherhood as Experience and Metaphor." *Studies in Short Fiction* 18 (Summer 1981): 287–92.

Gelfant, Blanche. "After Long Silence: Tillie Olsen's 'Requa.'" *Studies in American Fiction* 12:1 (1984): 61–69.

Gottlieb, Annie. "Feminists Look at Motherhood." *Mother Jones*, November 1976, pp. 51–53.

———. "Yonnondio." *New York Times Book Review*, 31 March 1974, p. 5.

Grumbach, Doris. "Silences." *Washington Post*, 6 August 1978.

Lester, Elenore. "The Riddle of Tillie Olsen." *Midstream*, January 1975, pp. 75–79.

McElhiney, Annette Bennington. "Alternative Responses to Life in Tillie Olsen's Work." *Frontiers* 2 (Spring 1977): 76–91.

McNeil, Helen. "Speaking for the Speechless." *Times Literary Supplement*, 4 November 1980.

Martin, Abigail. *Tillie Olsen*. Boise, Idaho: Boise State University, 1984.

O'Connor, William Van. "The Short Stories of Tillie Olsen." *Studies in Short Fiction* 1 (Fall 1963): 21–25.

Park-Fuller, Linda Marguerite. *Tillie Olsen: A Phenomenological Study of Consciousness with Implications for Performance*. Ph.D. diss., The University of Texas at Austin, 1980.

Rhodes, Carolyn, and Ernest Rhodes. "Tillie Olsen." In *Dictionary of Literary Biography Yearbook: 1980*, ed. Karen L. Rood, Jean W. Ross, and Richard Ziegfield. Detroit: Gale, 1981.

Rohrberger, Mary. "Tillie Olsen." In *Critical Survey of Short Fiction*. ed. Frank N. Magill. Englewood Cliffs, N.J.: Salem Press, 1981.

Rose, Ellen Cronan. "Limning: or Why Tillie Writes." *Hollins Critic* 13:2 (April 1976): 1–13.

Rosenfelt, Deborah. "From the Thirties: Tillie Olsen and the Radical Tradition." *Feminist Studies* 7:3 (Fall 1981): 371–406.

Rubin, Naomi. "A Riddle of History for the Future." *Sojourner*, July 1983, pp. 1, 4, and 18.

Schwartz, Helen J. "Tillie Olsen," In *American Women Writers*, ed. Lina Mainiero and Langdon Lynne Faust, vol. 3. New York: Ungar, 1981.

Shulman, Alix Kates. "Overcoming Silences: Teaching Writing for Women." *Harvard Educational Review* 49:4 (November 1979): 527–33.

Stimpson, Catherine R. "Tillie Olsen: Witness as Servant." *Polit* 1 (Fall 1977): 1–12.

Symposium: Tillie Olsen Week, The Writer and Society, 21–26 March 1983. Sponsored by St. Ambrose College, Davenport, Iowa; Augustana College, Rock Island, Illinois; Marycrest College, Davenport, Iowa; Scott Community College, Bettendorf, Iowa; Black Hawk College, Moline, Illinois. Contains seven essays: Winifred Farrant Bevilacqua, "Women Writers and Society in 1930 America: Tillie Olsen, Meridel LeSueur, and Josephine Herbst"; Mary K. DeShazar, "Tell Me a Riddle"; Sally H. Johnson, "Silence and Song: The Structure and Imagery of Tillie Olsen's 'Tell Me a Riddle'"; Sara McAlpin, "Mothers in Tillie Olsen's Stories"; Kathleen McCormack, "Song as Transcendence in the Works of Tillie Olsen"; Violet Olsen, "The Writer and Society"; and Vicki L. Sommer, "The Writings of Tillie Olsen: A Social Work Perspective."

"Tillie Olsen on the Privilege to Create." *Radcliffe Centennial News*, July 1979, p. 9.

Index